PHILOSOPHY OF THE SOCIAL SCIENCES II: SCHEMATA

Also by J.O. Wisdom in the Avebury Series in the
Philosophy of Science

Challengeability in Modern Science

Philosophy of the Social Sciences I: A Metascientific
Introduction

Philosophy of the Social Sciences II: Schemata

J. O. WISDOM
University Professor Emeritus
of Philosophy and Social Science,
York University, Toronto

Avebury Series in the Philosophy of Science
Aldershot · Brookfield USA · Hong Kong · Singapore · Sydney

Published by
Avebury
Gower Publishing Company Limited
Gower House
Croft Road
Aldershot
Hants GU11 3HR
England

Gower Publishing Company
Old Post Road
Brookfield
Vermont 05036
USA

ISBN 0-566-05158-3

Printed and bound in Great Britain by
Athanaeum Press Limited, Newcastle-upon-Tyne

Contents

Figures

Preface

The notion of weltanschauung was claimed to be basic to natural science in my earlier book, *Challengeability in Modern Science*. It can be wide or narrow. A brief account of it is given here. In this book it takes specific forms which I call schemata. Some 20 of these, such as functionalism or psychologism, are examined in Part I.

The claim is put forward that most schemata either presuppose one another or can be seen to be one-sided; though of all of them it can be said that 'there is something in it'. Discussion of these leaves us with only two that are independent and include all the rest of the exponents. On them I have tried to base all ideas in the social sciences. These are individualism and holism. When neither of these is found to be reducible to the other, a 'bipolar' model is put forward to encompass the two, to form a basis on which to provide empirical societal theories.

The book should be within the compass of all senior undergraduates, and above, though it is written primarily for social scientists.

I owe a great deal as usual to Sir Karl Popper, though I do not follow him in regarding individualism alone as equal to the task of underpinning all social theory.

I wish to acknowledge the customary help I receive from my wife, Clara, with her background in social anthropology as well as in philosophy of science, also from my old friends Professor Ian Jarvie and Professor Jagdish Hattiangadi. I am also indebted to my students at York University, Toronto. I have in addition received much aid from the care taken by my publisher's editor. When I dropped the ball, which was very frequently, she proved an excellent scrum-half.

I go against the usual printing convention of italicising foreign words, in order to retain italics exclusively for emphasis. I have requested that all foreign words should be printed in roman type. Also I write German nouns without capitals.

Wilmont House   J. O. Wisdom
Castlebridge
Co. Wexford

10 December 1986

Acknowledgements

Certain chapters have been published before: the chapter and associated appendix on situational individualism have appeared twice before. Once was in *The Listener*, 1966 (two talks on the BBC Third Programme 18 August, 223–5, and 25 August, 265–6; *The Listener* does not restrict reproduction). They then appeared as a chapter in *Explanation in the Behavioural Sciences*, editors Boiger and Croffi, 1970. I wish to acknowledge permission to reprint by the Cambridge University Press.

'Situational individualism and emergent group-properties' originally appeared in *Explanation in the Behavioural Sciences*, Cambridge, 1970, 271–96. I thank the University Press for permission to reprint.

'General explanation in history' appeared in *History and Theory*, 1976, *15*, 257–66. I wish to acknowledge the agreement of the Wesleyan University Press which first published the paper.

'Science versus the scientific revolution', *Philosophy of the Social Sciences*, 1971, *1*, 259–84. I acknowledge permission of author and editor to reprint.

'Schemata in social science: structural and operational' appeared as Part 1; 'Schemata in social science: metatheoretical' appeared as Part 2, *Inquiry*, respectively, 1980, *23*, 445–64, and 1981, *24*, 3–19. I thank the editor and publisher for permission to reprint both.

PART I
FORMS OF SCHEMATA

1 The role of weltanshauungen – schemata

Weltanschauungen have a special importance in the social sciences and in the philosophy of the social sciences. The idea is all the more interesting because it is the only definite contribution made to the philosophy of the social sciences by the social sciences themselves. All else has been absorbed either correctly or incorrectly from the philosophy of the natural sciences. It happens that my own introduction to the notion came by discovering its position in natural science but, having found it, I also quickly discovered that it was recognised, though not fully utilised, by the social sciences, sometimes under that name, sometimes other names such as 'frameworks', 'orientations', 'general outlook on life', and so on. The simplest shorthand metaphor for conveying the notion is that of spectacles which have two functions: one being the way in which one sees the social world, and the other being the way in which one sees the social sciences – the two go together.

There is a positive benefit in having located the notion in the understanding of the natural sciences, for it shows one more important parallel between the activity of structure of natural science and that of social science. Moreover, those natural scientists who wish to preserve the myth of natural science as 'hard science' permeated by no mushy metaphysics, or social scientists who think either that they cannot emulate the natural sciences in method, or that they ought not to do so because they ought to pursue an independent line of their own – all those who follow either of these lines of thought are in a position to look once again at the matter. It is salutory to find that, in every period in history, every natural science theory lies within the confines of some weltanschauung. It is still more salutory to recognise that a weltanschauung is inherently unprovable and un-disprovable. It is possible to shake a weltanschauung, to undermine it by *persuasive* arguments, but this is a far cry from producing a definite refutation. If this should seem somewhat puzzling, it is only necessary to realise that, when a particular empirical theory is refuted, this does not ipso facto refute its weltanschauung, for it may be possible to construct another empirical theory — a better one perhaps — within exactly the same weltanschauung. It should not be overlooked, moreover, that there can be sub-weltanschauungen, two of which may live side-by-side and live under the umbrella of a broader weltanschauung embracing both.

The appearance of weltanschauungen in science is not due to weakness of the intellect, nor to subjective bias. It is an inherent necessity of the progress of the science at any given time, and of its evolution and tradition. A scientist must work within the existing weltanschauungen, although occasionally, if he is lucky, he may be able fruitfully to find or invent a new one: however, this is not readily done at will and, if it does occur, it will be because of the influence of the existing weltanschauungen and the need to come to terms with them. For one thinks and works only with the problems, theories, and information that we have and that is what we have inherited. Thus, Newton could no more have thought in terms of the weltanschauung of Einstein's theory of relativity than he could have gone to the moon — and, by the same token, Einstein could not have developed his weltanschauung had he not been nurtured on Newton's theory and its own weltanschauung.

The significance of weltanschauungen lies mainly in their influence on the empirical theorising that takes place under their umbrella. They do not dictate specifically what new theory shall be explored. It is more that they restrict the kind of theory that can be con-sidered, that is, they lay down limits to the kind of theory that can be dealt with, and thus, metaphorically speaking, act as reins which prevent current theorising going off on a tangent from the current tradition of thought.

If one does not have to be over-conscious about weltanschauungen for the development of natural science — although there are certain key places where it may be necessary to reflect on them — the position may well be very different in the social sciences. In fact, I think it is so. One of the reasons for the importance of weltan-schauungen to the social sciences is the dearth of specific empirical theories in this field so that, apart from gathering information and

4

discussing method, there is nothing for the social sciences to do except consider weltanschauungen. Once the point is made explicit, it will, I think, be recognised that there is a great deal of argument in the social science field over weltanschauungen.

There is reason to suppose, I would contend, that weltanschauungen constitute one of the forms that metaphysics can assume and always has assumed. There are, it is true, various forms of metaphysics, but one of them is that. And it is salutory to reflect that so much of science and, even more emphatically, of social science, consists of a form of metaphysics. For there is still a hangover of the attitude that preponderated earlier in the century, both among natural scientists and also social scientists, that there was something not quite decent about metaphysics, playing a part in serious thinking. This attitude is part of the positivist legacy, for positivism recognised no part in science for philosophy. However, if we face the fact that philosophy or, more specifically, a branch of metaphysics, is a natural part of all science, natural or social, and if we face this fact overtly, we can study the nature of its role and consider how we may cope with it in view of the difficulty that we can neither prove nor disprove it. Does this fact render science and social science irrational and hopeless, or is it on the contrary of some value to discovery?

In the field of the social sciences, I prefer to introduce another term for weltanschauungen, namely 'schemata', which seems perhaps more appropriate because it sounds a little more specific and less vague than weltanschauungen and suggests slightly sharper and slightly narrower boundaries.

Concentrating on the notion of schemata in the social sciences and in the philosophy of the social sciences and, indeed, of empirical theorising in the social sciences, there are two main tasks in this sequel. One is to inspect the schemata that currently exist and those to be found in social science history insofar as this is alive. It is surprising to discover how many of these there actually are. Having charted the map of schemata, we need, in the first place, to find out how far they are mutually dependent and how far they are mutually exclusive. Such an investigation will bear on the bitter attitudes that exist in social science between different schools of thought, which are often so overwhelmed by their own schemata that they cannot see the social world or social theories from the point of view of another schema at all, and are so preoccupied with their exclusive validity that they fail to make progress with empirical theories. If some progress can be made with this enterprise, there will then arise the question of unearthing what problems really are telling in the clash between various schemata. For after needless clashes have been removed, there may nonetheless be some inherent and basic clashes of schemata to be investigated. The latter enterprise is, of course, additionally difficult in view of the fact that there is no known way of setting about proving or disproving any specific schema.

In general, it will become plain that there are other controversial matters periodically discussed, such as the influence of positivism, the need for stressing individual experience, and the need to understand cultures or societies in their own terms, from their own point of view, that is, within the framework of their own schemata. Such controversial matters become clarified, easier to discuss, and less emotionally riven by the attempt to fly a flag, once we have managed to locate them under an appropriate schema. They will sometimes be found to be basically different from the kind of clash first considered, for in some cases they hinge on fashion, or on misunderstanding of opponents, or even on misunderstanding the nature of science altogether, and the nature of what constitutes a problem and where a problem arises.

The first task is to draw the map of every available schema. Before tackling that explicitly, however, it may be more useful to discuss the attitudes, beliefs, and prejudices that exist about a number of specific doctrines — such as the attitude to natural science by social scientists and the attitude towards logical positivism — and to discuss the broad issue in current controversy of cultural relativism.

2 Phenomenology and allied forms of individualism

Although phenomenology *could* just argue that its central tendency was not one hundred per cent individualistic; the point will be taken up in due course.

In the hands of its urvater, Husserl, phenomenology has no bearing on society or the social sciences. His immediate successors, Schutz (1962) and Merleau-Ponty (1962) applied it in these ways, though with a large philosophical infusion remaining. From them have evolved several branches which are almost purely societal. These differ markedly, at least on the surface, from one another (and it might be an interesting matter to speculate upon what their grandfathers would have thought of them, or for that matter their fathers). I will in the first place consider two main descendants, the first close in spirit and execution to the ancestral line, the other not. One of the simplest, clearest, and best representatives of the first is given by Berger and Luckmann (1966). Let us begin by stating the sociological problem.

I take individualism to be a basic schema in the social sciences, and the phenomenological approach to be one of the most significant and indeed extreme, of these. The overriding aim is to interpret all sociological happenings in relation to the individual experiences of individual people. Such a programme gives rise to a fundamental problem, namely, how do subjective meanings, that is, the individual experiences private to each individual, lead to or produce a world of objective things? Or, otherwise expressed, how is a world of social reality constructible? Or, as Allan Cobb puts it, how does consciousness of social reality develop from a collection of individual consciousnesses? This problem has exercised various phenomenological authors of recent years.

The Construction of Social Reality

The sequence goes somewhat as follows.

The Construction of Social Reality out of Roles

An individual person begins with the phenomenological experience of his own body; this he can see and touch (he can also have not only experience *of* it but experience *with* it). The experience is readily widened to include phenomenological experience of the world immediately around him, which consists of inanimate objects such as the table in his study, animate objects such as the fly on the window pane, and other individuals such as his children who have invaded his study — all which become parts of his immediate experience.

The next extension is to consider things round the corner, that is to say, things that are outside what actually confronts him. He has to be able to relate the table in the dining room, the fly on the dining room window, and his wife setting out the lunch table in relation to his present experience. If this is not too difficult a task — and it might be for it brings in the *social* idea of a wife, not to say his knowledge of her as traditional or as liberated — he is then confronted with further extensions of a more difficult nature.

Round the corner, though in a metaphorical sense, lie ideas, theories, values, and what not; and these have to be brought into relation with his immediate experience. As Berger and Luckmann put it 'society exists only as individuals are conscious of it' (p. 73) (in the same context they mention other important factors but these will concern us later).

Thus far we have a sketch of the entities that have to be brought within the purview of phenomenological experience, but now we must recognise a characteristic feature of some of these entities. It is universally accepted that the world around us and the world round the corner contain institutions as part of social reality. To reach unto an account of these requires an intermediate step and this is achieved by considering the phenomenology of roles. The contention is that roles mediate subjective meanings and their objectifications in society. Let us now turn to the conception of role.

This important conception has become prominent since the earlier writings of Sartre (and in some measure by G.H. Mead) in which he gave graphic descriptions of the nature of a role and its functioning in ordinary life, in ordinary phenomenological or existential experience. The now hackneyed example is that of a waiter in a café who plays the role of being a waiter: he is the epitomy of obsequiousness and docility, endeavouring to please, and frustrating himself with the utmost humility though there may be slender indications of a hardly betrayed smouldering resentment and contempt for his customers. A role thus depicted takes the waiter's personality to consist of this role and to exclude other roles or other personal characteristics. So far as he accepts this role, adopts it, plays himself into it, and so far as his customers pin it on to him (and indeed their attitude of thinking of him exclusively in terms of this role may facilitate the tendency in him to think of himself solely in this way), the waiter's personality becomes equated with this role alone. His role of a father, of being an enthusiast about playing dominoes, and other role activities fade out of the picture and thus his personality becomes reduced to the residual role of waiter. However, sociologists or humanists having dinner may show an interest and even enquire after the waiter's other roles or it may even occur to the casual diner without enquiring that the waiter does do other things in life. In this context the waiter becomes a congeries of roles, maybe even significant ones. The question arises at this point whether a man is a sum of roles or whether his personality is something over and above the sum total of all his roles. This is, I think, equivalent to the question whether a man is exclusively a societal creature or whether he has in him an individual characterisation not interpretable in terms of societal relationships alone. Without attempting to sort out this question now, it might be well to keep our options open by allowing the possibility that a man has an individuality other than what is made up only of societal relationships, that is to say, an individuality over and above the sum total of his roles. Nor are we concerned at this point, important though it is, with the pejorative idea of a man conceived merely as a role, so well brought out by Sartre in connection with bad faith — bad faith on the part of the waiter and of his customer in cutting him down to less than life size.

The problem arises, once the notion of role is clearly before us, of understanding how social roles develop out of the phenomenological experience of the individual, and perhaps it goes something like this. The population of a village is evacuated as a result of war, eruption of a volcano, or whatever. It is sent temporarily to a place with almost no facilities, the children play around but they have nothing to play with, and there are no tasks for people to engage in. Emergency rations are somehow made available and the population is for a short while left to its own devices. Then some adult, either a man or a woman, thinks it would be a good idea to provide the children with a little help over something to play with. He looks around for cast-off cardboard boxes and a few bits of string and, with the children, makes a few toys. He finds this acceptable and useful and extends his activities more widely next day and thus continues. The other adults recognise in this a useful benefit to the community and tacitly or overtly express their approval. The innovator has thus become recognised both by the children and by the adults as having a role: thus far a role, his 'thing', has become habitualised and recognised. I am reminded of a metaphor introduced by Popper, though in another connection: a man walks through the undergrowth for some purpose or other and in the course of doing so he tramples down the grass, so when others who have a need to go in that direction see the slightly trampled down grass they tend to go the same way and trample the grass down further. In this way a path becomes beaten out. A very real example of this has come from one of the new campuses of North America, carpeted by snow. The designers decided not to make foot-paths in the first year but to leave the virgin snow to be trampled down by the students. The students intuitively selected their most convenient routes across campus and in this way trampled out a satis-factory set of pathways, whereupon when the snows had fled the designers installed orthodox pathways in the places beaten out by the students in the snow.

Now a role, so far as it is simply carried out by an individual in a habitual way and although recognised, is thus far only partially a role; something else needs to accrue as well. The organiser of games for the children may get influenza or may die and then there is consternation both among the children and among the adults; they all agree that here is a real need and they invite someone else to take over the role temporarily if the man is ill, or permanently if he is dead. Later they may form a council and pass a legal enactment that such a role shall persist. It is evident therefore that roles need to be given persistence to be fully roles, and it would seem that this may be achieved in one or other of two ways — one by tradition, developing, growing in the way described and the other by legal enactment. But it is necessary to realise that legal enactment, though important for some of the greater roles in the society, is not an inherent necessity for a role as such, which may develop simply as a result of tradition. (And indeed some of the most important great roles in a society are a result of tradition and not actually enshrined as such by law; thus the British Constitution is an example, for though it contains many laws its basis lies largely in tradition.)

The question may be articulated, whether a role, fully developed in this way out of the individual experiences of individual people, really

10

does afford a link to something objective in social reality. It should, I think, be conceded that the example of the regular footpaths built where the snow tracks lay and the example of tradition do show in part how permanency, and thus objectivity in a social sense, arise in connection with a role. The problem may thus be seen to concern the progression from a role as a spatial activity at one time towards becoming an activity solidified through time. And a significant part of the answer lies in the alternatives, tradition and law, or a combination of them.

The transition to institutions is not far to seek, for an institution is conceived from the phenomenological angle as a set of roles; and Berger and Luckmann's account of institutions in terms of roles is a noteworthy achievement.

Are Roles Purely Individualistic?

We may now raise the question, has the phenomenological approach achieved its goal of seeing social reality entirely in terms of relationships to and between individuals?

One obvious limitation to this can be seen at the sophisticated end-result, namely where the role is enshrined by law; for the conception of law is itself a societal reality and therefore would have to be explained in terms of individualism if it is to provide content for the notion of role. Let us, however, see whether this is so in connection with tradition. It certainly looks as if the repetitions carried out by children and adults to ensure the persistence of a playgroup organiser consist simply in individual experiences crystallised into a role by repetition. But doubts are alerted at this point: might it not be that the adults, in their consternation at the loss of a playgroup leader and seeking a replacement, are expressing their *combined* sense of responsibility for the children or at least, if they are not so far advanced as this, a *corporate* sense of anxiety to get the children off their backs while they see to something else? In either case the grown-ups are seeing themselves as a band, that is as some sort of social group. They stick together, work together, have certain aims in common and this is a piece of social reality. So after all it does look as if the individual role is in part created by a piece of social reality stemming from the adults as a whole.

This point is not intended to be a fatal criticism of the phenomenological approach in the sense of showing that the approach is quite wrong-headed: it is intended to show only that there is something societal over and above the individual phenomenological experience. In other words, the phenomenologist has to recognise a duality in society: namely individuals, and roles or institutions as constituted by

11

individuals but also by something different. This structure is exactly parallel to one position attributed to Popper's form of individualism (the Watkins—Agassi version of this), though Popper himself recognises that institutions have something over and above the experience of the individual. The phenomenologists have not perhaps overtly considered this question in their own domain, but if they did so or were pressed I think they would have to settle for an additional irreducible factor with a family resemblance to Popper's.

There is a further highly interesting feature of the phenomenological approach, which has, I believe, been almost completely overlooked — a fundamental principle or premiss it shares with classical British empiricism. Classical British empiricism has always held that the basis of experience is pure observation out of which the rest of the world is somehow to be constructed, notably by induction. Classical British empiricism does not go in for the nuances of immediate personal experience in the way that phenomenology does; it is simply concerned to note broad observations and provide a scientific or metascientific apparatus for building up further knowledge upon them. The phenomenologist differs in going in for refinements concerning the immediate experience of the individual; and he gives a broader account of the experience of the individual by introducing a theory of intentionality. A further difference is that the classical British empiricist is concerned with the construction of the physical world for our *knowledge* whereas the phenomenologist is concerned to construct our *social world* (not excluding the physical world but this is not the focus of interest here). Strangely enough, although the phenomenologist has the aim, in large measure like the classical British empiricist, of taking the whole world of other persons and social reality for his province, nonetheless he has a logical problem in passing out to these further realms from his own immediate experience (at least Husserl would have this problem, though not Sartre or Merleau-Ponty). Phenomenologists have recognised that there is a real problem in obviating solipsism. This they attempt by giving new interpretations of experience, which however centre on intentionality. The notion of intentionality has the great merit of enabling the phenomenologist to go, or at least attempt to go, beyond immediate experience and therefore to jump a hurdle which the classical British empiricist was never able to surmount. In fact the intersubjective experiences of intentionality are regarded as involving a social reality that is wider than the sum of individual experience. This amounts to a theory that may very well not answer to the immediate experience of the individual. It must thus be an assumption. If so, the claim may very well beg the question, or rest upon a mediate inference about existence outside experience, or need testing in the Popperian manner. For the phenomenologist must divide up the intentional experience into the immediate experience to which he attaches intentionality and the further ramifications achieved by the intentionality; and there is no inductive process by which he could validly pass from the one to the other. In that case he is in the same logical impasse as the classical British empiricist and fundamentally shut up within the circle of his own experience. He is, however, free to use the Popperian method of testing which is not open to the classical British empiricist, who is restricted to operating with sensations; for the phenomenologist can apply the testing procedure to the object of intentionality.

We may, then, summarise the two main features of the conception of a role. One is that it constitutes mostly genuine human complexes of individual experiences which form an intermediary link in developing social institutions. The other occurs when roles of individual people become degraded, that is to say when a person becomes equated either with too few of his roles, or even equated with all of his roles but with no personality ascribed to him over and above his roles. This dehydrating of the personality has become known as 'reification' which means turning something human into a thing (it is not to be confused with the much older concept of reification in the philosophy of natural science, which was the classical procedure in science of treating abstract conceptions as realities and was a perfectly correct and normal procedure). Moreover it might be held that, though the phenomenologist has brought a wealth of illuminating commentary and detail to bear on the individual and social situation, he cannot tackle the problems of social reality in terms of individual experience alone. In other words his individualism, like other individualisms, are a most important part of any social schema we adopt but cannot be accepted as the sole basis for the social sciences, that is, as an adequate schema.

Role-conservation

So far the phenomenological enterprise is concerned with the establishment of roles and institutions as existents in relation to individual human experience. The phenomenologist is next concerned with the conservation (known in the literature as 'legitimation') of roles and institutions through time, and a good deal of attention is given to the conceptual machineries of social reality maintenance. This is carried out effectively by considering quite a number of social activities and pressures, both deliberate and unnoticed. It should be observed once again that all such procedures of conservation, whether of roles, institutions, or any feature of social reality, presuppose that the people involved in effecting these consolidations, whether deliberately or through unintended consequences, do so in the capacity of being linked into a social whole where *social reality is presupposed in this very enterprise.*

If these aspects of the phenomenological approach are dealt with fully and in simple language by Berger and Luckmann, they are in effect accepted by Holzner (1968) who handles the matter in a slightly different and briefer manner. The Berger and Luckmann exegesis is admirably suited to the beginner; Holzner's is not. Although his writing possesses a certain distinction of style and does genuinely focus on its subject matter, he does not keep the reader well signposted so as to let him know exactly where he is at any one phase of the discussion. He is, however, concerned to take the phenomenological investigation further (and in the course of doing so adds some scholarly assessment of other writers); and he uses a wider framework. One might add that these authors are concerned to develop the phenomenological construction of reality solely: they do not raise problems to be solved — simply phenomenological tasks to be accomplished.

One of Holzner's most important extensions concerns the conception of *work*. He goes into the phenomenological factors involved in the conception (not forgetting Schutz on work). He notes for example that a work-role, when differentiated from other work-roles and from other activities, establishes a degree of authority (or perhaps autonomy) and that there is a tendency to increase this authority further. Indeed he considers that work, or rather the work-role, may well be a main spring that contributes to reality-construction or to the formation of social reality. This is all in line with what has been said above, for work clearly marks out roles; but let us not forget once again that work or the work-role as socially recognised is a product of a previously existing social reality. The work-role not only builds by adding social reality but also is sustained by it.

As an addendum to the above discussion of the phenomenological approach, it is interesting to note the assessment given by a very different writer. Cohen's (1968) work in modern social theory is concerned with the overall field of sociology, aiming to depict the types of problem, to state systematically the explanatory ideas that have been propounded, and to discuss and criticise these in a systematic way. Here, however, I am concerned not with Cohen's discussion of the entire field but with his comments relevant to the present theme. He is not a phenomenologist but he does ascribe great value to what he refers to as the 'interaction approach'. One merit he points to is that it follows up unintended consequences. Cohen is surely right in drawing attention to this little-noticed feature and it is certainly a merit of the approach. Another merit is that it avoids reification, which is apt to occur with the over-stylised approaches of some classical sociologies. A third merit is that it links part of a system together, something which other approaches hardly touch. And fourthly he gives it an outstanding accolade in crediting it with giving an account of social change (one might also add that it gives an account of social conservation). This fourth achievement is most important. What it seems to me to do, however, is to provide a genuine account of one important factor in social change (and conservation) but this factor concerns individual activities only. What it does not do is establish that this is sufficient to account for social change (and conservation). It still remains an open question whether there is not also a societal factor over and above the activities of individuals and their unintended consequences.

If we consider another of Cohen's questions, namely, what holds society together, it is more than doubtful whether the phenomenological approach has anything whatever to contribute to the solution of this problem.

Dialectic

The foregoing account of the phenomenological approach would be slightly one-sided and partially inaccurate without bringing in the notion of dialectic. Neither Berger and Luckmann nor Holzner say very much about it, nor do they make very much use of it in these works. Nonetheless one can see that it is present. The term itself in this context is, I would think, debased currency. It has little or nothing to do with dialectic as understood by Plato or dialectic in a quite different sense as understood by Hegel or in the somewhat related sense used by Marx. It has to do quite simply with the inter-action between people (and doubtless also things), somewhat in the following way. One person initiates action: he does not simply follow through with an entire course of action oblivious of its effects on other people (perhaps also on inanimate objects). For these effects on other people evoke from them reactions which in turn influence or modify the further implementation of his initial course of action. Technical terms are essential tools for some jobs but in this case we have one or two perfectly good terms in English, such as interaction or interplay. The word transaction is sometimes used in this sense, but this is to give it a technical meaning which it does not bear in its ordinary usage. Need one really go beyond the word 'interplay'?

If we now look back over the account given above of the phenomenological approach we can see that beating out a path through the snow, which initiates the formation of a role, involves interplay between persons and so on right through. If Berger and Luckmann say 'society is a human product, society is an objective reality' (p. 58) and '. . . society exists only as individuals are conscious of it' (p. 73), we must not overlook the other half of these quotations, which are 'man is a social product' (p. 58) and '. . . individual consciousness is socially determined' (p. 73).

Thus, it would be an inadequate portrayal of their view to depict it as asserting that roles, institutions, and social reality are constructed simply out of individual experiences. Although they would hold this view, they also hold that the interplay or, if you like, the feedback (to draw on a concept from cybernetics), is vitally involved in the construction of social reality. And the reason why it is so important to do justice to this point is that, on the phenomenological thesis, the interplay (or dialectic) would be regarded as taking care of the problem of constructing social reality out of the experiences of individuals alone, without taking into account an independent societal factor as well. It may be questioned whether even the interplay thus conceived does the trick, but at least it should be made clear that the phenomenologists put it forward for this purpose, and even if they are wrong it is not with the object of evading an issue. In my opinion they are not sufficiently alive to the issue, that is to say, they do not press home the question upon themselves whether the interplay is sufficient to explain the coming into being of social reality without resort to a further societal factor.

It will be seen that on the foregoing interpretation the phenomenological approach is fundamentally an individualism. I have called Popper's schema a *situational individualism*; the phenomenological version (which is very closely allied to his and, as far as it goes, should be acceptable to him) I would call *interplay individualism*.

Interpretative Interactionism

There are two versions I wish to consider here: (a) a doctrine called 'symbolic interactionism' due to Blumer (1969), though he claims only to have put in a new form certain points made by numerous authors; and (b) a doctrine called 'ethnomethodology' due to Garfinkel (1967), but which in effect fairly subsumes the numerous works of Goffman (see Posner and Craig). I find Blumer's designation not expressive of what he wants, and I have substituted one that does some justice to his view. The same title, I think, captures a central part of what might be called Garfinkel's and Goffman's 'street-corner' sociology.

16

Interpretative Interaction. Blumer's first point could hardly arouse any opposition, though he seems to have thought he had to struggle for it: that things — inkstands or pennies — are what they *mean* for us, and we act towards them on the basis of those meanings. Strangely, he says '. . . this simple view is ignored or played down in practically all of the thought and work in contemporary science and psychological science' (Blumer, 1969, p. 2), though later he alludes to unconscious motives and mentions several other approaches that surely share the above view. The strangest fact of all is that, among the long list of ancestors he names for his approach, he omits the two most influential — Freud and Malinowski — for whom meaning was the first item of paramount importance, the one in the psychology of the individual, the other in anthropology.

What Blumer is getting at is that a thing has no meaning in itself outside a human social context. A visitor from Mars might regard a penny as a wedge, a bullet, or nothing more than an oddity of nature. This leads to Blumer's second point which, for some, will modify the first: the meaning of a thing arises from *social interaction* — a penny being offered for a box of matches or being given in change for too large a payment. There would no doubt be philosophers for whom the meaning would be given by one person alone, but for Blumer this is not so.

Next, Blumer does not regard the world as consisting solely of such meanings; they are subject to change, being modified interpretatively by a person dealing with the things (meanings) he encounters. Thus a motorcycle, which has the meaning of a method of getting about quickly and less tiringly, may later acquire for its owner the further meaning of something dangerous or something that gets one a ticket from a policeman and a fine. Thus, in addition to the meaning that arises through the interactions of social processes, a person *handles* these meanings in the light of his situation and the direction of his action. Moreover, a person, in handling meanings, is *interacting with himself*. So it would seem that, in developing the meaning of his motorcycle and thence getting a fine, the reception of the fine is part of himself with which he is now interacting.

Wider Groups. So far we have Blumer's development of interpretative meaning. It is a small step for him to compound social interaction and various lines of social interaction and their interconnections into the notion of a human group, which involves a reference to other persons and indeed also to their situations. Thus 'fundamentally human groups or society *exists in action* [author's italics and grammar] and must be seen in terms of action. This picture of human society as action must be the starting point' for any empirical scheme. He puts it very succinctly: 'Joint or collective action is an outcome of such a process of interpretative interaction' (Blumer, 1969, p. 16). Broadly, culture and social structure are 'derived' from what people do. In using the term 'derive' I presume that Blumer has in mind that groups, society, culture, structure or whatever are, so to speak, complexes of social interaction; but I believe that this would be better rendered not by 'derived' but by 'constructed'.

Having reached a construct of society, Blumer considers other matters that fill out the basics of human behaviour. Thus, '. . . social interaction is a process that forms human conduct instead of being merely a means or a setting for the expression or release of human conduct' (Blumer, 1969, p. 8). He does not explain why it should not be both, though in that case one could understand why he would wish to place predominance on the former. He also cites Mead, in the context of gestures, on the fact that people take on each other's roles (this is the nearest he comes to recognising what psychoanalysts know as 'projective identification' and 'introjective identification') and speaks, too, of 'possessing a self', thus turning the self into an object for oneself, much as Sartre might put it. Also somewhat reminiscent of Sartre, he considers that people do not *react* to other's actions but 'define' them, that is, mediate them by inserting an interpretation between stimulus and response.

Blumer's Metascience.   Blumer (1969, pp. 26—33, 91) goes on to make some mostly well directed attacks on various forms of metascience, with the apparent objective of producing another prop for his own view of individual and collective activities. This is therefore a convenient point at which to turn to his individualism.

Like Popper, he holds that 'collectivities' emerge from joint action, without identifying the individuals. Thus interpretative interaction

> . . . sees social action as consisting of the individual and collective activities of people who are engaged in social interaction — that is to say, activities whose own formation is made up in the light of the activity of one another. (Blumer, 1969, p. 54)

> . . . the essence of society lies in an ongoing process of action — not in a posited structure of relations. (Blumer, 1969, p. 71)

> There is no empirically observable entity in human society that does not spring from some acting unit. (Blumer, 1969, p. 85)

And he denies that action stems from shared values (here, I presume that means that this is not the basic explanation of action, for one would suppose that some action can arise in this way). However, this is subsidiary to the thrust towards individualism at this point, as has been illustrated in several quotations (Blumer, 1969, pp. 6, 16, 54, 71, 85).

The qualification to be made to his individualism lies in the *social* interaction that endows things with meaning — much as we saw that the pure phenomenologist, in his turn, presupposed a *context* at some point that encompasses more than the individual. Nonetheless, like the phenomenologist, the interpretative interactionist places the main weight of his social construction upon the individual.

Ethnomethodology or 'Street-Corner Sociology'

Preliminary account of ethnomethodology. Garfinkel (1967) put forward an approach under the banner of 'ethnomethodology'; the term is not explicitly explained, but it appears to refer to a methodology, in the sense of an orientation or ideology (rather than metascience), that focuses on the activities of people (all people, races). Be that as it may, he is at odds with Durkheim (Garfinkel's treatment of his ideas comes over to me as outmoded lumber), on whom is pinned (though without conceptual discrimination about what he had in mind and perhaps more importantly, what he was excluding) the doctrine of the unqualified *objective* reality of social *facts*.

The contrast made lies in the orientation or weltanschauung that '. . . the objective reality of social facts *as* an *ongoing* accomplishment of the concerted activities of daily life' (Garfinkel, 1967, p. vii, my italics), i.e. the essence of a social fact lies in its being 'observable and reportable' (Garfinkel, 1967, p. 1); the author wants to substitute 'indexical' expressions — which act as signposts to other related expressions in a context — for 'objective' expressions which the author takes to be 'context-free'.

Illustration. Garfinkel writes at great length, in sentences which are objectively clear, of considerable length, and highly abstract. It is impossible to know what it all means without an illustration; most 'writing workshops' would insist that one should be put near the beginning. But there is no need to despair; when the reader may have given up all hope, suddenly and unexpectedly there appears a good, clear, full and adequate illustration (although it is doubtful whether many readers — apart from the indoctrinated who will not need to do so — will resolutely turn back to re-read what the illustration should endow with life). In the left-hand column is a report of a commonplace conversation, in terms of what was actually said, say, about a member of the family on returning from a visit to the shops. Its main characteristic is that it is constantly *allusive* or elliptical, for the hearer will automatically mentally supply some of the details required to make full sense of it. Reference to a parking meter may reveal to the hearer an actual gap and he may wish to ask which of two shops was visited first. Students may be given the exercise of filling in a full, or fuller, account in the right-hand column, to include what the hearer automatically supplies (Garfinkel, 1967, pp. 25–6, 27, 38–9).

To do this is apparently to do ethnomethodology. It is perhaps not reasonable to expect to be told how to rank students' abilities: one would have difficulty in distinguishing a B, B+, and A student; indeed anyone capable of getting into a university should score a B in ethnomethodology without trouble. Nevertheless, if the mysteries of society can be laid bare with great ease, that should be applauded. Still, it would be interesting to see what the different answers scoring a B and an A+ would look like!

The Messages. What, however, do we learn from ethnomethodology? Students learn that the spinning out of a report never succeeds in completing it, no matter how much it is gone over and added to; gaps simply multiply. The moral of this discovery is not explained.

They also learn to distinguish *what* was actually *said* from the *content* that was in fact *talked about.*

> *What the parties said* [which could be picked up by a tape-recorder] would be treated as a sketchy, partial, incomplete, masked, elliptical, concealed, ambiguous, or misleading version of *what the parties talked about.* (Garfinkel, 1967, p. 27)

To do this it would be necessary to use one's knowledge of the parties, of their shared backgrounds, of their relationships, and of the parties' *situation.*

Now Garfinkel is not satisfied with this account and suggests another which concerns exclusively *how* the parties were speaking; he suggests that in being asked for ever more descriptive fillings, the students were in fact being asked for an 'adverbial' answer to describe the manner in which the parties spoke. Thus 'your shoes need heeling' may be said narratively, metaphorically, and so on. Hence the appropriate image of a shared understanding is not overlapping knowledge but a process.

What Street-Corner Sociology Concludes. Ethnomethodology is the study of practical actions: to search among an infinity of possibilities to locate the project of an action, after leaving aside standard categories of discourse, to present the project in a recordable, reportable or, in a word, *accountable* way.

I would venture to sum up ethnomethodology as the adverbial elaboration of the accountability of what actually happens in the social world.

What is it for? It is a sociological end-in-itself, which brings out that social reality is an *ongoing process* — this is a fundamental phenomenon.

Since the term 'ethnomethodology' is a misnomer, I suggest instead 'street-corner sociology' since, whatever sophisticated areas it may be applied to, it begins with verbal interactions in the home or the marketplace.

Comments. Garfinkel (1967, p. viii) disclaims any interest in other methodologies and their quarrels with ethnomethodology; he considers the sole interest these may possess is as phenomena for ethnomethodological study. In this, he is being quick on the draw, for it is probable that several other sociologies and psychologies would immediately react in this way, and regard ethnomethodology as having so little content and to suffer from such other major defects, that the sociological or psychological problem is to understand how ethnomethodology ever got a footing, let alone a place of distinction, in the learned world (if that is indeed the world into which it gained an entrée).

Gellner (1975) has taken the trouble to bring all his big guns to bear on it and its cognates. Goffman's numerous works would seem to do no more than add to the same, with no difference of idea, only style (though it must not be overlooked that in this half of the twentieth century style often counts for everything). The interested reader may be referred to two extremely able and opposite critiques of Goffman (Posner, 1978; Craig, 1978).

Here I have merely three points to make: a general evaluation; an analysis of its central approach; and its failure to attain the status of a sociological theory — of hardly counting as sociology at all.

1 Street-corner sociology (Garfinkel, Goffman) does well to emphasise the complexity of social rubbing shoulders. Certainly too many sociologists and psychologists have disregarded it — even been oblivious of it for too long. What it has achieved, however, need not be exaggerated. To say 'parturiunt montes rediculus mus' would be a most unfair exaggeration; but it would be reasonable to say 'parturiunt montes sterilis mus'. Moreover, from the sociological point of view, street-corner sociology is essentially

absorbed, or could be made an additional chapter in Blumer's interpretative interactionism. From the viewpoint of other social sciences, there is nothing in street-corner sociology that would come as a surprise to Freud or to Malinowski: after all Freud's method of asking for associations to dream-items was an overt admission that he did not know the context of such items until the patient told him. And Malinowski's whole work, centring on functionalism, was in effect contextualism.

2 As with phenomenology and with interpretative interactionism, street-corner sociology is fundamentally individualistic. Certainly, there is a context, and it is a social context; there is a situation, and it is a social situation, in that all the unalluded-to components of meaning shared by the parties are part of a social context. Each could perhaps be given an individualistic reduction, or explained in terms of other people's actions, but there always remains a social setting. Nonetheless the emphasis in street-corner sociology is heavily on the side of individualism.

3 The most important point made was to characterise street-corner sociology mainly as a species of individualism. The most important criticism is that it ends where a science of society begins: having found out in great detail *what actually happens*, to reveal what is shared in interpersonal experience, the real problem opens up — as with Blumer's interpretative interactionism — of seeking a sociological theory to explain such findings. It is not a sociology but social experience in search of a sociology.

Social Exchange

This is virtually a school, or sub-school, that bases itself on the notion of exchange. This could be questionable if this schema were restricted solely to individualism; but we will return to that after explaining the notion and its development.

Social exchange probably originated in Simmel (1950). He was individualistic in that he mentions the possibility 'that ultimately it is the human individuals that are the true realities'. But, although he does not accept this, he continues: 'Groping for the tangible, we find only individuals; and between them, a vacuum, as it were' (quoted by Blau (1964, p. 11) from Simmel, 1950). Simmel's intention of constructing social reality by means of exchange between individuals would seem to be given expression in:

> All contacts among men rest on the schema of giving and returning the equivalence [? the equivalent] (quoted by Blau). Exchange is the objectification of human interaction. (Simmel, 1950, p. 388)

If Simmel founded the line of thought, it was widely stressed by Homans (1950) who, however, does not seem to have abstracted its main ideas. The clearest presentation, often with neat formulations, though the work as a whole is turgid and inordinately long for its purpose, is that given by Blau (1964), and I will follow his account briefly.

Exchange is any kind of social transaction in which, when one person facilitates another in some way, this is followed by a return of the favour in however different a form by the other person. Thus if a man gives a lift to a colleague for a few days while the colleague's car is out of order, the colleague may take some of his workload off his benefactor. The 'repayment' has to appear intuitively to be roughly equal to the original service. Presumably negative favours work the same way, as in vendettas.

The individualism involved comes out in this:

> To speak of social life is to speak of the associations between people . . . (Blau, 1964, p. 12)

Blau's task is to derive the social processes that govern complex societies from the simpler ones that govern individuals and their inter-personal relations. His approach would thus seem to be strongly individualistic; but this is considerably modified by his contention that there are significant *emergent* properties of social life, which cannot be reduced to individual behaviour. The task of the exchange schema is to explain social phenomena — social relations and, in particular, power. Thus:

> Forces of social attraction stimulate exchange transactions. Social ex-change, in turn, tends to give rise to differentiation of status and power. Further processes emerge . . . that lead to legitimation and organization . . . and to opposition and change. (p. 14)

Thus:

> . . . exchanges of benefits shape the structure of social relations. (p. 18)

> The simpler social processes that can be observed in interpersonal associations and that rest directly on psychological dispositions give rise to the more complex social processes that govern structures of inter-connected social associations [for example, political or in the factory]. (pp. 19—20)

Further there exists the power to command compliance:

> A person can establish superiority over others by overwhelming them with

benefits they cannot possibly repay and thus subduing them with the weight of their obligations to him. (p. 113)

Moreover:

Exchange processes . . . give rise to differentiation of power. (p. 22)

Blau elaborates on what happens when a recipient has nothing to offer when an exchange-repayment is appropriate!

Collective approval of power legitimates that power. (p. 23)

On the other hand:

There is a strain toward imbalance as well as toward reciprocity in social associations. (p. 26)

In addition, Blau has an interesting commentary on groups and the relations of a group to its members, in particular new members.

In developing how social phenomena are produced from individual exchange, Blau distinguishes his results into the development of integration, differentiation, organisation, and opposition; the first two arising unplanned, the second two from organised efforts promoting collective objectives. In sum:

Social exchange has been defined by two criteria, associations largely to extrinsic rather than purely intrinsic rewards and reciprocal rather than unilateral transactions. (p. 328)

He adds that he considers that the whole process involves an element of 'dialectic'.

Every detail so far spells individualism; every social phenomenon is depicted as growing out of individual exchange. However, there are explicit denials to the contrary. Thus, according to Simmel (1950, p. 54),

One [problem] is the fact that the individual has to function as part of a collective for which he lives; but that, in turn, he derives his own values and improvements from this collective. The other is the fact that the life of the individual is a roundabout route for the purposes of the whole; but the life of the whole, in turn, has this same function for the purposes of the individual.

Homans would probably agree. Blau is also explicit that:

> Emergent properties are essentially relationships between elements in a structure. The relationships are not contained in the elements, though they could not exist without them, and they define the structure. (p. 3)

If this qualification reflects a real part of his view, then it is not pure individualism — it has a partner. Although I include the present schema under individualism, I do so with some hesitation therefore; but I do so because it is not made clear at what point, nor how, the notion of emergent property is actually used. (If I should be mistaken, then there would be one less individualistic schema than I had thought.)

Comment

1   There is no doubt that the notion of social exchange picks out an enormously important element in social life. It clearly characterises social life universally. Indeed, one can scarcely conceive of social life without it.
2   If so, the inherent nature of social exchange becomes *a theorem* about social life, which renders it a defining characteristic or — more reasonably — a logical consequence of more basic characteristics. And Blau hints at such a conclusion when he discourses on exchange arising out of attractive qualities in persons (in the sense of being likely to provide benefits) (Blau, 1964, pp. 19, 20, 21, 33, 43, 57). Perhaps human exchange is better thought of as an *aspect* of human interaction, though not the overriding characteristic of it.
3   If so, such potential benefactors can be recognised by individuals *by previous experience*. By previous experience where? In social life. Hence the notion of social exchange would seem to *presuppose* that of social life.
4   Hence social exchange, while undoubtedly of considerable explanatory power, itself requires social explanation.
5   Moreover, social life (as a whole) would seem to be conceived of here as a holistic, perhaps emergent, property not derived from the actions and so on of individuals — certainly not from the individual exchange relationship without a circle in the reasoning.
6   Of the various, and moderately numerous, forms of individualism, there is no way provided for accepting the exchange schema rather than one of the others. They may indeed not really be rivals, but may presuppose, or at least require, one another. Thus social exchange must surely presuppose social meaning as portrayed by Blumer's interpretative interactionism.

I would make two points in closing. First, although it is no part of my objective to assess the relative merits of those schemata, I have the impression that interpretative interactionism seems to be the best of them, since it is presupposed by all the others; though it would be strengthened by an infusion of each. Second, they do not seem to function completely on their own, without presupposing, though not very explicitly, an emergent or a holistic type of schema.

References

Berger, Peter and Luckmann, Thomas (1966), *The Social Construction of Reality*, Doubleday, New York.

Blau, P.M. (1964) *Exchange and Power in Social Life*, Wiley, New York.

Blumer, Herbert (1969), *Symbolic Interactionism*, Prentice-Hall, Englewood Cliffs, New Jersey.

Cohen, Percy S. (1968), *Modern Social Theory*, Heinemann, London.

Craig, Ian (1978), 'Erving Goffman: Frame Analysis', *Philosophy of the Social Sciences*, *8*, pp. 79–86.

Garfinkel, Harold (1967), *Ethnomethodology*, Prentice-Hall, Englewood Cliffs, New Jersey.

Gellner, Ernest (1975), 'Ethnomethodology: the re-enchantment industry or the Californian way of subjectivity', *Philosophy of the Social Sciences*, *5*, pp. 431–50.

Goffman, Erving, any work of.

Holzner, Burkhart (1968), *Reality Construction in Society*, Schenkmann, Cambridge, Mass.

Homans, G.C. (1950), *The Human Group*, Harcourt Brace, New York.

Merleau-Ponty, Maurice (1962), *The Phenomenology of Perception*, Routledge, London.

Posner, Judith (1978), 'Erving Goffman: his presentation of self', *Philosophy of the Social Sciences*, *8*, pp. 67–78.

Schutz, Alfred (1962), *The Problem of Social Reality, Collected Papers I*, Nijhoff, den Haag.

Simmel, Georg (1950), *The Sociology of Georg Simmel*, Free Press, New York.

3 Kuhn's thesis of incommensurability

In 1962 Kuhn produced a work of small size but of considerable importance which opened a new chapter in the philosophy of science in general. However, in the face of a barrage of criticism, he retracted various aspects of his thesis, which served only to weaken his work, make it less interesting and, I would think, less valuable. I propose to adhere to the original version as the one most worthy of discussion. Kuhn has also had followers — perhaps more properly described as colleagues — who wrote about the same time. But apart from other possible considerations, on the grounds of accuracy or scholarship alone, it seems to me that Kuhn provides the most viable presentation of the general point of view involved and I shall restrict myself to it. Moreover, Kuhn has personally had an influence far outside science and the philosophy of science in that his work has been taken up by numerous social scientists, and it is precisely this that makes his work relevant here. Such an outcome may be surprising in view of Kuhn's history for he began as a physicist; he was a real practising scientist in the hardest of the 'hard' sciences. He understood very well what it was like to be a real scientist and therefore took account of features of real science as it is actually practised in a way that is usually totally absent from writings by historians and philosophers of science in general. So much for various factors that render Kuhn of considerable importance quite apart from the problem that occupied him and his thesis. What then were his problem and his thesis?

Like many another, Kuhn's attention was attracted to the fact that one great theory may reign for a long time and then fall into disrepute, decay, or failure, and become replaced by another great theory. The great contemporary example of this is, of course, the replacement of Newtonian celestial mechanics by Einstein after a reign of 239 years. Like many another, Kuhn probably assumed initially that the outgoing theory was found wanting and that it was therefore given up on rational grounds by all scientists. Such an approach would have been reinforced by the fact that the new meta-science emanating from Popper (1959) had gained considerable influence in quite a short time (for although Popper's work had originally been published in 1934 it was not translated into English for many years and the English-speaking world was relatively ignorant of Popper's views and sometimes knew of them only in a somewhat distorted form). At this point, we are not concerned with the detail of Popper's views; what we are concerned with is a very central contention in his metascience, namely that scientific theories (that is, general theories) as contrasted with all non-scientific ideas, can be characterised quite accurately and precisely as *empirically testable*. This means that deductive chains of reasoning can be constructed from the theory under consideration, ending up either in empirical generalisations or in straightforward particular observations which can be checked by observation or by experiment (that is, by the observation made during an experiment). In short, scientific theories are testable by observation. Following on this contention is its cognate that testability consists, in fact, not in verification or in confirmation — which according to Popper serve no useful purpose at all — but in refutation or falsification. And that completes the central statement of Popper's revolutionary idea. Thus, to be scientific, a theory must have the seeds of falsifiability within it. That is to say, if the theory is false, it must be possible to show this by observation, and if the theory is not false, it is necessary to be able to show what situation *would* disclose its falsity *had* it actually been so.

With these factors, the general behaviour of scientists and Popper's influential metascience, Kuhn faced a world of science in which the changeover from one theory to another was accomplished by giving up a false theory in favour of a new one that offered better hopes. Now, Kuhn came to doubt this version of scientific progress, and, although he does not explain why, I will provide a possible conjecture about what influenced him, which may help the reader even if it may happen to be wrong.

Living in the world of great science Kuhn would have realised that theories live long after they had been shown up as false. Sensing that scientists did not like to give up theories, he would have further realised that they would go to considerable lengths and indulge in some very hard work to patch them up and save them. He would also have realised that eminent scientists would go to very bizarre lengths at times to invent circumstances of a wholly unknown kind that would be such as to save the theory, and came to see all this as 'a stage of crisis'. After the crisis had been around for some time, with no such satisfactory resolution appearing, a sense of dis-illusionment would set in and sometimes a new theory would appear that would solve the problems of the old theory or at least offer considerable promise of doing so. It might produce new problems in its turn; nonetheless, there would be a new sense of optimism or progress and the success of the new theory was certain to oust the old one, with the new one becoming increasingly accepted on 'a bandwagon effect' and the old one becoming a mere matter of history. As Kuhn portrays it, this changeover was not based on a fully rational consideration of evidence, in the sense of one theory being rationally weighed against another; it was sociological — that is, a development in the sociology of science — in which a number of scientifico-sociological factors influenced the minds of the principal scientists of the day (and the minds of those who joined the band-wagon in their wake), although rational factors would also be taken into account.

It is convenient to summarise this development and way of looking at scientific matters as a modern version of the conventionalist approach. Conventionalism is quite an old doctrine of metascience in which defects in a theory are cured, not by developing a new theory but by altering the conventions under which the terms and meaning of the theory as a whole are understood. Proof, on that view, is a matter of convention and one obtains serviceable theories by manipulating the conventions. Kuhn's theory is perhaps more extreme than the classical version for, according to him, scientists simply replace one theory conventionally by another one in what would appear to be a slap-happy fashion.

Because of its relation to the social scientist, I am calling this the conventionalist aspect of Kuhn's theory for convenience and for its conventional spirit, but it does not reflect the whole of Kuhn's own view. He is not entirely happy with the conventionalist approach because he does retain, at the back of his mind, some degree of belief that rationality does ultimately play a part in science and in the acceptance of scientific theories. Kuhn tries very hard to show how the rational factors can, in fact, play a part, although in this he is not, I would say, terribly successful. He has the inordinately dif-ficult, if not logically impossible,[1] task of marrying rationality to social influence. There is a real problem here: it is a very deep one, and it would be unfair to cavil at Kuhn for not having found the answer to so formidable a question. In his attempt he is faced with a dilemma. Either the rationality factor totally determines the outcome of a conflict between an old theory and a new one, or it does so only partially. If the former, then he has not added a new metascience at all but would be following the scientists' classical procedure and Popper's metascience. If the latter, then so far as rational factors do not dominate, what is it that does determine the outcome? The answer is the only other possible factor that he is discussing, namely the sociological one; and then, in the event of a clash between the rational factors and the sociological factors, if the latter are the ones that gain acceptance, then the decision is one that finally clashes with rationality. Kuhn seems to find this dilemma wholly insuperable. I will call this aspect of Kuhn's theory for convenience the 'democratic criterion of scientific truths'.

These two aspects of Kuhn's metascientific view have not carried equal weight in the sociological world of social scientists. This world is one in which, in accordance with most contemporary thought, is happy with doctrines of cultural relativism, non-absolute truths, the feeling that science is arid and inappropriate to the understanding of human beings, human nature, and society, and in general one that is quite glad to see real science put on one side. Thus Kuhn's work has apparently proved a godsend to social scientists who have somehow got the message, that is the first message, which I have called the conventionalist aspect. It would be interesting to investigate how this has won such widespread acceptance. For not many of those who have been influenced by Kuhn have actually read him, at least with care and understanding, so presumably the influence stems from those few who have read him — perhaps with understanding, perhaps without — or possibly the influence has stemmed simply from a perusal of reviews. But there is no indication that those social scientists impressed by Kuhn are in the least aware of the depths of his scientific education and scientific understanding. Moreover, there is no indication at all that social scientists are aware of the second component which, for convenience, I have labelled the democratic criterion of acceptability. In other words, they do not seem to realise that Kuhn struggled very hard to preserve objectivity in science, failed by only a short head, and possibly would not be willing to concede that he had really failed — and that his intention was to save rationality for science. The overall impression is that social scientists find Kuhn a very convenient stick with which to beat science.

We turn now to wider developments. I think it is fair to say that the most important implication which is drawn from Kuhn, both by himself as well as by social scientists, but certainly by social scientists themselves, is that theories are *incommensurable*. This is another way of expressing the conventionalist approach to science. For if one convention is in principle as good as another one, so that it is only a matter of adopting the convention that happens to suit, then there is no way in which two conventions can be compared — that is to say, compared for actual *truth*. Truth as a real goal of science simply does not figure in this approach. A broader way of expressing this effect is that one may hold any theory that appears satisfactory to oneself, and that there is no way of criticising it, because there is no true view against which one might attempt to compare and criticise it. And so in the end it comes to being a case of 'anything goes'. This slang slogan reflects a widespread attitude found in many countries in the contemporary world, attacking infringements of citizens' rights, corruption, Watergate, or in times past, the Lord Chancellor Bacon's acceptance of bribes. There can be no argument about most of these occurrences. The banner that claims to stand up for them goes back far in the history of philosophy: it stems from the days of the Greeks, when Protagoras enunciated the doctrine 'Man is the measure of all things', which Feyerabend transforms into 'anything goes'. We have interestingly progressed, in 2400 years, from Protagoras' 'Man is the measure of all things' to Kuhn's and Feyerabend's 'democratic conventionalism' more popularly known as 'anything goes'.

The reason why this appeals to some social scientists is that for a considerable time in the past, though I think it has disappeared for several decades now, it was the custom for the western world to look down on backward peoples as savage, uncivilised, immoral, having no sense of decency even, as a kind of children who had to be educated in western ways. Such a view began to disappear in the first decade or two of this century when Malinowski went into the field and found out what primitives were actually like, and gradually most, perhaps all, of these pejoratives have been dropped. This was achieved long before supposedly emancipating conclusions emerged from Kuhn. There would seem to have been a further reason for the current development, rooted not simply on ignorance of the achievements of social anthropology but rooted also in a political wish to have a stick to beat ourselves with, or at least our élite. The incommensurability thesis enables a social scientist to say that we are no better than they in any respect whatsoever. We cannot compare our way of life with theirs or rather compare their way of life with ours. Theirs is equally valid; and behind this lies the motif that so far as there is any incentive to criticise primitives that only adds fuel to the surge of criticism of our own establishment.

In criticising the doctrine of incommensurability, it is proper to add one further value which has accrued as a result of it; namely, that it may make the paperback reader at large more aware of the relatedness of man to man whether the other man is a primitive or a western millionaire. As social or political propaganda it may have played a useful part. As serious sociology, that is another matter.

The question finally arises whether the intellectual claim of incommensurability can be substantiated or criticised effectively.

Incommensurability means that circles of values that form one whole cannot be compared, contrasted, or criticised by another circle of integrated values. Expressed thus, in a very general form, the doctrine looks overwhelmingly obvious. It seems, for example, that there can be no meeting point between the capitalist West and the non-capitalist East. But when one considers more modest circles of values, the same notion of incommensurability is supposed to apply, though it may not then appear to be so convincing. For instance the circle of values that animates women's liberation is different from the circle of values that has hitherto animated men. Are they merely incomparable? Men have given way to argument and to force and done so in practical ways. If they understood the value system of women's liberation as little as they understand the values of the dinosaur this would clearly be unlikely. Or take the value system of the trades unions and the value systems of the entrepreneurs. These two have clashed, criticised one another, come to terms, separated again, clashed again, and had to work out differences, but had to admit in practice some overlap of values — some commensurability. There are in the world today some very striking admissions of commensurability between some of the world's great religions which had hitherto looked upon themselves as completely incommensurable with any other. Is classical music incommensurable with jazz? If so, strangely, there have been many people who have enjoyed both without appearing to be obviously schizophrenic.

The general question raised is whether there is any conceptual system in the world at all that is or has to be accepted by everybody no matter what other different value systems or incommensurable systems he believes he has (Popper, 1959; Kuhn 1962). Put this way it looks as if we can only give way to despair. How can one ever find anything upon which all people necessarily must agree? You might say everybody must agree on the principle of non-contradiction. Indeed personally I would think this is so; but if you try it out you would find a certain number of social scientists who will, through a misunderstanding of one kind or another, claim that it is untrue, that there are important systems of sociology in which it plays no part. Although I think they are unscholarly in this claim, and making an intellectual mistake, nonetheless they do make this sort of claim.

For good measure I will put forward a unifying framework to serve as a weltanschauung for universal acceptance. It is: 'change occurs'.[2]

Notes

1 I would think that the two factors, rationality and social influence, cannot be combined into a single determinant, if they are treated as parallel influences on the same level; but that they could be, if one is regarded as contributory on a different level, that is, contributory to the other taken to be decisive.
2 The learned may point out that there has been a highly distinguished Greek philosopher to challenge even this, namely Parmenides. But there is reason to doubt that he meant what we would mean by it. So I think it may serve.

References

Kuhn, T.S. (1962), *The Structure of Scientific Revolutions*, University of Chicago Press, Chicago.

Popper, K.R. (1959), *The Logic of Scientific Discovery*, London and New York.

4 The interpersonalist revolt against positivism

The recent movement of the social sciences, or more particularly of sociology, rooted in a humanistic approach is not altogether surprising. It assumes several different forms to which brief allusion may be made. Broadly speaking, the emphasis is on people and inter-actions with other people, and the most pervasive philosophical approach underlying this is phenomenology. Although phenomeno-logy began as a philosophical doctrine with Husserl and is best known these days from the work of a more recent philosopher, Merleau-Ponty, it has become detached from its philosophical moorings in detail though not in content, and is being developed by sociologists, notably by Berger and Luckmann and by Holzner. Their aim is to show how society can be phenomenologically built up, conceptually speaking, from the experiences of the individual human being. Another line from Husserl develops via Schutz to Garfinkel's ethnomethodology. A further variant here is symbolic interactionism, developed notably by Blumer. These developments place a huge amount of emphasis upon the interaction between human beings as contrasted with the more classical phenomenology, which, though it did not leave this out of account, laid the most stress upon the experience of each individual. If Blumer's work is more theoretical, the lived day-to-day experience of interplay between individuals is depicted in numerous contexts by Garfinkel and also, though differently, by Goffman. The term, *interpersonalism*, which I have chosen, is now clear: it *represents the stress on the interplay between various persons*. The reason for the stress is that while traditional sociology does often and importantly concern literal interactions between persons such as stealing a pocket-book or passing the salt, most forms of interaction are more personal, and according to the new trends constitute a different world of reality from that depicted by traditional approaches.

The current emphasis on the notion of class-conflicts indicates a somewhat different direction. It is concerned with conflict; it is concerned with conflict as a group- or community- or societal phenomenon; it holds that this is an inevitable feature of society; and it holds this as something not necessarily to be deprecated but that may be creative. This development in sociology is more societal in its approach, that is, in dealing with systems of people rather than in being purely phenomenological and rooted in individuals alone; nonetheless it pays great attention to what happens to individuals in all this. It therefore shares with the phenomenological approach and that of symbolic interactionism the attitude of taking human beings seriously. Whatever may be the deficiencies of any or all of these approaches, they are surely right to bring in fully the significance of the role of the individual and the significance of interplay between individuals, and the significance of conflict not only between individuals but when individuals become grouped.

Because the overall movement or the family of movements seems to be somewhat wider than that of phenomenology alone, but involves a broader notion — a sort of humanist interactionism — that I have used the wider title of interpersonalism. This is a deliberately vague term though not, of course, so vague or wishy-washy as, say, humanism; it is the nearest general name I can find that contains reasonable specificity to cover the broad approach that I have just attempted to describe.

Now this approach doubtless owed something to boredom with the kind of sociology that had been going on for some decades, which sometimes gave the impression of investigating social phenomena for no particular reason, in the light of no particular theory, to establish nothing outside itself beyond the factual information it unearthed — and throwing no light on the fundamental problems of social structure, social change, and so forth. The most important source is the sense that the world constituted by interpersonalist relations cannot be studied at all by traditional procedures. Thus there is opposition to natural science. But one very great influence that has stimulated this approach was opposition to logical positivism; and as we shall see this is a clear case of a weltanschauung leading to a whole new development in the sociological field. However, it is lugubrious to find a plethora of misunderstanding of logical positivism in the minds of many sociologists. This is not to say that logical positivism can be vindicated, for it cannot; but the kinds of misunderstanding involved lead to a considerable expenditure of time on misunderstandings and on discussions of a scholastic nature. And more important even than this is that the misunderstandings can and do hamper proper scientific investigation in the social field. We may consider this first.

Logical Positivism and Science

The most insidious mistake of all is that *logical positivism is quite widely taken to be the approach of natural science*, in other words logical positivism is taken to represent 'hard' science, to leave out persons in actual fact, and to leave them out inevitably — in principle. At least their humanity is left out; they are simply cameras, recorders, or calculators. With this is coupled the scientific stress on objectivity; and as a result objectivity gets a bad name. The quick conclusion arrived at by many social thinkers of humanist bent is that objectivity stands in their way and must be thrown overboard in any living investigation of the vital nature of social relations in human society.

As regards the justice of their view they certainly have a point: for they have picked out something of the weltanschauung of logical positivism and have even picked out something of the weltanschauung of traditional natural science, even though the conception of logical positivism portrayed could hardly be picked out in an identity parade by philosophers who know that field. Taking logical positivism to represent the nature of natural science is damaging, because it actually would prevent natural science from being applicable to human beings, when natural science itself is quite easily adaptable so as to apply to human beings and society without in the least depersonalising them.

To bring out all these features requires a statement of twentieth-century logical positivism. It began in Vienna in the 1920s with the simple aim of undermining all metaphysics and theology — undermining them not merely to render them false but as *meaningless*, making no sense at all. That summarises the negative aim; the positive aim was to replace the stream of hot air that was accounted metaphysics by a positive natural science account of phenomena.

The notion of positive is somewhat perplexing, but I think it can be understood against the body of metaphysics and theology that logical positivism was out to sink: metaphysics and theology, whatever else they may be, are concerned with and presuppose entities that are altogether beyond the reach of sensory knowledge. In liquidating such studies, a replacement by contrast was almost bound to consist of whatever is present in sensory knowledge — what is, in one form or another, counted as observation. Here logical positivism reverted to an Aristotelian adage which was iterated repeatedly in the Middle Ages, and which was at the centre of the empirical philosophy of Locke and most particularly of Hume. It is often expressed in the form, 'nihil in intellectu quod non prius in sensu'. What was positive, then, was the front face of experience, so to speak: it was believed that whatever doubt could be raised logically or philosophically about the existence of the inside, say, of an apple, no doubt could be raised about the experience of its front presentation — this was what was positive. At one time philosophers made an occasional reference to Comte, the sociological innovator of sociological positivism, but they said little about this, because there was really hardly any connection between logical positivism and Comte. However, sociologists now tend to mention Comte more often, so presumably there is a question in people's minds about the possible relation between Comte and logical positivism. My impression is that the only connection is that both were positive, both were concerned with the front face of experience — the logical positivist from the point of view of logical and philosophical investigation, Comte from the point of view of society. For Comte, like Bacon, would have begun with the literal observations that one could make about society and social behaviour and would eschew dark speculations about the nature of society, social contract, and so on.

If logical positivism was by no means original in its emphasis on observation, it did introduce a more or less original doctrine of meaning, though even this is not quite original for it is virtually explicit in Hume. Hume's *Enquiry* concludes with a magnificent purple passage of prose in which he asks of any claim to knowledge, does it consist of mathematics or matter of fact in which case it receives his imprimatur, but if not 'commit it to the flames for it contains nothing but sophistry and illusion'. If for sophistry and illusion we substitute meaningless nonsense, then we have the doctrine of logical positivism. Incidentally, Bacon's war on 'idols' and superstition amount to the same thing — as also does Kant's attack on metaphysics.

Now we approach the central criterion of meaning versus meaninglessness. The important goal for the logical positivist was to be able to drive a wedge between the meaningful and the meaningless and devise an appropriate criterion by which one could discriminate the one from the other. Positivism did this by means of the verifiability theory of meaning. In outline, a statement is meaningful if it is verifiable and a statement is meaningless if it is unverifiable by observation.

It will add a little flesh and blood to this account to indicate very briefly the sort of filling out that was developed for this criterion. The earliest formulation was to the effect that the meaning of the statement consisted solely in its method of verification. Such an idea falls strangely on the ears at first until one gets used to it, for it cuts right across one's intuitive notion that the meaning is one thing, and that the verification is another, having to do with the truth or falsity of the statement. The idea is further confusing because, instead of being linked with the truth of a statement, the verification is linked with truth or falsity, because for a statement to be meaningful it does not matter whether it is true or false — even if it is false it is meaningful. This will become plain with an example. Suppose we consider an object straight in front of us and make the statement, 'that is an inkstand'; the logical positivist verifies this by taking a look and seeing that there is in fact an inkstand, though in this case the statement would also be true. If however, no inkstand is present and we look around the room without finding one, we verify in the positivist sense the meaningfulness of the statement 'that is an inkstand' though not its truth.

This example serves to bring out the next point, which is that, for an observation to constitute a verification, we must know what it would be like to make the relevant observation; thus if there is no inkstand present the verification consisting in the observation of no inkstand counts for the logical positivist just because we *know what it would be like* to observe an inkstand. This development leads on to a consideration of objects, say, in the next room; 'there is a table in the next room' is meaningful if we go into the next room and find that there is a table *or* that there is not a table, but we need not do this because the statement is meaningful since we *know what it would be like* to observe the table there. We take a step further, moreover, when we consider the case 'there are mountains on the other side of the moon' (this example actually comes from Ayer (1936), written at a time when the other side of the moon had not been visited). This statement is said to be verifiable simply because we know what it would be like to go to the other side of the moon and observe mountains there.

The next development concerns generalisations such as 'water boils at 100° C'; this is verifiable because we can take a single sample of water and boil it and measure its temperature, and whether it is right or wrong the statement is verified (it would in fact be true at normal pressure though false on the top of a mountain).

All these examples functioned relatively satisfactorily after certain difficulties had been smoothed out, simply because they are of a type that are amenable by their very nature to observational verification.

However, the logical positivists ran into trouble when they sought to extend the principle of verifiability to high-level abstract theories, that is explanations of empirical generalisations; for these are not directly verifiable, they cannot be, because they involve unobservables, that is, entities very like the dark metaphysical entities that the positivists were initially so keen to eliminate. Thus the theory of gravitational force would be one. The theory of electromagnetic fields would be another. And there are quite a number of these which constitute the acme of scientific achievement. Since the principle of verifiability by observation did not work for these, a further development of the principle, or an elaboration of it, was required to bring such theoretical statements into line. This was done, for example, by Ayer by means that might be called the principle of verifiability by deduction. If a theoretical statement was such that, from it, (with technical props added as appropriate) it would be possible to deduce through however long a chain of inference an observation-statement, or indeed an empirical generalisation which is verifiable, then the theoretical statement would be verifiable in this extended sense and would be meaningful. By contrast, if it should be impossible to deduce an observation-statement, or for that matter an empirical generalisation, then the theoretical statement would not be verifiable in any sense whatever and would be meaningless.

This elaboration, while apparently completing the edifice satisfactorily, actually failed because it was shown that any attempt to drive a wedge between the meaningful and the meaningless either did too little or did too much. It transpired that a principle that would admit the higher reaches of abstract science as meaningful would allow back metaphysical and theological statements also as meaningful. On the other hand, any principle strong enough to exclude metaphysics and theology as meaningless would also exclude the abstract theories of science. And so the programme broke down.

As a result of this deficiency and perhaps of others, soon after World War II, logical positivism was regarded as dead, that is to say, practically no positivist philosopher overtly admitted holding it any longer, though the spirit of it survived for a long time and still does in a few quarters. It was replaced in philosophical circles by a new movement of linguistic analysis (and later by a more attenuated form of philosophical analysis), which seems to have been a compromise-formation between, on the one hand, an attenuated version which accomplished none of the aims of logical positivism whether one sympathised with those aims or not, but at the price of containing no doctrine at all, while, on the other hand, it often argued in a way that looked like logical positivism surreptitiously brought to life in another guise. However this may be, the logical positivists' principle of verifiability, originally designed to show how to hive off the meaningful from the meaningless, was 'officially' given up by virtually all philosophers.

Now, although the criterion of meaning was the central feature of the doctrine, there were certain other features as well. With the emphasis placed upon observation it is clear that huge importance was attached to the physical sciences, rather than to the psychological sciences or to any science dealing with persons. In this connection there arose the doctrine of the unity of science, which claimed that all knowledge could be expressed in terms of one fundamental science, and, since physics was the one opted for, this became the thesis of physicalism: namely that all truths and all knowledge could be expressed in terms of the language of physics. And it hardly needs emphasising that, with the completely dominant role of observation, and observation seems to be the most objective thing there is, the whole tenor of logical positivism was set up to make objectivity a paramount value. In view of these two contentions it is easy to see that humanist interactionists would have been much put off by a dehydrating philosophy, and they would have turned away both from physics and therefore from natural science in general and also from objectivity. The irony is that of all the natural sciences, physics has the *least* to do with observation.

There is yet another feature of logical positivism which is certainly worth attending to, though in its own context it was relatively minor; that is, that the whole enquiry of verification is conducted by one philosopher as if no other people in the world existed; all that is required is an observation and that observation can be made in principle by one philosopher without consulting another, and more than that without any kind of interplay between persons. Indeed, in the early days of the subject, Carnap spoke of methodological solipsism, which meant not that no other people in the world existed except the philosopher conducting the enquiry, but that from a metascientific point of view the existence of other persons need not be taken into account, and further that the existence of other persons would be verified by the same sort of procedure as the existence of tables, inkstands, and so on, in terms of verifying observations carried out by the philosopher in question. Although this adjunct of logical positivism was far from central from its own point of view, it is by no means merely peripheral to a sociologist who takes the relationships between persons to be of fundamental importance.

However, whatever may be the shortcomings of logical positivism and whatever may have been the misunderstandings of its position, the gravest aspect of the matter involved in the attitude of interpersonalists is their taking logical positivism to represent natural science. They often take it for granted that whatever deficiencies there may be in logical positivism are, ipso facto, deficiencies in the nature of natural science itself: that is to say, if logical positivism precludes the interplay between persons, then it is held that such personal relationships are also precluded by the nature of natural science itself (and this I consider is wholly untrue).

Popper and logical positivism

To come to grips with the nature of natural science and its relation to interpersonal relationships, it is first necessary to point out that there exists an account of the nature of natural science that is fundamentally at variance with logical positivism, and that is the metascience of Popper. There is, alas, a widespread impression among sociologists and perhaps still more among some Marxists, at any rate those among them who are not particularly well up either in Marx or in Popper, that Popper is just another logical positivist or as near as makes no difference. And the same view is held by interpersonalists. This matter is, though it should not be, a complicated one. From the earliest days of the Vienna circle which promulgated logical positivism, the charge has been constantly made, and made within philosophical circles themselves, that Popper was a logical positivist. The external history gives no grounds for this, since Popper made a constant attack, sustained over 50 years, on one after another of the tenets of logical positivism. That he was not attacking without a substantial ground of difference may be easily seen in the following way. First of all, many, indeed almost all, of his criticisms, have in the end been adopted by logical positivists themselves — I do not say accepted from him for they acquiesced in the criticisms only after discovering them within the positivist circle. Secondly, the metascience that Popper puts forward is quite obviously significantly different from logical positivism. Comments on these two points will be in order.

First, the reasons why Popper has been charged with being a logical positivist. The fundamental work in which he set forth his own metascience appeared at the end of 1934, published in Vienna in German. English readers are not notorious for reading philosophy in foreign languages. However, there were two very able philosophers with a first class knowledge of German, and the knowledge of Popper seeped through to English-speaking philosophers as they portrayed it. His book was reviewed in the premier journal of philosophy, *Mind*, by Max Black who wrote appreciatively of the work but gave the impression that it was from the logical positivist school though with considerable originality of its own. Anyone reading this review would take it that Popper was just another fairly intelligent positivist with an interesting variant on the theme. No one would know that he was attacking positivism root and branch. Soon after, indeed less than two years after, there appeared Ayer's book *Language, Truth and Knowledge* which focused on the verifiability theory of meaning. Dealing with certain difficulties in this doctrine, Ayer mentioned the variant due to Popper, that instead of statements being verifiable they should be falsifiable. This reading of Popper's work would convey exactly the same impression namely that Popper's criterion was just a variant. Ayer nowhere pointed out that the criterion, falsifiability, was not a criterion of meaningfulness at all, but a criterion with a totally different function. In general it might be said that the positivists, who were the main ones who charged Popper with positivism, did so because they looked on Popper not as an opponent but as a sort of erring member of their own fold, and they sometimes gave the impression of not being able to understand why he was being finicky and making a fuss.

We may turn now to the question of what difference it makes that the criterion due to Popper of falsifiability is not a criterion of meaning. Whether Popper was right or wrong is not the issue here. The issue concerns his departure from logical positivism. His problem was not one of meaning at all but was the problem of finding a criterion to discriminate between science and non-science or, if you like, between science and metaphysics. This he located in his criterion of falsifiability: that is to say, a statement belongs to science if it is in principle falsifiable by observation (with however long a deduction linking the statement to the observation); and if the statement is not falsifiable by observation then it belongs to metaphysics. Now the vital point here is that, while at that time Popper took little or no interest in metaphysics, this criterion does not interpret metaphysics as meaningless; for all Popper knew, metaphysics might be meaningful and might even be true; all he was concerned with was that metaphysics was in a different compartment from science.

Popper and Natural Science

Popper was aiming at giving an account of scientific procedure, and this account was, in short, that science consists of problems, that a problem is solved by a theory, but that there is no procedure available for obtaining a theory (simply that if one is lucky one may hit upon a theory); further, an attempt is then made to test the theory empirically, that is, to deduce from the theory an empirical observation (or, on a fuller account, an empirical generalisation) which would be capable in principle of falsifying the theory. That is to say, if the theory should happen to be false, the observation would not turn out as anticipated, or, more simply expressed, a theory is falsifiable if it can lead to a prediction that, if not substantiated, will show the theory to be false. Moreover, it is forever impossible to verify a theory at all: however many correct predictions turn up, they constitute no evidence whatsoever for the validity of the theory. They carry punch only if they could have refuted the theory; hence all we shall have achieved after testing is a theory that might have been refuted by a stern test but in fact survived the refutation attempt.

The significance of this different criterion of Popper's lies in various features. One is that there is no way by which a scientific theory can be built up by making observations; the theory is arrived at in a totally different manner namely by making a guess (an informed guess if you like) at an answer to a problem. Moreover, there is no explanatory power in a theory unless its predictions could show it to be false.

A most important feature of Popper's view of science is that it does not build up theories upon observations at all and thus is not restricted to what is positive, that is, the front surface of what we perceive in this world; on the contrary it permits the making use of invisibles, unobservables, theoretical entities, that is to say what is hidden, as a means of explaining what is not hidden − of explaining what we have observed. Thus logical positivism and Popper's meta-science are, in one basic respect, polar opposites: positivism makes observation central to building the structure of science upon abstract entities or unobservables (although it has trouble in reaching them): Popper's approach starts from there. And physics, the paradigm of natural science, thrives on them.

Thus Popper's metascience had little in common with logical positivism: they shared a lack of interest at least in metaphysics (though with positivism it is actually stronger than lack of interest) and they both put a premium on scientific procedure; however, Popper's metascience permits a wider kind of scientific theorising, for it finds no difficulty in allowing scientific theories to be rooted in highly theoretical entities. Thus Popper's metascience does not provide too narrow a framework for real science to be squeezed into.

The Relevance of Popper to Social Science?

Even granting, however, that Popper's metascience is true to the nature of science, this may still not appear to give the interpersonalist all he wants. For how, it may be asked, can natural science, even with the Popperian interpretation, be applied to theories and hypotheses about human beings? More specifically, the problem is, how can a theory or a hypothesis about human beings be tested, empirically that is, be made to yield by deduction an observational prediction that could refute it; more briefly, how from a theory about persons or hidden aspects of persons is it possible to deduce an observational prediction (which shall function as a test)?

I suggest that this can be answered fairly simply by considering the following example. Suppose you are sitting on a committee whose members are on the whole well known to you. Old so-and-so puts forward a suggestion. You have a pretty strong hunch about what you think he really wants and that this does not accord with his actual proposal; in other words, you conjecture that he has an ulterior motive and that you know what this ulterior motive is. Since you are not involved, you carry out a small investigation. What you do is to suggest a variant to his proposal, expressing this in a form of words that gives him what he has actually asked for, but subtly contrived to deny him what you conjecture he is really after. You predict that he will perhaps hum and haw, frown, and find some slight difficulty about your suggestion. You then go off on a different tack with the second half of the experiment: you speak to the effect that, since your proposal did not find favour, you would propose another one, and you formulate what will give him what you conjecture he really wants but formulated in such a way as to deny him what he verbally said he wanted. You predict that he would be wreathed in smiles and after making some covering-over remarks agree that your proposal would meet the case — to save face he would have to divert attention from the fact that your proposal goes against what he actually said he wanted in the first case. Now in these two broad experiments it is clear that the scientific conjecture was about an unobservable, yet it is possible to deduce observable consequences that would test it. In general it should be perfectly possible within the framework of natural science, and within the framework of metascience as depicted by Popper as representing natural science, to form hypotheses and theories about societies, groups, human beings, all being beyond the level of observation and yet to find empirical observation and tests for them.

Such a procedure has not found favour, partly because virtually no one has deliberately set out to use Popper's metascientific method, for this method does not seem to be in the bloodstream of social scientists, although it is well-nigh universally in the bloodstream of natural scientists.

Why has it been so difficult for philosophers to see the possibility of deriving empirical observational tests for a hypothesis about persons or something hidden and unobservable? One reason lies in the way in which we have been wedded to a principle absorbed with our mother's milk for hundreds of years that a scientific proposition must surely have instances of an observable kind. What is wrong with this view is that it overlooks the possibility of deriving an observation or test by means of a chain of deductive inferences: this makes all the difference.

The Traditional Character of Natural Science

These considerations lead us to reflect on the nature of natural science itself; to ask whether, after all, there may not be something in the nature of natural science that is inimical to the kind of testing just proposed. I would hold that, from the time of the Renaissance and the great physicists — namely Copernicus, Descartes, Kepler, and Galileo, up to Newton — the pattern of scientific procedure consisted of three characteristics. First, it was hypothetico-deductive in the way Popper describes; second, that it was certain; but the third and most important characteristic was that science was mechanistic: in other words, its weltanschauung or framework dictated that all connections in nature (that is, natural laws), were mechanical or mechanistic in nature. It is not too surprising that this is so. First of all, Renaissance science triumphed because of just this; it replaced the philosophisings of the scholars by a mechanistic scientific outlook. And secondly, and especially interesting in this context, all the problems involved were in their very nature mechanistic. The importance of this point is that it shows why science achieved excellent results — because it was dealing with just those things that would yield to the mechanistic weltanschauung. However, it is clear in recent times that something other than the mechanistic weltanschauung may be necessary, not that it is wrong so far as it goes, for it has yielded some admirable results, but only that it is too narrow and may preclude a whole host of equally admirable results obtainable by adopting some other weltanschauung. And, in fact, all that is needed is to realise that the mechanistic weltanschauung is not a necessary feature of scientific enquiry: there is nothing that tells us that all connections in this world must be mechanistic. Once we have realised that the weltanschauung is at our disposal and is not immutable, we can replace the mechanistic framework by a personalistic framework as required by the problem in hand. It is therefore clear that the method of natural science can be applied to unobservable entities forming a social science theory, and that this may be tested by the classical scientific procedure as depicted by Popper in such a way that an empirical observation-statement may be deduced which is capable of testing it.

Thus the procedure of natural science classically understood is perfectly capable of yielding results in the social sciences. This has not caught on, partly because almost no academic social scientist has thought of trying to operate in this way, but more because until recently the only social scientists who intuitively operated in this way, namely Freud and Marx, were anathema to the university social science faculties which, by contrast, pinned their faith or research activities on making observations and seeking to build up on those, according to the entirely classical (Baconian) misunderstanding of science.

It should be noted that science thus understood as hypothetico-deductive remains an endeavour concerned with objectivity, but it is clear that this would be in no way deleterious nor would it prevent us from achieving testable knowledge of human relationships. It is clear that by not attempting to follow the procedure of natural science, the interpersonalist is losing the possibility of obtaining scientific results.

Two Approaches to Social Science

There is another distinct way of looking at this controversy. We could rightly say that, among social scientists, there are two broad schools of thought about the way in which we should conduct an investigation (I do not say science). One is by aping the methods of the natural sciences and the other is by going it alone; let us consider these.

Many social scientists have attempted to do natural science by aping what they conceive to be its method, but all they have succeeded in doing is to imitate the inessential features of natural science, such as attempting to quantify results instead of copying the really central feature of forming high-level abstract theories and seeking to test them. But those in the social sciences who have aped the natural scientists have done so by attempting to imitate the method of Bacon and Mill consisting in making huge numbers of observations and believing that there is some mechanical procedure by which generalisations can be obtained from them. Although it is impossible to carry this out, one can approximate to it. Such attempts have merely produced results which are bordering on the vacuous.

The other alternative is to attempt to go it alone, adopted not only by interpersonalists in general, but also by psychiatrists, anthropologists and psychologists. The trouble here is that this orientation very often leads to interesting theories but denies the possibility of testing them empirically, that is, by the procedures of natural science. In principle this might not matter, for it might be possible to find an alternative to natural science — an alternative method of obtaining knowledge — but since no one has ever succeeded in bringing this about, it does not seem a very good horse to back. I call those who imitate the wrong features of science, parascientists, and those who attempt to go it alone, imagining that there is some alternative road to knowledge other than via natural science, I call transcientists. Neither parascientists nor transcientists realise the possibility of a genuine application of the methods of natural science in the social fields.

The moral of the tale so far would seem to be for social scientists to forget about positivism, let the dead bury the dead, and do some science.

Interpersonalism

However, for nearly a decade, a new approach has been attempted — the interpersonalist derivations from phenomenology. These contend that the objectivity and the concept of 'truth' in science, whether in natural science or in traditional sociology, are irrelevant to an interpersonalist approach; their conceptions of objectivity and truth assume a different form. They contend that scientific objectivity and truth bear on a world of reality that is not the world of interpersonalism, for the methods of science shape the conclusions and observations made under their aegis. And they advocate the interpersonalist alternative of finding how things look to the experiencing subjects themselves (there are different ways of going on from here, according to the form of interpersonalism followed).

In sum, the disillusioned — those disillusioned with science — have been disillusioned with the potpourri of natural science, logical positivism and Popperian objectivity through testing hypotheses, each of these being wrongly equated with each other. In their place — or is it places? — they have sought to substitute, in a whole variety of ways, some form of interpersonalism which would afford them objectivity and truth about human individuals in a richer and less turgid way that would bear on the actualities of real living.

References

Comte, Auguste (1865), *The General View of Positivism*, London: Trubner.

5 Twin bogeys: science and objectivism, and the flag of interpersonalism

The various forms of phenomenology and its progeny seek to isolate what really belongs to the social world of the persons involved (whether by 'bracketing', by building up from individual experience, by seeking the 'meaning' of an observation, by filling up ad infinitum lacunae in the common observations of interacting persons). Then the question at once obtrudes: What is the difference between the real world as so portrayed and the objective world of natural science? The answer appears to be fairly simple: the objective world of science contains no infusion of the personal, is not about persons or human life, is abstracted therefore from real life, and is therefore as it were frozen or statuesque. An objective piece of the world for science would be the 'cold fruitless moon'. On the other hand, what is 'meaningful', sharable, susceptible to being elaborated between human beings and is constructed out of individual experience can pulsate and lead to an elaborate interplay between the personalities of those involved. There is no pulsation between two physicists inspecting a photographic plate; there is construction, reconstruction, re-elaboration, filling in, no pulsating as when two people are going over a shopping list.

I would put the difference in the following way. The scientist is constrained within a weltanschauung of 'mechanism' — or, if this is slightly too comprehensive, of 'inert mechanism'. The sociologist in revolt eschews such a weltanschauung — even if on rare occasions it might be appropriate to him, such as when his car gets a slow puncture and he recalls enough physics to consider pumping it up. Instead he seeks the drama — usually in a somewhat undramatic form — of confrontation from mutual teasing at the dinner table to the minutely dissected detail of whether a certain shot in a game was validly judged or not.

It is not realised that the mechanistic weltanschauung can be replaced without damaging the hypothetico-deductive method of natural science.

Let us turn, now, to the bogey of objectivity.

Objectivity

Objectivity can refer to objectivity in general, but tends to be equated with objectivity of observation. There is, however, objectivity of theory: thus, the Einstein theory of gravitation is objective for all observers in all places at all times. There is objectivity of natural law: thus in the same way, water is a compound of hydrogen and oxygen. And there is objectivity of observation: thus, the barometer reading is the same for everyone in the laboratory. This latter example may be conceded even though observation can be ticklish in that what is seen under a microscope can be a matter of interpretation and therefore of dispute and, more importantly, observation is uncertain if we accept the view that all observation is theory-laden. This last, of course, does not mean that an observation is subjective — it is relative not to observers but to theories. However, this restriction on the objectivity of observation is not what concerns social scientists — though it well might. What, then, is it that makes social scientists question the objectivity of observation?

It is, I think, that objective observations are very difficult, if not impossible, to arrive at. A great deal of Garfinkel's time is devoted to elucidating the gaps inevitably left in an observation-report, in that it has to be filled in very greatly if not endlessly, the report is couched relative to the background knowledge of the recipient, and it has to be filled in by reference to that knowledge and that recipient. Now it is true (and I am indebted to Dr Robert MacKay of the University of Toronto for stressing this) that Garfinkel is striving after objectivity; his very efforts to fill in observation-reports presuppose this. But such elaboration, which can have no absolute end but only an end that satisfies reporter and hearer, may well seem to imply that there is no absolutely objective observation. However this conclusion is hardly different from Popper's thesis that observations are theory-laden. And yet the Popperian view does not hamper his metascience of the hypothetico-deductive system.

So, what is it that needles the social scientist? I think that in part it is the impossibility of getting at the truth of social happenings. Take a prison revolt; or take a mild storm in the nursery containing only two or three children and one observer. It is next to impossible to find out 'what really happened' (I would hate to be a judge on the bench trying to arrive at a point of fact). Maybe with enough radio-television cameras we might do better. But in the end there is a large ingredient of interpretation. And the interpretation depends on *who* you are and what *view of human nature*, what *weltanschauung*, you adopt. Hence, it is easy to suppose that there can be no such thing as an observation-in-itself. The conclusion that really follows, however, is that an observation is relative to a weltanschauung (value-system, system of prejudices, and so on). But this fact, however sobering, in no way precludes the possibility of investigating the weltanschauung, to consider whether the observation is distorted. We should be in a position to state an observation with some precision but with sufficient vagueness for it to function neutrally in a discussion. Thus every physicist knows that to a certain extent, a measurement is approximate, loose and vague. But he (usually) knows the *limits* of error. Thus he does not state the distance from Toronto to Montreal correct to a millimetre; he states it to the nearest kilometre (or perhaps half kilometre) with limits of error stated as being plus or minus half a kilometre. Such vagueness, or rather looseness of the garment, renders the measurement highly accurate and objective. An ultra-precise statement is almost bound to be wrong; an imprecise one can be virtually absolutely true.

One last point. That an observation is what it seems to the group making it, and not just what it seems to the visiting scientist, is important. In other words an observation is largely what it *means* (to its own people). But it is still a scientific question why they see it the way they do. So the disparagement of science and observation can end up as meagre knowledge unless we use science and an objectivity weltanschauung to study why people see their own observations as they do.

Have we really got to the heart of the matter yet? I doubt it. I think that what really upsets the social scientist is that there seems to be no standard way of settling a disputed social observation. To illustrate: I was once waiting to disembark at Fishguard harbour. While the gangway was being lowered and fixed in position, passengers were standing on a companion-way; there was relative silence. A small boy was holding a newspaper (objective!) which I suppose was rolled up (retrospective conjecture), and on the next step down stood another small boy, presumably his brother. Suddenly, out of the blue 'for no reason at all', the upper boy hit the other on the head with the newspaper. Now, is this an objective observation of aggression out of the blue? If so, it is of great interest to a psychologist. But do we know that the boy below provided no provocation, a whispered barb? For children can be adept at making quick, almost unseeable 'flips' at their fellows. To collect 'evidence' from the bystanders would (usually) get us nowhere. On the look-out for a similar eventuality in the future, we might install television cameras with soundtrack and after many weary vigils in which nothing happened, we might get a recording with sufficient detail to justify venturing an interpretation. And then we would seek further checks. The point here is that steps *could* be taken, *on occasion*, to refine the mode of observation so as to make a result possible. But, allowing that such a refinement would sometimes be possible, we could not hope to cover all unexpected observations; we simply could not be adequately prepared (with cameras, tapes, bugs).

So, it would seem that we can occasionally make a fairly reliable social observation; but we are helpless before the impossibility of making observations just as they turn up, and we forever lack the power to exercise command over social observations as we need them (whereas the physicist is virtually never in this plight). And, cognate with this, for many social scientists, real people are *not objectively minded*, and objective conclusions are nearly impossible — for example, in a family quarrel.

This constitutes a genuine obstacle to research in the social sciences, although I doubt if it is what really obstructs progress in the field for two reasons. First, if we work with a theory, we can specify what observations we need to make to test that theory. All this can be worked out in the armchair and we have all the time in the world to plan how to make the requisite observations in which case we can plan to build in refinements for observing (cameras, and so on). The second reason is that the starting-point of research is (or rather should be) the careful development of an empirical theory; and the lack of all attempt to do this (with its implied general ignorance of meta-science) would seem to be a much more serious obstruction to the development of social science.

The Relation between the Bogeys

We have seen that, in the minds of many social scientists, the world of natural science is a world governed by 'mechanism' or 'inert mechanism', and that it is a world held on the tight rein of objectivity. There exists between these two a simple relation: objectivity could not exist without science, and science could not exist without objectivity.

Both seem to have, however, a deeper relation: they *seem* to live in a setting of impersonalism. In the mechanistic world there is, and can be, no life. In real life, lived by real people, comforting each other over human situations, there is an interrelationship that cannot be reduced to scientific or objective treatment where such is conceived to be mechanistic; it would become petrified in the process. Underlying the social scientist's disvaluation of science lies not an achievement in human knowledge, not an emancipation from a myth, but a flag — the flag of interpersonalism; he fails to see that interpersonalism can flourish alongside science — and indeed would prosper more with the aid of science.

The Lure of Interpersonalism

The attack on science, wrongly understood in terms of logical positivism, however grossly it misunderstands the nature of science, must rest upon some other approach to the world. And this other approach, whatever it is, may well be interesting, perhaps also valid in its own right or partially so, even though it uses science as a scapegoat and the attack on it as a rationalisation to prop itself up.

I think one can see at least two strands in science that may reasonably arouse the emotional righteousness of some social scientists.

One, which is true, is that science has no relation to values (cf. Skolimowski, 1977). This is undoubtedly an inadequacy — showing how primitive our science really is. For we have not even begun to look for a theory to unify the fundamentals of science and values. The inadequacy here does not, of course, 'invalidate science' but only demonstrates that science must develop (perhaps with a modification of approach) or else that values should become amenable to scientific testing. However, the thrust of the general attitude — before the possibility is disproved — is that it cannot be done.

The other strand, and this is the main one emanating from the progeny of phenomenology, is that science has no relation to what is personal and is indeed impersonal. This, of course, may be contested validly; for the greater part of psychoanalysis, both classical (Freud) and post-classical (Melanie Klein, Fairbairn, Bion) is very much a matter of personal relations. Against this there is the well-nigh universal opinion that psychoanalysis is not scientific. I do not accept that conclusion and indeed have underwritten its claim to be scientific (Wisdom, 1966, 1967). If science could not encompass the personal, it would be a grave defect; and one that would have to be rectified or some major change made (whether in science or in the personal).

In getting excited over the personal, however wrongly they approach the matter, social scientists are surely right (though not if they regard the personal as the *sole* basic factor). They recognise, at least for the first time in academic history, that interpersonal relations constitute one of the most important items in human life. Indeed one can understand social scientists getting so involved in the question of interpersonal relations that they can think of nothing else and make the personal the centre of all else. It is regrettable that the approach should be, as it seems, the enthusiasm (the enthousiasme in the older French sense) of an acolyte. Though it may stimulate, that is not the path to knowledge.

Apart from not being able to justify, or in any way prove, that the personal is the sole basis of social science, there is the question of possible damage done by the approach, on account of the seductive appeal it seems to have. The main possible or probable damage would accrue from forcing other features of human existence into this one mould — self-defeating in the long run maybe, but a wasteful abuse of scarce resources (human intellectual power).

A specific piece of damage is the widespread lure of the contention that other cultures can be understood in their own terms which, although true, all too easily leads to the conclusion that they are incommensurable and cannot be compared with ours. In short, we have slipped, almost without realising it, into cultural relativism.

References

Skolimowski, Henryk (1977), 'The Twilight of Physical Descriptions and the Ascent of Normative Models', *The World System*, ed. Laszlo, Inter Lib. of Systems Theory and Philosophy, George Braziller.

Wisdom, J.O. (1966), 'Testing a Psycho-Analytic Interpretation within a Session', *Ratio*.

Wisdom, J.O. (1977), 'Testing an Interpretation with a Session', *Int. J. Psycho-Analysis, 48*, 44—52.

6 Social isolation in cultural relativism

Cultural relativism is rife in this century. It has several sources of inspiration, some of them very different from one another and not closely connected. Weber, that great advocate of the view that the social sciences, qua science, are value-free, has come to be regarded as misguided and put on the shelf.

The first strong influence to be noted is the Marxist social philosophy, which has led to the perhaps unintentional consequence that laws of society hold only for certain epochs; on this construction there would be an economics of the feudal system, of the capitalist system, and so on. It is easy to show that this is based on a misunderstanding of generalisations and laws of natural science, which, when they are found to be restricted in their applicability, are restated with appropriate conditions attached, so as to render them universal. The same can be done with laws of economics or any social science; given the appropriate conditions attached, they can be stated as universal, and simply do not apply to certain groups of societies. For instance generalisations about witch doctors, with conditions attached about beliefs concerning witch doctors, may be accepted as universal social laws with restricted applicability; they simply do not apply in the western world. However the misunderstanding involved has been sufficient to give a very real boost to the notion of cultural relativism, that is, to the notion that knowledge is relative to an epoch or to a culture.

A very different boost has come from the realm of social

anthropology as a result of fieldwork. When social anthropologists went into the field, that is, lived with strange people in strange cultures and began to find the strange significance of all sorts of customs which would be unintelligible to, or wrongly interpreted by, western man, they naturally developed the notion of functionalism, that is, that customs had a function whose meaning was understandable only within the system of the culture they were studying. This is a most important — and indeed also a right-minded development, in that it enabled social anthropologists to carry out a considerable component of their task, namely to understand a culture in its own terms. Whether they need have gone further and held that there were no other terms in which it could be understood as well is another matter, but it is hardly surprising that they were so imbued with this approach as to universalise it and make it exclusive of other forms of social understanding. Thus the fieldwork carried out in social anthropology by the functionalists has been one of the bulwarks of cultural relativism.

Another influence stems from modern psychiatry. The psychiatrist is concerned to understand his patient in his own terms, not simply to write off the ravings of a lunatic as having no rational significance but to understand them in terms of the patient's own attitudes and way of seeing the world. This can reach the length that, if a patient complains of being spied on, the psychiatrist may not be concerned with whether this is actually true or false in the ordinary sense, that is, whether anyone is actually following the patient or not; he is only concerned with the patient's attitude, how the situation feels to him, what attitude it fits in with, thus seeing it entirely from the patient's point of view. Now this procedure, like the first two mentioned, is of course rooted in humanism, and therefore (as with the other two) is likely to lead to its being applied universally and to an exaggerated degree; for some psychiatrists may easily overlook the practical fact that there are times when they should be concerned with the truth or falsity of the patient's belief as well as his point of view in his own terms. For instance, the psychiatrist may need to know whether there is any truth in it, especially since his aim at getting the patient ultimately to see for himself whether he is sometimes being spied upon and sometimes not presupposes that there is another circle of ideas, or framework of truth and falsity, altogether: it is in reference to this framework that the patient's overall attitude in his own terms is to be assessed as either realistic or unrealistic — in other words whether the terms in which he sees the world are in fact true or false.

These three historical developments, deeply rooted in humanism, have understandably given rise to an attitude of cultural relativism, which is in fact a philosophy of life held by great numbers of social reformers and even social scientists.

At this point certain distinctions become relevant. The humanist tendency just noted of psychiatrists and anthropologists marks firm progress. No one should minimise its importance. Its theoretical importance is equally great; for, seeing symptoms or customs from the angle of the possessor or practitioner reorients the theoretical problems involved. All this is fast becoming properly recognised and is obviously bound to lead us to note the very sharp cultural differences that exist. This is nicely brought out by Ethel Albert (1964), and duly emphasised by Nowell-Smith (1971); to their criticisms have been added those of Jarvie (1975 and 1976) and Popper (1976). In addition, there is a new major assessment by Jarvie (1984).

Now there are two very broad differences of interpretation to be noted. The factual point here, so strongly in evidence, is what Nowell-Smith (1971, p. 1) appropriately calls 'cultural diversity'. The other interpretation, understandably inferred or somehow processed from this, however invalidly, is 'cultural relativism' which may be divided into two main forms.

One form is 'cross-cultural opacity', meaning that members of one culture cannot *understand* another culture. Certainly the difficulty encountered by psychiatrists in trying to understand their patients has been formidable; and the difficulty social anthropologists have had to contend with in trying to understand primitive cultures is scarcely less. But they have both in some measure succeeded. So total cross-cultural opacity is factually a myth. There may be a residual question of whether some matters may not be so deep as to make the outsider despair of gaining comprehension; that would be an important practical matter, but it would not support cross-cultural opacity in any significant way.

The second, and more important, form of cultural relativism allows that mutual understanding between cultures is possible; what it denies is what I might call 'right of judgment' to an outsider. Nowell-Smith (1971, p. 2) gives a sharp fourfold characterisation of this. Basically it is:

1 *the denial that there can be cross-cultural moral or value-judgments.*
2 It is an obvious consequence that there can be no absolute, no universal, moral rules or moral values.
3 It is also a consequence that the mores of a society are necessarily right for that society.
4 A consequence of this is that a member of that society *ought* to conform to its mores (in other words obligations are absolute *within* a given society).

I will describe the position maintaining some or all of these as 'judgment-relativity'. It would be logically possible, though awkward, to maintain (3) and (4) without (1) and (2). It may be noted that the position (3) and (4) precludes social reform within a society by its members. We may continue to speak of 'cultural relativism' in some contexts, in which it is clear whether we mean cross-cultural opacity or judgment-relativity. The most important form distinguished by Nowell-Smith is (1) — the denial of cross-cultural moral or value-judgments.

Relativity and Social Reform

By and large it seems to have escaped notice that the notion of a social reformer is apparently fundamentally incompatible with the notion of cultural relativism; for cultural relativism implies that everything that occurs in a culture is acceptable within that culture. Hence it cannot contain an incompatible sub-culture. There is therefore no room for criticism and a fortiori no room for reform. What seems to have happened, however, is that many cultural relativists tend to stifle criticism of certain foreign societies, while wishing to retain the right to criticise their own cultures. Thus they wish to prevent sophisticated western man from criticising primitive men or 'disadvantaged' societies, while at the same time they wish to criticise western society on all sorts of grounds. Sometimes it is used to undercut criticism of western ideas: while criticising western society they sometimes even protect a sub-culture within it from criticism. To criticise western society is of course perfectly in order; what is not clear, what is not overt, however, is the point of view or the framework presupposed from which the criticism is made or from which it is desired to introduce reform — and the outcome is not faced that cultural relativism may well make it difficult for a social scientist to know from what angle he can criticise his own society.

In the foregoing I have not been concerned with a very real practical difficulty involved in cultural relativism, to do with the drawing of the boundaries of a culture. Intuitively it may be very plain; western culture is one thing and primitive culture is another, but there is probably just as great a difficulty in the meeting of minds or meeting of cultures between various sub-cultures in western society. For instance, how far is it possible for Harvard University to understand Eastside New York from its own point of view? How far is it possible for America to come to grips with the viewpoint of Europe? Followed to a logical conclusion, we might find ourselves reduced to sub-cultures the size of villages which could not communicate with one another, and an iron curtain between group and group, and then find ourselves reduced to sub-cultures of family-sized units or maybe even to an iron curtain between individuals. In fact this has largely happened, as expressed in the doctrine of the generation gap, in which it was held for a short while that it is impossible for the over-30s to understand the under-30s and vice versa — and then there were hints that the over-21s could not understand the under-21s! No one can deny that there is a huge problem of communication in practice, and it has come to the fore in the almost universal phenomenon of loneliness. This has been elevated into a principle of incommunicability, and indeed this may be one of the contemporary roots of cultural relativism.

Cultural relativism as a rational position may, then, be inconsistent; for it seems to undermine the possibility of human knowledge altogether. Human knowledge is something that is social; if we invert this fact — since we do, in fact, have a great deal of commonplace human knowledge — it would seem to follow that cultural relativism is false. The individual intellectual problem consists solely of finding out what universal framework for knowledge there must be to embrace widely different cultures which, in the heat and disillusionment of the twentieth century, are seen within their own terms to be cut off from one another. East is east and west is west; nonetheless there is a conception of certain values such as justice, which, however differently applied, are universal. Opposing cultures very seldom meet at this level, and this is part of the reason why a possible channel of communication is overlooked. If we have to go further than political philosophy for a unificatory framework, we may find it in old-fashioned ontology, for all mankind accepts the ontological truth of the proposition 'change occurs'.

A suspicion of inconsistency arises in other ways as well. It may be agreed that institutions (including mores and so on) can be explained by social structure. In so far as this is so, at least for certain institutions, would not the theory of social structure have to be a piece of objective science? A further inadequacy, pointed out by Clara Wisdom (1980), is that it is a function of customs to be problem-solving but that, while the solutions may be culture-relative, in that each culture may deal with a problem in its own way, *the problem itself* may well be common to all, that is, may be universal. It is not likely, however, that the above considerations would weigh heavily with a relativist.

The foregoing discussion may be summed up by saying that cultural relativism is to be greatly valued for its stress on humanism and on the importance of seeing things from the point of view of the individual or the society under consideration, but that it may be inconsistent with the idea of reform of a society from within, and that it may undermine the possibility of human knowledge, which in turn is relevant to the further growth of humanism.

That, of course, is far from the end of the matter. A relativist may reply that the idea of human knowledge as having universal validity begs the question, or that that is the issue itself albeit in another form. It would be a strong reply.

Cultural Solipsism?

Can we come to grips with the issue? Cultural relativism has been strongly opposed by Nowell-Smith (1971), Jarvie (1975), and fiercely by Popper (1976) — let us take it that their target was judgment-relativism. What it all adds up to, however, is *a cogently argued undermining*. But refutation? That is another matter.

Can we set forth the relativist thesis in more specific form? It would require some proposition such as: 'We have a long-standing custom (e.g.) of killing off our old people, in order to ensure the economic survival of our society.' Further, our informant, backed by our own relativists, holds that 'we' must not criticise the practice of gerontocide. It may, however, be noted that, though the practice is not excused, there is a hint that it is a condoned form of killing, but that killing is not in general condoned. If so, we immediately have a precept — uncondoned killing — that this particular society shares with ours. Nonetheless, the relativist will not be impressed, for he will point out that the *role* of the killing in that society is not common to our society.

The discussion in the above form, and the very idea underlying relativism — that we have to see things from the angle of the other party — both presuppose that we *understand* the proposition about the internal role played by a custom within a different society. And understanding can include any intellectual comprehension but also empathic grasp.

Given that much, someone from another culture can understand the society that practises gerontocide as well as can the indigene, that is also, a native of England can understand head-hunting in New Guinea as well as can the indigene. Hence he is in the same position as a New Guinea reformer if he criticises a custom. Indeed, some people who disapprove of murder would have sympathised with Crippen (i.e. understand his point of view while rejecting his action).

Thus we can reduce the problem of relativism to the problem of whether the notion of reform is meaningful *within the framework of judgment-relativism* (where 'relativism' is not so extreme as to *preclude understanding* of another culture — and neither the theory of Marx, nor of Freud, nor of Malinowski would lend themselves to this extravagance, that is, to cross-cultured opacity, which factually is plainly false or at least exaggerated).

What, then, is the position of the reformer with respect to relativism? Either his views are part of the culture he is criticising or they are not — or, in his spectrum, his views are at the radical end of the spectrum or they are not.

If they are part of the culture, if they are not at the radical end of the spectrum, there is no disparateness of framework. Hence what he can criticise and propose reforming can also be criticised and put up for reform by a native of a different culture; for not being radical to the culture it would not be disparate to that culture if put forward from the outside. The real problem for relativism arises, however, if the criticism comes from the radical end of the spectrum, forming a split. For example, atomic scientists who belong to a culture but also feel a loyalty to science and therefore pass secret information to another power.

We have already noted that, in this case, an iron curtain would descend between culture and subculture, between village and village, between group and group, between man and man. But the iron curtain of relativism may extend even further. For if the reformer's views are not part of the culture — or if his radical proposals at one end of the spectrum of his views are not part of the culture — then the whole problem of relativism breaks out for him within his own personality, because he may identify with the culture while attacking it.

In other words, judgment-relativism holds only for a closed society, closed in the sense that in principle no social reform is thinkable within it. A more graphic way of putting the matter would be that judgment-relativism implies a set of 'solipsistic' societies, for each of which each alone exists. Is not this a reductio ad absurdum?

References

Ayer, A.J. (1936), *Language, Truth and Logic*, London, Gollanz.
Hume, David (1902), 'Enquiry concerning the human understanding', ed. Selby-Bigge, Oxford, Clarendon.
Popper, K.R. (1945), *The Open Society and Its Enemies*, London, Kegan Paul.

Note on some Recent Literature

Relevant writings have been cited in the preceding chapter. But there are some other writings. Attempts have been made to devise some dodge to get round the standard argument due to Hume, Kant, Moore, and Hare, showing that value-judgments (in particular moral judgments) do not follow from empirical statements ('ought' does not follow from 'is'). Such attempts to circumvent this now classical argument, which logically cannot be gainsaid, would seem to be designed to give relativism a chance of survival, for the classical argument underlies objective ethics.

There are also miscellaneous papers (all focusing on ethical relativism rather than cultural relativism), with different objectives. I note three.

Searle (1964) was concerned, with due deference to Hume, Kant, and Hare, to derive 'ought' from 'is'. To this end he constructs an apparently valid counterexample to the classical argument. However, the 'is' statement is not in the *indicative*, stating a fact, but is a concealed imperative of the form 'X promised Y'. Of course this can be done (in less than a 15-page paper), but it is wholly irrelevant to the Hume—Kant—Hare argument which is concerned with an indicative statement of fact. I cannot believe the author would deny the fatuous outcome; nor do I believe he could not have discovered the outcome for himself. The paper is a striking example of how a competent philosopher can apparently use his interest, time, and energy, in the service of a wish-fulfilment fantasy.

Harman (1975) has defended moral relativism. But he does so by defending an uncontentious form, which is irrelevant to the substantive issue. It is late in the day to peddle an igoratio elechi.

Williams (1975), who is perhaps better known and who occupies a position of status, attempts an appraisal of moral relativism. Of his 13 pages, the first *six* are taken up with qualifications which would not bother anyone really concerned with the problem. The next *four* are not quite outside the issue; they concern a distinction of real versus notional options. The last *three* come to an end, giving the impression that the subject has not yet started. But he does apparently state his thesis, more or less without drawing attention to it, pp. 225— 6. The thesis appears to be that, in a purely notional confrontation (that is, not a real option), questions of appraisal do not arise. Does this mean that in *un*important matters, moral judgment is not involved? And does this mean that, in significant matters, he is back at square one, which strictly speaking he has never left?

What is the relevance of these three papers to moral relativism, cultural relativism, and their contribution to human knowledge or philosophy?

References

Albert, Ethel M. (1964), 'Facts and Values', *The Range of Philosophy* ed. Titus, H.H. and Maylor, American Book Co., New York, chapter 19, pp. 250–64.

Harman, Gilbert (1975), 'Moral Relativism Defended', *Philosophical Review*, *84*, pp. 3–22.

Jarvie, I.C. (1973), *Functionalism*, Minneapolis, Burgess Publishing.

Jarvie, I.C. (1975), 'Cultural Relativism Again', *Philosophy of the Social Sciences*, *5*, pp. 343–53.

Jarvie, I.C. (1984), *Rationalism and Relativism in Search of a Philosophy and History of Anthropology*, Routledge & Kegan Paul, London.

Nowell-Smith, P.H. (1971), 'Cultural Relativism', *Philosophy of the Social Sciences*, *1*, pp. 1–17.

Popper, K.R. (1976), 'The Myth of the Framework', *The Abdication of Philosophy: Philosophy and the Public Good*, Open Court, Chicago.

Searle, J.R. (1964), 'How to Derive Ought From Is', *Philosophical Review*, *73*, pp. 43–58.

PART II
INDEPENDENT SCHEMATA

7 The notion of weltanshauungen

It is assumed for the present that there are in the social sciences innumerable societal facts and that, however interpretive they may be, they are in a certain sense objective. Thus, when the janitor of your building opens the door and helps you with your parcels, he is not, the moment you have passed, going to plunge a knife in your back. It is assumed moreover, again for the present, that there are generalisations about the social world, that is to say, generalisations in the social sciences just as there are in the natural sciences — though these may be, and mostly are, statistical rather than absolutely universal. For example, in nearly all classes held in the Faculty of Arts of any university it will nearly always be the case that at least 25 per cent of the students attending will be unreachable. It is further assumed that in the social sciences there can be in principle, even though there may not actually be any examples of them to date, theories in a deeper sense which involve entities not open to observation and which explain a number of empirical generalisations. This phenomenon is very well known in the natural sciences though widely overlooked; thus, the Newtonian theory of gravitation, which involves the notion of gravitational force, itself not open to observation, explains numbers of generalisations such as those due to Kepler about planetary motion. Also the fact that this theory is known to be slightly false through and through does not in the least interfere with its being a theory, and, indeed, a highly effective one. There are maybe five to ten such instances in the natural sciences;

the smallness of their number does not mean that they are unimportant, for they are each so powerful as to occupy the study time of a specialist for many, many years.

Theories in the Social Sciences

No similar example in the social sciences comes readily to mind, and the one or two cases that have been proposed have turned out to be generalisations and not theories of this sort at all. One of the few places in which one may hope to find any examples whatever is in Freud, who, until lately, would not have been regarded in the social sciences or in the university as being a serious candidate for study. But whether his theories are right or wrong there can be little doubt that he did propose a number of empirical social science theories. Another possible exponent of such theories — again one who until lately would not have been acceptable in universities as a genuine social scientist — is Marx. But beyond these two, among the academicians who would have been acceptable in the universities and studied in the social sciences, it is, I think, well-nigh impossible to find examples, whether one looks in Plato, Machiavelli, Montesquieu, Comte, Durkheim, or Weber. On the other hand empirical generalisations and theories form the commonplace structure of natural science, and, for long enough, it has been customary to suppose that this inventory constitutes this kind of structure.

A New Factor in Scientific Structure

However, by chance I happened to light upon a further factor in the structure which appears to have been largely overlooked (though not completely, for it was occasionally alluded to in a rather unexplicit way), and this is what I call the weltanschauung of a theory.

Examples would be the notions in Newtonian celestial mechanics of an infinite absolute space possessing an absolute centre; again the notion that all bodily changes are due to physical causes; or the view that matter can be neither created nor destroyed; and many other such. These weltanschauungen are chiefly characterised by being unprovable and undisprovable, in which respect they differ from the contents of an ordinary empirical theory in natural science which is capable of being refuted by observation or experiment. Weltanschauungen have the function of facilitating or blocking the progress of empirical theories within natural science. For instance the last example mentioned would prevent the development of the notion in recent astronomy of the spontaneous creation of matter. The weltanschauung of witches in the western world of some hundreds of years ago, not so very long ago either, was deleterious to the development of modern medicine. The weltanschauung of Pasteur has meant that for a hundred years medicine has thought almost exclusively in terms of germs. In recent decades a change has been made in this weltanschauung in that the development of endocrinology has led to another pole in modern medicine consisting of hormone therapy. Indeed, one could say that contemporary medicine consists of germ therapy and hormone therapy, with, of course, the addition of vitamin therapy. Moreover, anything that lies outside the scope of the accepted weltanschauung is usually rejected without serious thought. (For a fuller treatment see Wisdom (1987, ch. 15.)

Weltanschauungen in the Social Sciences

Now although I happened to light on this idea from the consideration of natural sciences — particularly physics — it turns out not to have been unknown in the social sciences. I wish to direct explicit attention to this fact because it is customary to maintain that metascientific development has arisen solely from the study of the natural sciences and that the social sciences over the years have added nothing to this field. This, indeed, I believe to be largely true; the social sciences have produced almost no insights into the nature of science nor added anything useful to the methods of scientific practice. This has been so much the case that discussions in papers, books, and conferences in the social sciences have been largely devoted to reporting observations of one sort or another and to discussing how theory construction should be carried out — in other words, discussing procedures for doing science. Since there were no theories to discuss, generalisations could be introduced or criticised but there was little else that could be debated. Nonetheless, it is an interesting truth that the social sciences have been alive to the existence of weltanschauungen for quite a long time. In fact, this word is found to be fairly widely used, as virtually an English word imported and naturalised into our language. Other terms have been used also with the conscious appreciation of the meaning or at least some facets of that meaning; for instance, the word 'orientations' is to be found in Holzner, the word 'set' is also used, and clearly the notion of a 'general outlook on life' is widespread in social science writings. Social scientists have been alive to the fact that weltanschauungen play a considerable influence in shaping a researcher's approach to his subject, on the research he does, and possibly on the result that he obtains or more accurately fails to obtain. 'Weltanschauung' does not necessarily include bias; but since bias is so natural to the social sciences and their practice, it is not surprising that it has been noticed and has enabled the notion of weltanschauung to arise. And though weltanschauungen do not necessarily include bias, they are quite likely to do so. Hence the articulation of weltanschauungen is important, for it enables bias to be detected.

The notion of weltanschauung has been presented here as a further category superadded to generalisations and theories. But it is independent of such a structure: those who try to develop the social sciences without them can readily, and in fact do, have a weltanschauung. Thus what we shall meet as 'street-corner' sociology may eschew generalisations and theories, but it certainly has a weltanschauung of subtle interpersonal interactions.

As an example of a weltanschauung in the social sciences let us recall the aura of a virtue that belonged in the Victorian era (and even later) to the practice of saving. It was not only a virtue of individual human beings to save money — and, indeed, at that time it possibly was a very good thing to do, although sometimes it was done at considerable cost through being carried too far — but it was also regarded as a merit by orthodox economics. If we compare this weltanschauung with its contemporary counterpart, a very young person or even a middle-aged person could not possibly understand their grandparents' social outlook on this matter. Today the weltanschauung is quite the opposite, mainly, spend while you can and borrow all you can in order to get all you want while you can; the weltanschauung is that it is just plain stupidity not to do so. It contains other supporting features too, such as inflation, and doubtless other factors.

Resolution of Conflicting Weltanschauungen

In this context our concern will be not for these smaller scale weltanschauungen but with the larger ones that dominate the social sciences. One of the most striking features of the various weltanschauungen is how numerous they are and also that there is no settled agreement, even a tentative one, among social scientists about which are the more important, which ones should be discarded and which ones kept. Nor is there any serious attempt to sort them out. Each type of social scientist pursues his own weltanschauung, generally considering that those following other outlooks are misguided and not to be taken seriously. There is a dogmatism and intolerance in the area of

70

weltanschauungen which is unknown in the area of empirical theories. Those who disagree about empirical theory can usually do so with genuine interest, but disagreement over weltanschauung is usually a matter of belligerence. In all this the situation closely resembles that of some of the natural sciences, say, of 200 years ago when, for instance, there was disagreement about whether there should be theories of one-fluid or two-fluids, say, in electricity or in heat. And the schools that followed the one were intolerant of the schools that followed the other, and of course were not on speaking terms partly because the weltanschauungen were at odds, but also because their theories did not make sense to those of a different weltanschauung. All this disappeared in the natural sciences in the course of time because in the end some *empirical* theory won the day over the other empirical theories simply by doing a better job. It won what was by and large an inter-Darwinian struggle by being successful, and the weltanschauung that it carried along with it then became almost automatically accepted, and the ones that were associated with the defeated theories simply faded away.

Ranking, Proof and Disproof

This is important to the social sciences now because it may be possible to short-circuit some of the disparateness of outlook by making a deliberate attempt to sort out the weltanschauungen, possibly by ranking them in some measure and possibly by finding out which ones really are incompatible with which others. Though it may turn out that, on examination, there is nothing like the same basic incompatibility between a number of them as there would appear to be at first sight.

One of the first questions that naturally arises is whether such an entity can be proved or disproved. Most examples show clearly that they can be neither, and that they differ from the empirical content of theories. In that respect this makes them very difficult to handle within a science and their appearance in science is perhaps most unfortunate; but if so that is an unfortunate reality. In the case of certain examples a little can be done to show compatibility or incompatibility between certain members. For instance, suppose one subscribes to the weltanschauung that one should not jump the queue. While this is not susceptible to any kind of actual proof, we may be able, in a context, to show how it is related to other weltan-schauungen; thus, if one or a large number of people subscribed to the weltanschauung that orderliness, in certain circumstances (while it may be somewhat frustrating and hold some people back) on the whole conduces to a pragmatic quick dispatch of minor chores; or even less ambiguously put, the advantage of having a queue and a ticket office is that people buying tickets do not have to be on the qui vive to see that nobody gets in ahead of them, and this makes life less of a strain. On the other hand, there are countries where the people prefer the excitement of a rush and, when this is the case, they have a different set of values or order their weltanschauungen in a different rank. Arguments in this sort of context then are mainly relative arguments. They serve to bring out which weltanschauungen come high and which come lower down, but there is no positive proof of the one or the other. When the weltanschauungen are in alternative ranked orders, then one could raise the question which is the better order to adopt. One could have much argument about the matter; but proof? — that is a different kettle of fish.

Whatever one's opinion about the value of one weltanschauung as against another one, it is highly important in trying to understand a society to find out what its weltanschauungen are. Otherwise one will be hopelessly at sea in that society. So it becomes fairly evident that one function of the weltanschauungen is to give an order to a society's way of life. It is possible to go a very long way in understanding a society or a country by studying the various weltanschauungen that are prominent and the relations between them — at least those that are held by large numbers of the community or by large sections of it. The really fascinating and most profound questions of society can then begin to open up; for it would be possible to explain an enormous amount of societal behaviour by means of the network of weltanschauungen which one has constructed. But when reaching the limit of what can be explained in this way, one has at last reached a societal problem for which a basic empirical societal theory will be required. And this is the level at which, so far, almost no societal studies have been carried out. Nonetheless, an attempt should be made to illustrate the meaning of such an endeavour. Examples, for the most part, would be found only in Freud or Marx, although possibly one or two others might be discernible — for instance, the relation between religion and the rise of capitalism might be an example of such an empirical theory to be found in Weber. I do not think there is an example in Machiavelli but there might be one to be found in Durkheim; however, the examples that may exist are certainly very few in number and do not constitute very powerful explanatory theories.

Why are Problems So Intractable?

There are two quite different reasons why a weltanschauung blocks one's thinking. One is the psychological effect on the individual person. To take a commonplace example, supposing one thinks that all germs are bad, and germs are everywhere, then one's life may be governed by trying to obliterate germs, right, left and centre. I have not been concerned with these sorts of psychological blockages, important though they are, but with what is our main concern here, another blockage that comes from epistemology, that is to say when the weltanschauung blocks certain ways of thinking about human knowledge that are inherent in the nature of the conceptual thought itself. A very simple historical example of this would be that it was virtually impossible for a physicist 400 years ago to think of the earth as a planet, because the weltanschauung of the ages, that is for hundreds or thousands of years, had been that the earth was the centre of universe. This blocked the whole possibility of developing physics as a system in which the earth was one planet among many, or revolving around the sun. Or to seek an example from the social area, when some students get the impression that the curriculum committees devise courses which are not sufficiently relevant to satisfy the student's interest. This deficiency supposedly leads the faculty to run things in a way that is simplest for themselves (there may of course, be more than a grain of truth in this at times). So far as there is some truth in a notion of this kind, it would block new developments in education, or rather, block conceptions leading to new developments. In short, the weltanschauung whether small or great, with a reputation at a certain time, may determine the initial fate of the content of an idea which may be trying to break through, or get a hearing. This applies very widely in science, but it should be emphasised that the weltanschauung's influence is on the initial fate, and also what it is influencing the initial fate for. What actually is explanatory, or ultimately influential in practice, is the content of a scientific theory, whether social or natural, and what the weltanschauung may do is simply to abort this. If an idea with content comes to birth, it is at once subject to a different kind of examination altogether by the ordinary processes of science, namely by testing it out, by experiment or by observation; that is an objective matter and the idea sinks or swims on its merits, that is by whether it is successful in answering a problem or by being applicable to some concrete practical situation. This latter part of the process has been well known for a long time; what has been grossly overlooked is the initial influence of the weltanschauung.

Weltanschauungen — Blinkers or Spurs?

The question that arises is whether a weltanschauung acts as blinkers or as spurs. To go back to the example of Copernicus, the weltanschauung of the Ptolemaic system acted as blinkers on those who might have thought of the sun as the centre of our system, but they were debarred from doing so by the fact that the dignity of man required not only that the earth was not a planet, but that it was at the centre of the universe — and this in its turn was held because the dignity of man required that man himself should be at the centre. Another piece of very general weltanschauung has been the notion — one of the two great notions of the nature of man that have come down to us over hundreds of years — that man is inherently selfish, will make no sacrifice for others, in no circumstances take the interests of others into consideration, in fact every man for himself and the devil take the hindmost. This notion which comes to us is generally attributed to Hobbes and has of course quite a lot of truth in it, but its exaggeration has put blinkers on the possibility of developing a different philosophy of man. One irritating defect about an exaggerated weltanschauung like this is that it leads to a revolt eventually, taking an equally gross form and replacing the old one by an extreme opposition; thus the next most important conception of man was that due to Rousseau, who looked on man as a kindly, gentle creature, who would never do a thing to hurt anybody if it was not for the ills that beset him and turned him artificially nasty. It is all very well to suppose that great scientists are above such limitations, but an examination of historical examples shows this is not so. Agassi shows that Newton, who is generally regarded as the greatest of winners, lost to Descartes over the behaviour of light in a dense medium. Newton concluded that the velocity of light was greater in a dense medium like water or glass than in a thin medium like air, by virtue of his corpuscular weltanschauung, which in turn rested on the weltanschauung of atomism inherited from the Greeks. Another fascinating example from natural science also comes from Agassi's discussions. He describes the old familiar story of Oersted who was working for many, many years on the relationship between electricity and magnetism. He thought that a powerful current ought to be able to deflect a compass needle, that is to say, a magnet, and he had his reasons for putting the wire carrying the current in the east—west direction. No deflection occurred; so, thinking that he had used too weak a battery, he increased the power of the battery, which was a natural and sensible sort of thing to do, and he kept on increasing the current, always without effect. Having a very strong interest in this experiment, Agassi points out quite rightly that Oersted was under the influence of a dominating idea which (as I am describing it) was his weltanschauung: in fact, it was a weltanschauung inherited from Newtonian mechanics which led him to think that magnetism was a form of electricity. One day when giving a lecture demonstration he was trying to show the results of an effective experiment; nothing happened and the audience was leaving the hall when, in desperation, he picked up the battery and turned it to its opposite extreme, that is to say, he put it so that the wire lay in a north–south direction. Immediately the compass needle deflected and a great electromagnetic result was successfully revealed. (Of course it can be obtained thus with quite a small current.)

One point that Agassi makes which is of considerable value to note, is that a laboratory assistant, a student, or a member of the public who knew little about the matter, would not have behaved in this way, he might have doodled in effect, just randomly trying the wire in different directions, and indeed might have been lucky in so doing. The phenomenon reveals that Oersted was not doodling, though this is a common enough conception of the way a scientist works, but was operating under a weltanschauung with a particular theory in mind. This is normally the way in which a theory is discovered or is not discovered.

However, to follow on in the same field, Faraday put forward a totally new conception of electric force which he could not get across to his contemporaries at all; and at that time there was a whole galaxy of first-rate specialists in the field of electricity and magnetism. His bizarre conception was of a force in empty space as contrasted with the preceding notion that force always had to be attached to some piece of matter. It is very interesting to see how he arrived at this conception but that is not our consideration here; he got it, and he made it work in experimental applications, but for years nobody understood it nor bothered to think it even interesting. His peers thought he got his great experimental results out of that mystery box called 'genius', but did not realise that he got them from this notion of his which they did not trouble to understand. Some years later, Maxwell and Hertz took Faraday's notion seriously; they had indeed great conceptual difficulty with understanding it, at least at first, but in the end Maxwell mastered it and applied it with such enormous success that he became the second greatest physicist known since the time of Newton (although his name has hardly ever become known to the educated public). Maxwell has transformed the whole study of electricity and magnetism, and his work remains viable to this day. Hertz did some of the laboratory applications. This is a case where Faraday's weltanschauung was so bizarre that even the distinguished physicists of the day had difficulty in coming to grips with it. Yet, although it acted as a blinker on his colleagues in his own day, with Maxwell in the end it acted as a liberating agent and led him on to very great discoveries.

Where do we look in the social sciences for examples of weltanschauungen that act as blinkers or as spurs? True to human nature, one often forgets that a very old notion of man consists of the idea that the mind is a 'tabula rasa', that is to say that the mind is a wax tablet receiving impressions but contributes nothing, or nothing much, itself. Thus, initiatives or technical dynamics are not, apart from a minor exception, to be attributed to it. Such a view vastly predates Locke who made it famous hundreds of years ago, but it dominated the social scene from his time until around the end of last century; indeed it is still around in full force, although it now has a rival. With this obviously naïve conception, Locke and his successors were able to make an attempt to explain how complex ideas were formed out of simple ideas in the wax of the tablet, although this development may not strike one as particularly exciting in throwing light on why man is simultaneously such a creative and such a barbarous animal. Nevertheless it was at least a sort of beginning, making a modest effort to explain a few elementary laws or to invent them. The weltanschauung behind it dominated psychology for centuries and even dominated the more modern type of psychologies that developed in Germany in the nineteenth century when experimental psychology was born. There is surely a lesson here because experimentalism alone really did very little, if anything, to improve knowledge because the experiments were all set within the weltanschauung in question. I suppose one could justly say that one or two sociologists — there had not been very many — went against this weltanschauung to a certain extent: for instance, when Weber probed the relationship between religion and the rise of capitalism, he was at least presupposing, even if he did not stress the fact, that man is contributing some form of *activity* in developing capitalism. (This example would need a detailed examination on its own merits if it were to be argued that religion developed the idea of capitalism on the passive wax tablet of mind.) Durkheim also seemed to be slightly restive at the old weltanschauung when, for instance, he discovered that the suicide rate in a society varied inversely with the degree of social cohesion, for it is difficult to think of social cohesion as other than some sort of *dynamic* notion. Even so, the amount of dynamism in these works is not very great, even if it is discernible in some small degree.

There were two figures who really introduced dynamism into the social field, and would have had no truck with the Lockean conception at all. One was Marx, and it hardly needs underlining at all that his notion, whether he was right or wrong in his detailed theory, was that the development of society was dynamic. That notion is not for a moment at stake; the point at stake is that he held a theory by which, dynamically, feudalism passed into, or necessitated a development into, capitalism by creating the market, then that capitalism would, in its turn, reach its limits of its capacity to operate, would decay and disintegrate, and for various reasons, which he discussed, develop into a state of socialism, but that socialism was but an imperfect form of final development, for it still had limitations for society and would in the end, from its own inner nature, dynamically evolve into communism. Even if Marx was wrong from top to bottom in his detailed theories, what makes him outstanding as a social theorist, and the most important since Plato, is that he transformed the weltanschauung completely into a dynamic one (incidentally, it might with some justice be claimed that Plato's sociology was in some measure, dynamic). The other, and only other, great example who also totally repudiated the weltanschauung of his time was Freud. This again hardly needs emphasis; any student who has read two or three of the early publications, widely available in paperback, shows Freud's thinking as being along dynamic lines; the disorders from which his patients suffered were not simply the results of implants on the wax tablets of the mind, but were the products of desires or fears or anxieties. He conceived of a mind which led to clashes and thence to symptoms. Here we have examples of weltanschauungen that acted as blinkers for not merely generations, but for centuries, and were eventually replaced by weltanschauungen that, when they did come about, acted as tremendous spurs; for the whole face of political thinking has been influenced by Marx even though much of it by opposition, and nearly all current psychiatric thinking discernibly owes itself to Freud's conceptions (often without realising the fact). On the other hand, it is not the only form of psychiatry around; for the time-honoured weltanschauung of Locke's totally passive mind still forms the basis of an alternative approach which is on the market, after being modernised by Pavlov and by his successors in England and America. These two weltanschauungen continue to clash.

Weltanschauungen as a Threat

A very old phenomenon which one can still hear repeated from time to time, is that such and such does not conform to what we have always known as science. This can indeed be written off as just conformity or conservatism with a small 'c' or unwillingness to change. I do not think however, that this is an adequate way of looking at it.

It certainly does involve considerable ignorance of the history of science that is very widespread, but I think it depends on other factors as well. It is overlooked that weltanschauungen are, in effect, reins. It overlooks that weltanschauungen are always present, just as when you ride a horse you need reins. The reins may hold the horse in so that it is badly impeded, a horse may be given loose reins so as to make a wild dash, or the reins may be managed in such a way as to exercise control, and indeed it may be an art to recognise where control lies, where impediment ends and the dash is restricted, and how far control extends in the middle between the two.

But the intellectual failure is to understand that a weltanschauung exists and inherently exists, not just as a blemish which scientists should not have allowed to creep into their work, but as a real factor to be used negatively or positively.

The question naturally raises its ugly head, why was it so long before the existence of such a conception came to be recognised? One would naturally suppose that the very notion itself was regarded as a threat. An interesting example is to be found in one of Shaw's plays, *Too True to be Good* which centred, among other things, on an atheist who had lost his faith. As Shaw depicted the disorientation of his situation the character became like one of the millions of contemporary people — he no longer knew where he stood. And this, I think, is one of the basic things that a threat to a weltanschauung does, it leaves people not knowing where they stand — it leaves them floundering. As regards the way fine thinkers are bound to their weltanschauung, it is well to remember that hell hath no fury like a weltanschauung scorned. The relationship between a weltanschauung and the theories that people develop is somewhat complicated. I think, though without knowing with any great certainty, that the sheer intellectual quality of a scientist's mind plays an obscure role. Undoubtedly, the importance of sheer intellect is vastly underrated in a society convinced that hard work, attending the right courses, in other words performing the right kind of social observances, will do the trick. Nothing could be further from the truth. Intelligence, intellect of the highest quality is a fundamental requirement, but having got that, what then? I think, though without being able to substantiate it, that quite possibly Faraday may have been no cleverer than his peers. They have been surpassed by his conceptions, and we may suspect that he was a bit superior to them intellectually, but it is quite possible that he was not much cleverer. They discovered important things, but minor laws within the same old weltanschauung as before; he did what is sometimes called breaking new ground, that is, he created a new weltanschauung, and of course, the intellect is required for pursuing the work within it. The weltanschauung provides no results, no theories, nothing except a new point of view. It provides the freedom or possibility of inserting new theories that would not have been possible under the old weltanschauung, but they had to be invented, and the intellectual work is required there. A further feature, which I think is of importance for the creative scientist who breaks new ground, is the value of being able to entertain alternative weltanschauungen. Well, you may say, why has that to be stressed? The reason is, it is difficult enough to think of one weltanschauung, let alone think of more than one. Also I suspect that there is a very grave risk of mental breakdown in developing a new weltanschauung, at least I would think so on psychological grounds which need not be elaborated now; but it is interesting to note that Faraday did, in fact, have a mental breakdown, and so did Newton. There also appears to be evidence that Ibsen also had a breakdown. Einstein, on the other hand, appeared to have had a rather untroubled life so far as his intellectual development went. He had troubles with his personal life, and troubles over his commitment to atomic energy, but that is not the same thing as being really troubled at having developed his 'crazy' notion about the behaviour of the velocity of light. I would consider that one of the first men to look madness in the face, was Aristarchus, who was the first to propound the theory that the earth was round: everyone knew, and it was good common sense that the earth was flat, so only a madman could have suggested that the earth was round; it would not have been only the unpleasant situation of being told he was mad by his colleagues, but *the fear in himself* that he was mad. The reward, on the other hand, is perhaps that scientists are playing with life and death in the sense of madness and sanity in trying to discover the nature of the world, whether the natural world or the social world, and it could be set forth in some detail why he risks himself and thus why he experiences the fascination of science, as a mountaineer may experience the fascination of climbing an impenetrable and unclimbable crag, or a schoolboy climb some dangerous trapeze. However, there is perhaps little that could be added on the relative weights of the content of scientific enquiry, and the weltanschauung containing it. Let us look back on Galileo. He propounded several laws of falling bodies which we now think simple. These can be checked, he might have been wrong, and there is a story that he did get one of them wrong, but found out his error; but even if the story is true, and even if he had had one or all of them wrong, he would have lost a gain. He would have been a bit depressed and mourned the disappointment, but his reputation would not, I think, have been very different from what it is now, because he would have broken new ground even though he had got the details wrong. What he did have was a new weltanschauung and that remains even if the details under it had been wrong. Again, Marx and Freud have introduced dynamism into their respective social sciences, and even if every single one of their detailed laws should prove to be mistaken, this dynamism remains more or less for good.

Handling Weltanschauungen

Weltanschauungen are hard to study; they are particularly hard to recognise and to pick out; even in historic examples of long ago, it is not always easy to specify the precise feature that constitutes a weltanschauung. Formulation can be a serious problem, because weltanschauungen tend to be a little bit vague; this is part of their importance and power, and one has to learn to be content to express great things in a vague way, but we want to find a formulation, as little vague as possible, but not over-concerned with a 'breakthrough' when not precise and compatible with what we know. A further difficulty is that there is no known test for weltanschauungen. Since Popper, we know how to test the content of scientific theories; we do not know since Popper or since anybody else how to test weltanschauungen. Indeed there is reason to believe, though I do not propose to go into it here, that it is in principle impossible to specify a way of testing a weltanschauung. If they are not provable and not disprovable, nor are testable, what then are we to make of this apparently irrational element creeping its way into all the sciences, not only into the social sciences where they have been recognised for a little while, but also in natural science where they have been hardly recognised at all? Is this the irrationalism of science that critics love to unearth if they can? One way of answering this is that you use a weltanschuung to foster discovery, even though it can never be corroborated; this is, of course, a sort of pragmatic procedure acceptable so long as it promotes discovery, and when it does not, you begin to reflect whether you can find another weltanschauung that may help to promote the development of more fertile empirical theories. Then of course, if you succeed in this, you have what one might call a fortuitous refuting procedure for getting rid of the old weltanschauung, the refutation consisting of the fact that the new one does better than the old one.

A further very interesting problem arises when trying to break through to a new weltanschauung. Does the new weltanschauung emerge first, before the discovery of empirical theories, or does the discovery of empirical theory come first and lead in its train, simply drag behind it, a new weltanschauung appropriate to it. What I suspect is that both procedures are possible, though, in nearly all historical examples that I am familiar with, the new empirical theory has come first, and brought the new weltanschauung in its train. At the same time a doubt comes up about this because one gets the impression at times that the two developments occur together. It may be that the scientist had a sort of split mind in which he was thinking about empirical theories in one part of his mind and thinking about weltanschauungen in another, and that somehow the two meet together at some point. It is not necessary to enlarge on or dogmatise about such matters here. I would simply add that, for the most part, a weltanschauung is best disposed of, or the anomalies in it ironed out, by thinking of a new theory with empirical content whose new weltanschauung displaces the problems associated with the old one.

Speaking of the two parts of the scientist's mind, one which may be developing empirical content and the other reflecting on weltanschauungen, the scientist who is not interested in the latter is not of the stuff of which the fundamental scientist is made. The scientist who is so constituted as to concentrate only on empirical laws will do useful research and add to details of knowledge — he may perhaps be described as the nine-to-five research worker.

Weltanschauungen, though Guidelines, are not Necessarily Restrictive

To turn to certain different kinds of topics or different features altogether of the notion of weltanschauung, it is important to know that the notion does not pre-empt any answer. It does not, for instance, in the natural or social sciences pre-empt the question of objectivity: there should be objectivity or should not, there may be a particular weltanschauung that fosters the one or precludes it, but the notion itself does not. This also holds for the weltanschauung of conventionalism or realism, or the fundamental role of observation. What is the truth about these matters is not settled as an issue about the role of weltanschauungen (though each is an issue about a weltanschauung); there will be theories within the weltanschauungen, but such an occurrence will not establish a weltanschauung. In this connection it is worth noting that a weltanschauung that does pre-empt a certain kind of answer, that is a narrow range of empirical theories, is common enough. Then it becomes in all essentials an *ideology*, possibly a political ideology. The point about political ideology is that it is a weltanschauung that does not allow you to think in terms of certain alternatives. A simple enough example would be that a capitalist economy would be a political ideology which would preclude most economists from taking serious account of, or trying to use any features from a Marxist political economy, and vice versa. Or take an individualistic weltanschauung which holds that the rights of the individual are sacrosanct and for which proponents rise up in wrath whenever any infringement of individual rights is threatened; for example, if it is suggested that seat belts should be made compulsory in cars. This can be opposed on the grounds of individualism. But an opposing ideology would say that we must take into account the accident-damage to as many people as possible, or the opposing weltanschauung would (or would not) take into account the fact that the requirement, if not a very big imposition, might be accepted. Another example is the question whether strikes should be permanently illegal. The *ideology* would be that they are damaging to the country on the whole, and that there are alternative ways of handling disputes. The opposing ideology holds that, not only have strikes been an absolute necessity historically, for obtaining even minimal human rights for factory workers, but that if that weapon is given up those rights will soon be eroded again. However, the fact in such a case is that the two weltanschauungen are not really so far apart, and their being held as absolutely irreconcilable indicates that distrust is what keeps them apart — that is to say the upholder of one weltanschauung will not take seriously, that is, in a sense listen to the other. It would be very salutary to write down on half a page a set of principles that would enable the two weltanschauungen to be resolved, or if this is in principle impossible then to put them in commensurable form and rendered discussible. The aim would be to obviate strikes, in all but the most extreme circumstances, enabling difficulties to be handled in a fairly simple, but above all in a fairly rapid, way. This would not be a great intellectual achievement, but the unwillingness to try to do it would seem to be an indication of the power of the two ideologies in question. I am not here concerned with ideology as such, I am concerned only to show that a weltanschauung can be restrictive, or may be unrestrictive. The restrictive kinds tend to be equivalent to ideologies, and indeed when scientists of different schools either discuss with one another, or more often, talk about one another behind their backs, they are taking up an ideological attitude. I would think, moreover, that just as it should be possible to write down a set of procedures for blending the ideology of strikes and the ideology of anti-strikes, so it should be possible for scientists from different schools of weltanschauungen to *study* in deadly earnest the other party's weltanschauung; for I would suspect that, if a scientist did so, he would learn something about his own weltanschauung which would not only prove profitable but also possibly iron out differences.

A Universal Weltanschauung? Relativism?

Naturally there arises the great question of whether there is such a thing as a universal framework at all, that is to say whether there is a universal weltanschauung containing within it harmonious sets of weltanschauungen. There is no, or practically no, such thing at present. I suppose there may be one or two vague examples, such as the weltanschauung that everybody on the earth is a human being, and perhaps just one or two others. But even this is not all that universally accepted, because certain human beings in specially touchy circumstances are not regarded as equal culturally and even humanly. Thus in the social world there was a time, and in some places there still is, when white men had an ideology that black men were not really quite fully human — probably they would not allow themselves to express it that way, but that is what it comes to — and until about 1916 men did not regard women as quite fully fledged human beings equal to men in all respects. From 1911 onwards, women have been busy providing various proofs that they are, but judging by their own success, which is considerable, and the limitations of their success, which are also considerable, they still have some way to go towards equality. Equality involves two goals. One is achieving the social realities of acceptability; and the other is the inner acceptance by men inside their own depths of thinking — not to mention inner acceptance of it by women themselves. So one of the obvious examples of a universal framework is not all that strong, and even if they could break down an academic barrier, the effects might not be all that useful in a social science context. Moreover, there is a widespread denial of the possibility of the universal framework because of the fairly ubiquitous contention of cultural relativism, which holds that all cultures are entirely contained within their own framework so that there can be no meeting ground. This notion of cultural relativism has spread, due to a curious and interesting development by a natural scientist now become a philosopher of science, namely Kuhn (1962). He, in effect, fathered the notion of cultural incommensurability between theories (though he may now have disowned paternity to some extent). Cultural incommensurability means in effect that there are weltanschauungen such that the different theories they house are undiscussable, and criticism between them is impossible. This process of polarisation in natural science (and even this process has been grossly exaggerated by some of Kuhn's readers and particularly by those who refer to him apparently without having read him), has had an immense boosting effect upon the notion of cultural relativism in the social sciences.

This effect is so marked that many highly intelligent men and women are prepared to forget all about the value of being able to argue against a position — to forget about the basic relevance of inconsistency. And if one forgets the relevance of consistency, one is committed (if consistent!), I suppose, to holding that inconsistency is allowable. And under the flag of inconsistency we should be living in an unconnected multiverse (rather than a universe) in the sense of interconnectednesses in which we would live under the domination of non-competitive ideas, or as I would put it, riding a horse without reins (see Wisdom, 1987). The curious point here is that the attack on the rationality of science which began in the first years of this century under the aegis of a great physicist has been promoted by several other great physicists and it has led to strange interpretations of science which do not allow it objectivity. Social scientists have taken up this attitude now that the final links in their argument are regarded as proven, with the result that these interpretations undermine the importance of social science and of consistency. Kuhn's influence apart, they have attained this position partly from psychiatry, but especially from considerations to do with social anthropology, brought to bear on primitive societies and ghettos. Interestingly, the attack on objectivity has been carried out at least in part by sociology — using the term 'sociology' to include social anthropology and those various considerations about science referred to. Now the question at once arises, is such a sociology *scientific*? Presumably it is — at least it is acceptable *knowledge*. If so, these social scientists are undermining the objectivity of science by their own sociology which can only be applicable if it is supposed to be consistent, scientific, and of universal application. If it is not scientific, what grounds do they offer to us for accepting it?

The Horse without Reins Hailed as Salvation

When we wonder why Kuhn's influence has been so great, we may want to know what in that approach seems to be *salvation* to social scientists. It would seem that Kuhn attributes the scientific establishment to young scientists on the grounds that, in the majority of cases, it is, or is believed to be, the young ones who make the new contributions. And among the younger generations (which I suppose, by now, means including those who are at least thirty or maybe forty), the social scientists have grown up in the belief that they are the first to attribute importance to people. By contrast, objective science is seen as dealing with objects in the world and as seeing people just as objects; this in turn is seen as inimical to the standpoint of the individual who is emphasised in many social science movements nowadays. This alone might not be so striking were it not for the fact that the same movements pay little attention to features of society other than the individual, or to objective generalisations of which they can hardly deny that some exist. So, although Popper's criterion is non-élitist, social science is replacing Popper's criterion of universal testability with the authority of the individual. All this goes far beyond Kuhn. Kuhn is effectively the Kerensky of the revolution; and you will remember that Kerensky was a moderate revolutionary, not out to arrest or ill-treat the Tsar, who, too liberal to last, was pushed aside by the first communist government of Russia. Likewise Kuhn's liberalism is not appreciated by those who use him but do not read him.

There is a strange feature of this emphasis on the individual. In the numerous versions that are assumed today, one gets the impression that its origins have been totally disregarded, not deliberately but just out of ignorance. For some social scientists have long respected the individual, two in particular being worthy of considerable mention. One was Malinowski who was the first to think it necessary to go into the field as an anthropologist and learn the language of the tribes he was studying, treating them not as objects or counters but as people to be understood, hearing their stories and what they made and understood of their own lives from the way they saw the world and expressed it themselves.[1] He was in fact doing very well what several contemporary schools of individualistic sociology are now doing (in a more superficial way). The other was, of course, Freud who was the very first of the school of modern psychiatrists who *listened* to patients and tried to understand what it was that they were saying meant to them themselves. Whatever other deficiencies there may, or may not, be in Freud, every subsequent psychoanalyst world-wide learns one agreed thing in common — to listen, and listen carefully, to his patients. But the social scientists' interpersonalist revolt against the chill and objectivity of science, makes no attempt whatever to understand the discipline.

In short, the somewhat artificial issue between schools of thought or rival weltanschauungen is, broadly speaking, between rationality on the one hand and a horse without reins on the other. It must be emphasised that those who ride the horse without reins do not realise that their weltanschauung, like all weltanschauungen that have preceded it, is also unprovable; so the riders lack an anchor, and dimly realise this. Because they cannot rely on an anchor and have no reins, they tend to use stirrups alone — and the stirrups they use is the Hegelian dialectic, often distorting it very grossly. But there is a real problem when confronted with weltanschauungen: how is one to assess the situation to which they pertain? I would suggest that the first thing to do is to ask what a weltanschauung rules out, for they may not be dispensable; at least we should know what would be ruled out before deliberately ruling them out. Then we should try to assess the weltanschauung by what job it can do and, of course, if we have several weltanschauungen we can try to tabulate what various jobs each can do, especially those that are specific to each.

Finally, one of the vital points to recognise is that a revolution contains the empirical content of theories designed to solve problems, and it *also* contains a weltanschauung. I would suggest, at the risk of being overbold or possibly overprovocative, that much of the new social science is a weltanschauung and a weltanschauung alone, with no empirical content.

Summary and Conclusion

The notion of a weltanschauung has been overlooked in natural science, noticed in some measure by social science, but not put to work. Unlike the empirical content of scientific theories, it can be neither proved nor disproved. It can, though it need not, block a scientific theory and preclude its invention; on the other hand, it may promote the development of new scientific theories. Psychological blockage is natural enough, but metascientifically more interesting is logical blockage. Thus metascientists who refuse to listen are not being merely stupid. One of the most important weltanschauungen to be held back in the social field was that of dynamism — in psychology and in sociology. Weltanschauungen have often been experienced as a threat — a threat to one's being and way of life, to knowing where one stands. 'Nuts and bolts' research does not require change of weltanschauung, but simply development within an existing one, but a 'breakthrough' in the theoretical field does require such a change. It puts its author out on a limb, threatens him with isolation, ostracism, and even madness. The reward is that, if it works successfully, it puts its author among the creative scientists. Weltanschauungen are hard to study, even to recognise and to formulate. And the absence of any means of testing them renders them suspect to scientists and makes scientists reluctant to recognise them. All we can do is compare rivals among them to see which does the better job and which is the least restrictive. Usually a theory with new empirical content comes first and this ushers in a new weltanschauung, but it may possibly work the other way round. When weltanschauungen occur in the political field, they are ideologies which thrive on controversy by exclusion. With a scientific weltanschauung, it is important to understand its rival; and opposition can be diminished or resolved by making one of them less restrictive. There may be technical details about the assessing and ranking of weltanschauungen. There is a further question whether there is, or can be, a universal weltanschauung or whether relativism must reign. The latter view is widespread nowadays in the social sciences, and seems to spell salvation for some social scientists, in that it gives them *an anchorage without an anchor* — but this attitude, too, is a weltanschauung, and a weltanschauung alone, lacking all empirical content.

Alternative Terms

A brief word about the term. Although 'weltanschauung' was the word I used first, which seemed appropriate because it had to do with a large outlook on life, and also seemed to emphasise the existence of a new unappreciated factor in the social sciences that was of considerable importance, nonetheless, in the social sciences, the word somehow seems to be inappropriate and I have decided to introduce another one in its place, namely the word 'schema'. I think for our purposes it will serve perfectly adequately and one of the first needs then is to bring order into the heterogeneous schemata that abound.

There is, as I use the terms, a slight difference between schema and weltanschauung in that schemata are specific to the social sciences and characterise ways in which social scientists see the social word and the sciences themselves. Therefore 'weltanschauung' will stand for something wider, to include schema, but will also stand for individual values held by individual people: thus the example I gave earlier of the Victorian propensity to save would be a piece of weltanschauung common to a great many people but would have nothing to do with the schemata of any social science, although it would figure in the nature of the society to be explained. To distinguish the two a little more clearly one has only to refer to one or two examples. Thus, customs in all societies mostly, and perhaps always, have a function. This gives rise to the schema of functionalism — or did in the hands of Malinowski. Other social scientists see the world in terms of the evolution by historic laws, sometimes called collectivism and known as historicism by Popper — a particularly important form of evolutionism. Another schema would be connected with the environment according to which it would be the natural environment that would determine all of human societal behaviour. On the other hand, examples of weltanschauungen, including these, would also include such further forms of general outlook as that everybody should take a cold bath in the morning. Another might be that one ought not to jump the queue. It may be noticed that these tend to have the status of values, mainly individual values, but values held by great numbers of people so as to be almost values held by a society.

In order to clarify the social sciences, emphasis in this field is to be placed on schemata.

Notes

1 Malinowski's diaries nonetheless show how his spirit rebelled. He found his savages and their ways revolting — yet he was capable of objectivity.

References

Popper, K.R. (1945), *The Open Society and its Enemies*, London, Routledge.

Kuhn, T.S. (1962), *The Structure of Scientific Revolutions*, University of Chicago Press, Chicago.

Wisdom, J.O. (1987), *Challengeability in Modern Science*, London, Gower.

8 Schemata in the social sciences: structural and operational

Introduction

The social science field is beset by an enormous number of different approaches which I shall here call schemata. To illustrate I may just mention a few of these at random. There are, for example, structuralism, functionalism, evolutionism, environmentalism, individualism, holism, symbolic interactionism. Such schemata permeate the social sciences, that is, at least those social sciences that deal with communities or societies, such as anthropology and sociology, and it is with these that I am concerned. They permeate studies in these areas in the sense that they determine the kind of work that is done and the kind of thinking that is considered irrelevant. Moreover, disputes between social scientists are sometimes reminiscent of disputes in a law court in which some fairly trivial detail is the focus for prolonged in-fighting. Yet the protagonists are not greatly concerned about the outcome so far as the trivial detail is concerned; what is at stake is the schema they are protecting in the background. In other situations social scientists with different background-schemata cannot even communicate with one another. One is reminded of the historical situation long ago envisaged, say, in the theory of heat or of electricity when physicists were at odds over the issue of whether to base their work upon a two-fluid structure or a one-fluid structure. In physics the issues were finally decided by the emergence of a theory with a satisfactory empirical content. That is to say, an empirical theory was found that was amenable to empirical test, was in fact tested, and found to be corroborated by experience — that is, by observation or experiment. In other words corroborated theories with empirical content won the day and determined what approach could be adopted, and this settled the issue of what kind of framework or schema was serviceable. In this respect, the social sciences are currently in the same unsettled stage as some of these physical studies 100 or 200 years ago. I have in fact made here a list of some 20 schemata, which sounds bewildering. But I do not think it is necessary to continue in a rudderless way, since the controversial realities can be reduced to reasonable dimensions. Here I am proposing a mode of systematisation to bring order into this uncharted sea although, even if my charts are accurate, it will not remove the element of disputation, however much this is reduced to tractable dimensions. To end the controversy completely would require the development of a new general theory with empirical content!

List of Schemata
> Individuals
> Institutions
> Ideals, goals
> History
> Tradition
> Evolution
> Biological needs
> God/gods
> Conspiracies
> Structuralism
> Functionalism
> Structural-functionalism
> Conflict
> Holism
> Historicism
> Epoch relativism
> Psychologistic
> Rule following
> Phenomenological/interpersonalist
> Situational (with feedback)

The Overt Societal Situation

To effect an entry into this confusion in order to try to sort matters out, I shall rely basically on the notion of *societal situation*. Though

90

the notion is not, of course, new (though the description of it may be), it does not seem to have been put to the fullest possible use. The notion is supposed to stand for something that is neutral as between nine schemata. I will display first the ingredients of the *overt societal situation* and it will then be evident that one particular schema or other is regarded by its exponents as the dominant one of these societal situations.

To this end I divide the constituents of society (individual people, institutions, goals, tradition, and so on) and the schemata or framework interpretations of societal behaviour into a small number of groups. Confusion may arise at the beginning because the same term can appear as a constituent and as a schema: thus evolution is both a constituent of society and is also a schema. But this is not a serious obstacle. I estimate that there are (at least) 20 schemata, which indicates the extent of the barrier that isolates one school of social thought from another.[1]

By imposing some order into this plethora of items, we shall be in a position to distinguish controversy about the rival possible constituents in a situation, and controversy about interpretations. When all this is done, we shall be able to reduce controversy to one basic issue about the nature of society, and to one controversy about method; and it may be possible to consider an additional item which in principle might make for a new interpretation or theory about the nature of the situation.

In laying out the first map (shown here as Figure 8.1) with groups of schemata, it should be borne in mind that most of the constituents are fairly obvious common sense constituents of the social map which would be taken for granted by any social scientist whether or not he thought some of them unimportant. But, in the second map, along with these will appear one or two non-overt factors which very few social scientists, if any, would include. These would be ascribed to the societal situation by some communities among mankind; thus the map of the overt societal situation is intended to include any kind of entity that actually is present for certain, while the second map will also include in the societal situation factors that might be ascribed to it even if they are sometimes disputed or would be widely denied.

Group I consists simply of individuals, that is, individual human beings, and they are denoted in the map by the usual symbols.

Group II consists simply of institutions denoted in the map by vertical blocks reminiscent perhaps of high-rise buildings. (Institutions should not, of course, be confused with physical buildings which may house them.) It should be remarked, however, that the concept of 'institution' is not really quite wide enough for the purpose in hand. Institutions typically include entities like governments, universities,

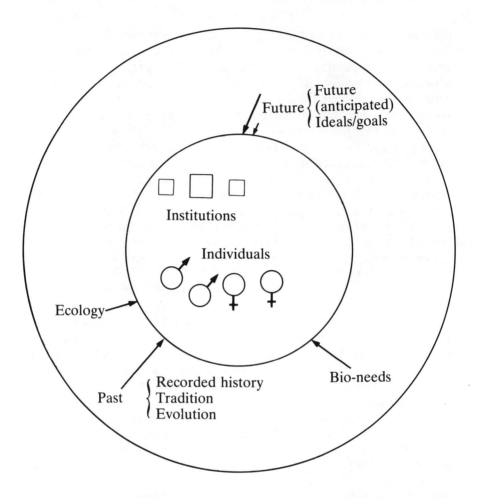

Group   I: Individuals

Group   II: Institutions

Group III: Environmental   { Physical circumstances
                                             { Biological needs

Group IV: Non-contemporary   { History, tradition, evolution
                                             { Future anticipations, ideals/goals

Note: Arrows denote influences upon individuals

Figure 8.1   The overt societal situation

weddings, football, and customs such as Christmas dinner; but there are also other entities to be included that would not normally be designated institutions such as living in houses, a drink before dinner, physical exercises to keep fit, reading a newspaper. Thus institutions range over a wider field of entities than is conventional, and in effect cover widespread *social habits*. Such an extension of the denotation of the term is of no significance in the present context, but it might be misleading not to mention it, since there would otherwise be a conceptual gap if social habits were not included somewhere.

Next comes group III, which consists of two constituents. The first is made up of ecological factors typified by the weather, pollution, or an abundance of edible wild crops. The second consists of man's biological needs. We know what these are typically, even if we have no very complete account of them, for we all recognise such needs as hunger, sex, human company, solitude, and so on. It is perhaps convenient to summarise this group under the heading of environmental or extrinsic determinants, or, if preferred, as non-societal determinants.

Group IV consists of non-contemporary determinants: that is to say, it is concerned with the past and the future so far as attitudes towards them affect present action. To the recorded history of the past, which consists more or less of what actually has happened, we must add tradition or myths about the past. Tradition is a part of history or it may involve a fantasy about history. Either way it is a potent influence upon human and societal activity. Another factor under this heading is evolution, meaning not physical evolution but the way in which customs, institutions, and so forth have evolved; and this clearly is likely to be a potent influence. As regards the future, our anticipations, however stupid, are likely to influence our present actions very greatly: for instance, the anticipation that something will turn up to save us from the effects of pollution lulls many of us into continuing to pollute. Another factor under this heading is goals. People in society and organisations have goals. Thus Hitler had the goal of peopling Europe with Aryans and generating a civilisation of Aryans designed to last for a thousand years. The Russian goal of society was to have government by the people. The Christian goal was ultimately to overcome all evil. Many revolutionary goals have been equality in one form or another. It is clear that anticipations and goals have a very marked effect upon human and societal activity, behaviour, and decisions.

At this point I wish to offer one comment; that the presentation of the overt societal situation given above in this form is intended to portray a fair number of social determinants in such a way that they can all be seen to belong together, and to bring out that some of the various schemata are no more than universalisations of isolated approaches, all or nearly all playing a genuine part. We may thus begin to see that numerous schemata are wrong only in claiming exclusiveness.

We now have a full map of the overt societal situation to inspect and may now consider how it may be typically used. The simplest way to begin is to consider it from the point of view of a predominantly individualistic schema. We suppose that an individual is confronted with the need to take some action or other; he cannot do exactly what he would like to do in terms of a complete wish-fulfilment fantasy, he is constricted by all sorts of realities, both physical and social, which, when spelt out, constitute the map in front of us (Figure 8.1); that is to say, he is constricted in his choice by the nine constituents that make up the various groups composing our map. It is perhaps well to underline the constraining effect of these nine constituents. Thus our man cannot grow crops in the winter; the environment sees to that. He cannot avoid paying some taxes; certain institutions see to that. He cannot go without food for a month; his biological needs insist on that. He cannot walk into his parliament and make a speech; custom, law, and procedure have evolved historically in such a way as to preclude that. The social tendency of the day is to demand and expect more and more in the way of health and social services. Our man may disapprove of all these things because he considers that they undermine the individual's initiative. He may write letters to the newspaper in protest but he cannot prevent these trends from being realised.

Thus we find two general features of his action when confronted with the need to take a decision/action. What he decides/acts is dependent upon the nine constraints, but this is qualified by the fact that these constraints, by virtue of being constraints, are negative; that is to say, they do not prescribe what he shall do, they give him limits within which he may exercise choice. (There would be occasional circumstances when the range of choice was so constricted that in effect he had no choice but, if this should ever be a reality, it is irrelevant here because he would then have no problem. The situation under consideration is one in which the man is confronted with a need to decide/act to the best of his ability with some latitude available to him.)

There are several reasons for laying out this map of the overt societal situation. It is possible to see the position of a man taking an action or a decision in terms of more or less common sense constraints, the existence of which would be more or less acceptable to all types of social scientists. We are then in a better position to consider whether there are any gaps in the map. It provides a jumping-off ground, enabling us to consider whether there might not be fuller maps of the societal situation. And we shall be in a better position to understand why certain kinds of social scientists have developed remarkable, deep, and abstract theories about the nature of social action.

We can, for example, pinpoint some social scientists as holding that the sole significant determinant of societal action on a broad scale lies in the environment. Consideration of the map, however, is alone sufficient to render such an approach extremely thin. Another kind of social scientist will hold that social institutions determine all, and maintain that individuals are powerless in their shadow — just puppets pushed here and there by them. Yet again there are others who will maintain that individuals can control all by taking enough trouble to control institutions and so on.

One overall point that is being made by this portrayal is that most or all of these constituents are sometimes taken by their authors to be isolated schemata, that is to say, to be exclusive determinants, very obviously giving a one-sided interpretation of society. All these schemata give reasonable feeds into a societal situation. They normally have an influence on society, and individuals taking decisions/actions are influenced by most or all of them. A considerable amount of totally unnecessary controversy could be avoided simply by seeing these schemata as parts of the societal situation — but as parts only. None of these schemata needs to be attacked or denied for they virtually all have some relevance to social decision/action. In short, they are wrong only in claiming to be exclusive.

The Problem Evoking Alternative Interpretations

If the foregoing seems straightforward and even commonsensical, one would wonder why there is need to say more. We know that deep and illustrious theories of society have been propounded; that there are notions like structure, functions, holistic forces. It seems to me that the problem arises very simply from one consideration, and that is that mankind, consisting of individuals, feels overwhelmed from time to time by its inability to alter or control events. It is one thing to be unable to go and plant the seeds for the crops just because it is raining, for the farmer simply waits until the next day. He wants a more comfortable bed so he gets hold of some soft material out of which he makes a mattress. Neighbours damage some of the things on his land so he puts up a fence. In short there are many things men can do either to make things better or more enjoyable, to satisfy them-selves on the one hand or to remove irritations on the other. However, situations do arise that overwhelm a man against his will and, no matter what he does, he feels he can do nothing about them. There may be periodic floods or even earthquakes but these are not the kinds of things that cause the greatest upset. Something can be done to defend oneself against these, if necessary by moving house. One example of the kind of thing that mankind feels beset by, at least in some phases, is war. Whatever efforts a man makes in concert with his neighbours or otherwise, there seems to be nothing he can do to prevent recurrent outbreak; and often the fear of invasion by neighbouring tribes was an age-old threat against which many communities were defenceless. Another modern phenomenon which man seems powerless to control is inflation, and a cognate one would be poverty in the midst of plenty. One that has beset every kind of second-class citizen from the dawn of man right up to the present moment is his powerlessness to protect himself against persecution. There is even the anomaly that if he gives in he is maltreated and if he defends himself he may be maltreated even worse. Broadly speaking, the problem seems to boil down to fairly simple dimensions, namely, that groups whether small or large smart under the treatment of the rest of society with greater power. One of the classic illustrations of early history is the persecution of the children of Israel by the Pharaohs; contemporary examples are too numerous to mention. It is this sort of situation that has led social theorists to look for something deeper to explain it than can be developed simply from the nine ingredients of the societal map. First, however, let us consider the class consisting of a group of two schemata believed in by a large part of mankind, though rarely by social scientists.

Mankind's Attribution of Personal Influences

This group consists of powers, human or divine — that is individuals or God/gods — and is illustrated by Figure 8.2. Most communities and societies have regarded God/gods as a significant determinant of much or all that happens and, while almost all have regarded these influences external to society, that is transcendent rather than immanent, they are allotted a place as part of the total situation. Alternatively, we could describe these as personal, whereas the third group consists of impersonal influences.

A basic distinction should be drawn here. The first three groups are conceived to be constituents that may operate blindly, or at least undeliberately without any personal plan, to affect human beings or society. This group, by contrast, concerns constituents that either do influence, or are believed to influence, the course of human affairs.

96

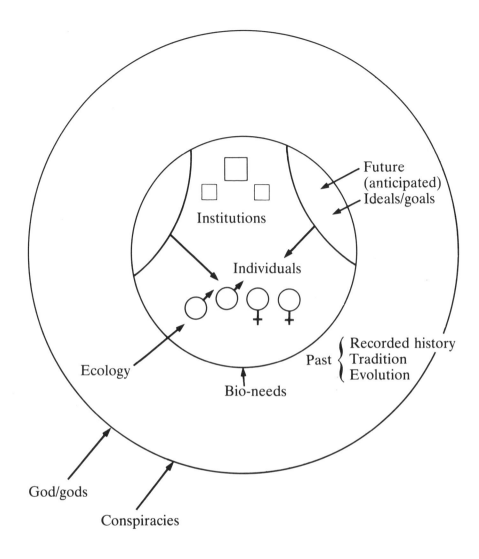

Mankind's interpretation

Group V: Personal   {God/gods
{Conspiracies

Figure 8.2   Mankind's interpretation of the societal situation

The influence of God/gods is felt to vary widely from society to society: in some, this influence is regarded as occasional; in others common; and in yet others universal. To take the early Christian view of society, for example, the opinion expressed in the *New Testament* was that not even the fall of a sparrow can take place except by the will of God. Since the Renaissance, however, the view has become more and more widely held that divine influence consists of creating the laws, both natural and moral, and leaving the world, both physical and moral, to operate in accordance with them except for very occasional interventions.

The other power that influences society and is of a personal kind consists of deliberate action by small groups of individuals. Popper (1962) has named this the conspiracy theory of society, which is very simply that groups of self-interested persons plot in secret how they shall attain their ends.

This theory needs explicit mention because of its enormously powerful influence upon large numbers of people, though only a small proportion of social scientists. It is a peculiarly uninteresting theory for a very simple reason. First let it be made clear that of course there have been plots throughout history from time to time, but the study of history would not suggest that there have been very many or that they have often been very influential. Minor plotting, of course, has always gone on fairly vigorously but that is not our concern; our concern is only with major plots which may have a decisive influence upon the development of societies. It seems probable that the Guy Fawkes 'plot' of 300 years ago was an invention by plotters who would have found such a 'plot' useful, for it enabled them to undermine their opponents. It is possible that one of the general elections in Great Britain in the 1930s was influenced by a forgery known as the Zinoviev letter. It may be that the Reichstag fire in Germany was a plot which enabled Hitler to assume greater policing power, ostensibly to protect the country, but actually to strengthen his own position. The Watergate plot was designed to ensure continuance of the reigning power and perhaps diminish the future power of the opposition.

The first point to notice is that there is no serious reason to think that major plots of these kinds have been major determinants through history.

But there is an even more significant point that drains the issue of all interest. It is very simply that such plots are of no avail unless they take place in a setting, that is, a social setting that is ripe for the kind of outcome fostered by the plot. In other words all that the plot does is either ensure or facilitate something that is likely to happen anyway. Thus Hitler was going to make sure he obtained absolute police control; the Reichstag fire was simply a shortcut to it. It is probable that the Watergate plot did not bring about a different result in the American presidential election. In the case of the British general election the forgery probably produced a hugely increased majority for the party that would have got in anyway. But of course there would occasionally be a plot that would just tilt the balance and therefore make for a great change that would have not occurred without it. However, the underlying point of social science interest is this. The social setting must be one to which the plot is relevant, and this is so whether the plot really ensures what would otherwise take place or on occasion alters it. Now in what general societal situation do plots thrive? It usually consists of a widespread social fear, whether a fear/hate/envy of Popery, of the Jews, of the blacks, of the communists, or whatnot: maybe it always consists of such a factor, though on occasion a plot may only look like self-seeking and self-aggrandisement (but perhaps this is a dubious exception). Taking the typical situation, however, the social science question of interest lies not in the plot at all, but in the nature of the societal situation, its meaning, origin, and so forth — the soil upon which the plot operates.

It is hardly surprising that many people have fallen for the conspiracy theory attributing all our ills to the machinations of a few cunning conspirators manipulating the rest for their own aggrandisement. However, as already indicated, the societal problem would be to understand why the problem of exploitation exists and not why there are sometimes malevolent people who will take advantage of it. The attribution of divine influence over us is not followed up by social scientists, even by those who have the belief, because they *cannot put it to work* in studying society. (The *belief* in it can of course be put to work and is obviously of immense societal influence.)

We are now in a position to begin considering the third class of schemata consisting of three groups of markedly different alternative interpretations or theories about the nature of the overt societal situation.

The Operational Units of Society: Institutions/Groups

Here, as illustrated by Figure 8.3, we meet the first of the three groups of interpretations of the nature of the societal situation. The group consists of four schemata, namely structuralism, functionalism, and structural-functionalism on the one hand, and 'conflict theory', which may be said to be of the same family viewed through the looking glass.

Structuralism has no very clear antecedents. Nearly everyone is a

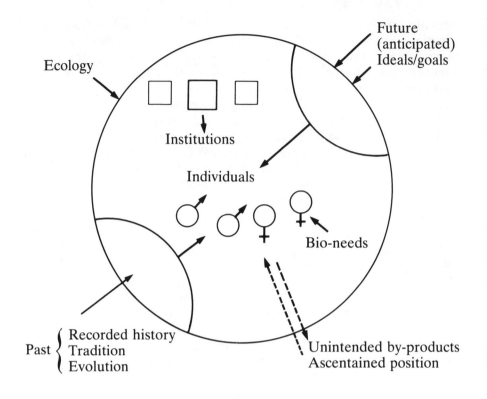

Social Science Interpretation

Group VI: (not shown)	Nature/Role of Institution/Groups	Structuralism Functionalism Structural Functionalism Conflict
Group VII: (not shown)	Holism (general)	Holism (specific) Historicism Epoch-relativism
Group VIII:	Individualism	Psychologistic Rule-following Phenomenological/ Interpersonalist Situational (with Feedback)

Figure 8.3   The societal situation with feedback (for situational individualism with ascertainable anticipations)

structuralist in some degree, everyone but the most out-and-out functionalist, and it is hard to see how even such a one could avoid being pressed into holding some structuralist view. But the structuralism that most people would hold would not be regarded as a powerful idea on its own. If we are determined on an ancestry we might conceivably mention Weber, Durkheim, and perhaps Plato.

Functionalism is associated par excellence with Malinowski (1944) and it continues to live on, though in a much weakened form. Structural-functionalism associated with Radcliffe-Brown (1952) is a position that attributes significant weight to both components.

The first point to notice, and this is a highly important one, is that these schemata are framework-theories about certain constituents of the societal situation only. Here is one advantage of depicting the overt societal situation, for we see at a glance that these schemata, so far from being theories of society in general, are but components of a possible overall approach.

Powerful criticisms have been levelled against functionalism by Gellner (1973) and by Jarvie (1973). Their heavy battery of criticisms aims not so much at annihilating functionalism as to elucidate it and especially to reveal a good deal in it that may be retained for limited purposes — thus performing not merely a cleaning up but also a rescue operation. All that is needed here, therefore, is a brief look at the numerous points involved, though a new point or two will be added.

Briefly we have structures, provided we do not mean any essential totally permanent unchangeable entity, since there must be some sort of structure to which we refer changes. Even if we were to follow Malinowski who, like Heraclitus, held that all is function, it should be urged that a function is a function of some structure. Likewise we certainly find functions, and it is about the conception of function that the following remarks will be made.

1   Functionalism as a schema is hardly controversial unless it is taken to be universalised. Malinowski made it his main plank that every custom, every habit, and so forth has a function. Obviously most do but universalisation may be and must be questioned.

2   As pointed out by Gellner (1958) and Jarvie (1964) it is a good metascientific prescription always to look for a function. This is wise because functions are a very important part of the social map. One could even go so far as to say they are overwhelmingly important, provided it is realised that there are other constituents that are also overwhelmingly important. (Usually when importance is stressed this is read as meaning sole importance.) In connection with these two points it is also wise to bear in mind

the possibility that there might very well be something or other in society that in fact had no function. This may be rare but it would be doctrinaire to exclude the possibility.

3   It is a fundamental objection to functionalism (as a universal schema) that it precludes the investigation of social change. The reason for this is that, if functions are the only components studied, what one is studying is the status quo, how society and its parts function, that is, function as they are. There is nothing in the conception of a function to bring about or to explain change at all. The attempt might be made to explain change in terms of consequences of interlocking functions and this might indeed be valid, but if so something would be superadded to functionalism as such.

4   An equally significant objection to functionalism is that it precludes studies to do with the evolution, history, and origin of society. This has proved the case in practice insofar as certain establishments in social anthropology have relinquished and even ruled out such studies. But the point is not merely a practical one. It is a theoretical consequence that the study of functions is the study of the working machinery of an ongoing society; and just as this has no bearing on change — that is, change in the future — so it has no bearing on change in the past, and would therefore exclude evolutionary change, historical change, and change in the form of origin or coming to be.

5   It is important to take note of the significant distinction brought out by Merton (1949) between the manifest function of, say, some custom and the latent function. According to him, the manifest function is not the subject of our interests; the latent function alone is the subject of social investigation. Thus if a tribe raids a neighbouring tribe and kills enemies or returns home with captives this may have the manifest function of self-protection. But the latent function may have to do with reinforcing masculinity, which is more significant. While this distinction is clearly relevant and while the latent function is the more important of the two, it would perhaps be a mistake to dismiss manifest functions altogether, for they too can give rise to problems. Thus we can initiate an entry into a great social problem if we raise the question why aggressive self-defence is needed.

6   This leads to one of the most important criticisms of functionalism: that functions do not explain, but constitute material requiring to be explained. This is a vitally important criticism and contains much truth; but at the same time too much has been made of it, and Gellner (1973), for one, has pointed out that it contains exaggeration. The detail needs to be elucidated somewhat.

102

Academic criticism of functions as explanatory has been given, for instance, by Robert Brown (1963). He makes what I would regard as one of his very few errors when he contends that functions are not explanatory, because they cannot be regarded as either necessary or sufficient causes. Thus, if we take the function of the heart to act as a pump, this is not necessary for producing pump-like effects, because they could be produced in a variety of other ways even though a pump is much the oldest and simplest. Nor is the function sufficient, because the heart could not pump without cerebral electroneural impulses, nor without input and output receptacles. There is obviously something wrong with this criticism; for there are all sorts of things in life that are most important in the causal role they play and yet they are neither necessary nor sufficient. This is intuitively so self-evident that it hardly needs to be pointed out. I think the objection stems from an overstringent conception of causation associating it either with the necessary or the sufficient, or a combination of the two. The notion that seems to be needed here is that of *'enabling'*. Though neither necessary nor sufficient, the heart has the function of enabling the blood to be moved from one place to another. It seems clear that enabling is a causal process neither necessary nor sufficient but of extraordinarily widespread occurrence.

It should be granted that a function can, in a moderate way, be explanatory. Thus if a man's wrist is slashed and blood pours steadily from it, the explanation of this lies in the pumping by the heart. Such explanations are low-level explanations and not interesting once we reach the higher reaches of theorising, but they form the staple diet of explanation in a massive way at the low level of generalisations, both in the physical and the social sciences. The point enables us to recognise that the most interesting problem about a function is to explain it itself; that is to say we want to know how it came to be, why such a thing is needed at all, and how it persists.

In brief, then, functionalism is false only as a universalistic schema; if restricted to certain needs of the social sciences, it continues to be most valuable. It is always wise to look for a function: functions are enabling; they explain at the generalisation level in a modest way; they constitute part of the social map of capital importance for understanding one's way around a society, which no journalist or ambassador could ignore; most of all they raise one of the great theoretical problems, albeit in a highly particularised form, concerning the origin, needs, and persistence of fundamental components in the overt societal situation.

Structural-functionalism is but a less doctrinaire version of the same thing for it overtly takes account of the significance of structures as well as functions. Thus Radcliffe-Brown (1952, ch. 3) was concerned not only with the functioning within the family of the kinship system, but he recognised that the kinship system was a basic structure. There again the same question arises as with functionalism: it is one thing to unearth the structure and its function — one of Radcliffe-Brown's great achievements — but in a sense the greatest problem arises only then — how do we explain it?

It would seem clear, therefore, that this interpretative group of components cannot be regarded as explanatory of societal behaviour to the exclusion of other schemata, that is to say they are not a theory of the overt societal situation. But they do constitute an important contribution to the theory of one constituent of this situation, namely social institutions. In other words what has been put forward as a schema for the understanding of society turns out to be one of the most significant *components* of the overt societal situation.

The point is sometimes made that functionalism is essentially conservative. What this means — even though the 'c' is small — is that what a function is for, what it does, is to conserve some wider system of which it is a part. The function may be efficient or poor or even deteriorate into a dysfunction, but still the system may keep going; however, if the dysfunction is bad enough or the function ceases, the system is gravely damaged and perhaps destroyed. Hence keeping things going is the keynote, restore things to their previous state, don't rock the boat — at least not outside recoverable limits.

Such a feature, if judged reprehensible, is not reprehensible in a specific function: it is the character of specific functions, even though not necessarily of systems, although it may be reprehensible when true of systems — that is, of functionalism. When it does not apply to whole systems, it provides the situation known as consensus (Parsons et al., 1951).

This consideration leads to its contrast. There may be much to be gained by sharply juxtaposing functionalism in its widest form with its contrasting schema which is 'conflict theory' (Dahrendorf, 1959). This schema is new in the form it assumes, though it has its ancestry in Marx, and even has its echoes in a very non-Marxist historian, Arnold Toynbee (1934), in his schema of challenge and response:[2] it seeks above all to explain social change, and to explain it by conflict. The conflict in question is between groups but may occur in any medium, economics, religion, values; it is envisaged not as an unfortunate evil but as the seminal germ of progress. It is a *dynamic* theory.

Conflict-theory is obviously one of the most important additions to our schemata. It is to be doubted, however, whether it has been adequately formulated. It covers several disparate situations under one misleading concept. One concerns tendencies that, if left to themselves, would go in different directions, but are *readily* amenable to coordination (such as the nervous system well coordinated by the old-brain, or the activities of secretary and chairman of a well-run club). Another situation concerns tendencies that are kept in uneasy harness (such as faculty and administration in many North American universities where there is no overt rebellion). And a third concerns worsening conflict (such as a strike). These might be described as encounter, confrontation, and dysfunction. It is, of course, perfectly legitimate for scientific purposes to take all these to be varieties of conflict; but a proviso is needed, that the theory shows up the different forms and what conditions make for one or the other.

A peculiarity of conflict-theory is that it may seem to be functionalism 'through the looking-glass', but this would be a sort of looking-glass mistake. Dahrendorf points out that a functionalist account can be interpreted as conflict: thus the function of a policeman on point-duty is to direct traffic; but, looked at the other way, he is a product of a conflict between the value-system of drivers, a war of all against all, and the values or needs of the drivers' employers and the public (and also the drivers) to expedite matters. Evidently the function here presupposes conflicting aims, so the conflict schema on this score would seem to be more basic. On the other hand, the conflict must remain an open conflict unless it can be harnessed functionally. So far, then, from conflict-theory being functionalism through the looking-glass, it is the other way round: functionalism is conflict-theory through the looking-glass, for functionalism omits certain vital attributes that render it bizarre. Its inadequacy, however, in no way detracts from the undoubted merits it does have in providing a map of the way things work, even though it does not reveal the identity of the unleashed forces that it harnesses. On the other hand, conflict-theory is typically concerned less with a policeman on point-duty than with a fair-sized clash between groups, which in turn depends upon a good many functions already formed and required for the very existence of the groups.

Dahrendorf himself has pointed out that conflict-theory and functionalism (he discusses it in the form of consensus) are complementary. But he is inclined to regard them as applicable to different, but parallel, situations: the one typically applies to strife (for example, a strike), the other to cooperation (for example, use of a personnel manager), so he lost the opportunity of placing them, not in parallel, but in layers (this notion will be developed in more detail next).

Reflecting further on the complementary layer relation between functionalism and conflict-theory, we note that functions are laws about what happens; but they are not in themselves dynamic (even though they may contain feedback mechanisms) — conflict-theory supplies the dynamics.

What, then, have we achieved so far? We have obtained a more or less agreed map of the overt societal situation with more or less agreed constituents. To this we have added a characterisation of structure and function which, with appropriate qualifications, may perhaps be accorded widespread acceptance; for it is appropriate to one of the most important constituents of the overt societal situation, namely, social institutions. This *full* acceptance of functionalism *restricted* to *institutions* or even functional *units* is vitalised when we add, *as its complement* the conflict schema (*functional* but *creative* conflict) as well as conflict as an underlying dynamic. The combination forms an integrated pair of schemata capable of taking account of 'routine', 'conservative' functions required in a system, together with sub-systems that may be loosely coupled, that may pull together in consensus, or that may be in a state of conflict; and an integrated pair consisting in one nourished by the other. There is, then, little that need be controversial or, if controversial, not in relation to the most fundamental problems. Subsequent investigation will concern interpretative schemata of high controversy.

In a further discussion we shall turn in particular to forms of extreme holism. The schemata just considered, notably functionalism, are sometimes considered as a form of holism. The reason it smacks of holism is because functionalism is *systemic* (whereas individualism is not). So functionalism does characterise whole units. Likewise conflict-theory is a systemic theory which, in Dahrendorf's form, is not holistic as it is in Marx. Neither functionalism nor conflict-theory is one of the 'blood-and-thunder' forms of holism that has been left unexamined above.

The main issue of schemata to have emerged so far is between some form of scientific structuralism and some form of anti-scientific, go-it-alone, personal interactionism. This controversy is concerned not with society in rerum natura, but with rival views of practitioners; it can therefore be understood to be ephemeral, for the schemata can all be seen to be required to belong together.

Notes

1   To give a tortuous amplification of this, in case it is of help to any reader, I divide the constituents of society and the schemata into

three broad classes with four groups in one, one in the second, and three groups in the third. The first class containing four groups will consist of nine *constituents* of the situation. The second is a group of two schemata of man's *intuitive explanations* of the workings of society, bringing in two more constituents. The third class of three groups will consist of *alternative interpretations* or theories in the sense of *frameworks* for the *nature* of societal behaviour given by social scientists and philosophers.

This makes 3 classes of 8 groups of 11 constituents and 20 schemata. If the reader finds the relation between constituents and schemata confusing, he need only bear in mind that constituents consist of the items obviously contained in, or widely believed to, form part of the societal situation, such as people, institutions, needs, goals, historical influences and so on, while schemata are ways of looking at these; the matter is confusing because the same names sometimes appear in both — individuals are constituents, individualism a schema.

2   Toynbee, however, was dealing with challenge and response of a whole society, not of subsystems within it.

References

Brown, Robert (1963), *Explanation in Social Science*, Aldine, Chicago, pp. 122—3.
Dahrendorf, Ralf (1959), *Class and Class-Conflict in Industrial Society*, Stanford University Press, Stanford, California, trans. 1972.
Friedman, Otto (1950), *Introduction to Social Psychology*, Sylvan Press, London.
Gellner, E.A. (1958), 'Time and Theory in Social Anthropology', *Mind, 67*, pp. 184—5.
Gellner, E.A. (1973), 'Sociology and Social Anthropology' in *Cause and Meaning in the Social Sciences*, Routledge & Kegan Paul, London, pp. 127—8.
Jarvie, I.C. (1964), *The Revolution in Anthropology*, Routledge & Kegan Paul, London, p. 188.
Jarvie, I.C. (1976), *Functionalism*, Burgess, Minneapolis.
Malinowski, Bronislaw (1944), *A Scientific Theory of Culture*, University of Carolina.
Merton, R.K. (1949), *Social Theory and Social Structure*, Free Press, Glencoe, Ill., ch. 1.
Parsons, Talcott and Shils, E.A. (1951), *Toward a General Theory of Action*, Harvard University Press, Cambridge, Mass.

Popper, K.R. (1962), *Conjectures and Refutations*, Basic Books, New York, p. 362.

Radcliffe-Brown, A.R. (1952), *Structure and Function in Primitive Society*, Free Press, Glencoe, Ill., chapters 9 and 10.

Toynbee, A.J. (1934), *A Study of History*, Oxford University Press, London.

Appendix: layered schemata

There is, however, a significant theoretical point to be taken care of. Are all these schemata, to do with institutions, environment, evolution, functions, conflict and so on, to be put together in one mix if they are included in one overall schema? The realities corresponding to them could go into one saucepan as a mix to be scrambled, but the schemata are conceptual and must not be scrambled but be kept in separate compartments, despite complexity in the realities. Friedman (1950, p. 171) rightly points to the complexity of factors involved in societal explanation, but the difficulty of complexity can, I think, be handled by realising that the very fact that the realities mutually influence or modify each other presupposes concepts that are unmixed. Indeed, he himself meets it rather in the same way; for though he uses no technically labelled schemata, he implies them, and, I think, implies them as conceptually distinct. For example, if faced with the task of explaining the British coal strike in 1974, he would no doubt draw attention to: the miner's sense of frustration at inflation; impatience at too slow improvement in wages; annoyance with the Industrial Relations Act; a sense of timing (get 'em on the wrong foot); the real hope of bringing down the government; employers' unwillingness to face a real showdown; the government's need to show that the act could work and prevent dislocation; the government's need to establish who governs; irrationality in the government's appraisals of the situation at various times. And certainly these factors would utilise at least these schemata: individuals, institutions, tradition, anticipations, goals, possibly conspiracy, and conflict. Moreover, he holds rightly that for a specified problem there is no general answer as to which factors are appropriate, that the answer can be found only by examining each case — common sense deciding on an appropriate selection. And to the wide variety of factors involved that would fall under our schemata, his individualistic approach takes into account a factor missing from all four meta-scientific forms of individualism to be discussed subsequently (Popper's, Wittgenstein's phenomenology, and psychological individualism), namely the *irrational* which may not play any part in some problems, but can find expression in all levels of social organisation (Friedman, 1950, p. 55).

Further, in regard to the need to keep the schemata conceptually distinct, in separate compartments, the relevant compartment depends in simple cases upon what question is asked. In less simple cases, instead of bemoaning that we cannot know the combined effect of biological needs, environmental factors, and tradition, we can reach limited results by taking them in phases: thus, given the needs and environment well specified, we can discuss the effect of tradition. A parallel is to be found in the approximate gas law that the pressure multiplied by the volume is proportional to the absolute temperature: we can hold the volume fixed as given, and discuss the effect of the pressure on changes in absolute temperature. In this way, we do not *disregard* the other factors, such as needs and environment, when we discuss the effect of tradition; there is only an appearance of over-simplification. Moreover, even when all the schemata are involved, corresponding to a pot-pourri in the real world, the concepts of the schemata remain distinct from one another. A pot-pourri in the real world does not produce a pot-pourri conceptually (except in the minds of those who allow it to happen). And the way to preserve conceptual distinctions is to keep most schemata temporarily out of the picture by keeping them (or concepts falling under them) constant, so that it is possible to ask a *simple* question about what are left.

Thus Friedman's healthy common sense differs from the present approach as regards method of handling complexity. Friedman gives all factors, so to speak, an equal hearing. Here the method suggested aims at avoiding being swamped by complexity, not, however, by evading it, but by imposing a layered order upon it.

9 Schemata in the social sciences: metatheoretical

Holism

Following various writers, I propose to use this term as a generic one for a group of views but conveniently also for a particular component view. Holism is of no interest unless it is understood in its most extreme form. That there are social wholes of importance, that the whole is more than the sum of its parts and so forth are trivia and are not significant in the great schemata of the social sciences.

This group of the interpretational class of *schemata* consists of three component interpretations, consisting of *holism* in the more specific sense of an *intuitive grasp* of society as a whole, historicism (in Popper's 1964, p. 3 sense), that is, an intuitive grasp of the historical carpet of society which unrolls, revealing the phases of society from past to future in a rigidly deterministic way, and *epoch-relativism*, or *restricted applicability* as I will call it for brevity, which is that the result of our studies of one culture has no relevance to, and cannot be transferred to, others.

According to holism in the specific sense, the only way of under-standing basic societal influences — social action, social change — is by means of intuitive insight into the nature or essence of society. As such, none of the ordinary procedures of science are applicable for this purpose. There is nothing in this view to preclude that natural science and similar procedures might not be used for obtaining generalisations and useful knowhow about the day-to-day realities of communities; it is simply that holists tend not to be very interested in this kind of thing, since what is really meaningful to them is an altogether different level of enquiry, namely the inner nature of society and the way it dominates social action and social life, and this is unaffected by what may be done on the small scale by paltry applications of ordinary scientific procedures. Thus if a God or gods on the one hand or a deep societal structure works like a steamroller, dominating the common lot of man, the fate of his immortal soul may override the importance of economic change; if he has a sense of helplessness, feeling either that his life belongs in the hereafter or that he has lost touch with himself as a human being, then it is of little avail to give him an old age pension or inject his children against polio. In Judaic historicism, the chosen people will receive their due, no matter what; in Christian historicism, good will triumph over evil, despite all the efforts of Satan; in Marx's historicism, efforts made by the individual do no more than facilitate like a midwife. Holism is perhaps an occidental version of an essentially oriental vision of the world in which the outer show bears little relation to the great inner, or underlying, reality.

Historicism in Popper's sense is closely associated with holism. Holism concerns the present in that the intuitive grasp of society is a current intuition, while historicism concerns the deterministic unfolding of the holistic picture from former phases to the present and future ones. It may be likened to a carpet unfolding inexorably, or to a cine film recorded from the beginning to the end of time. The greatest exponents of holism and historicism have been Plato, Hegel, and Marx, to cite individual thinkers; but there have also been great social movements, namely Judaism and Christianity, not to mention the Nazi dream of an Aryan world.

Popper (1964) has launched a colossal attack upon these positions, using a great deal of rational argument which does much to undermine them. It is questionable, however, whether he has succeeded in annihilating them, or what is the net result of his attack. It is difficult to see that any kind of empirical observation could tell against such schemata. Nor have a priori philosophical arguments proved decisive against such positions. To this I would add that the very fact that they are *schemata* precludes all possibility of their being proved or disproved by any ordinary means. It has escaped notice that they are in fact schemata and it has escaped notice that schemata are not amenable to ordinary modes of proof and disproof. However, we shall have made progress if we recognise that they are schemata, at least if this means that no straightforward method of disproof is possible; while it is equally the case that their exponents have no means of proof at their disposal.

A word should be added on epoch-relativism or restricted applicability which is a very influential view and manifests itself in different forms, such as ethnorelativism, cultural relativism, and so on. Another description of it was historicism in the older sense, not the one used by Popper. What it amounts to is the metascientific view that universal laws as found in natural science do not exist in the social sciences. Something like universal laws (but not really universal because they are circumscribed) may apply in a given society or a given period; thus 'laws' obtained by ordinary scientific procedures would be epoch-relative. Stated in this form the position is rather uninteresting because it contains an elementary fallacy. In natural science itself laws are stated as if universal; since it is then often found that they do not hold universally, it would be therefore perfectly possible to articulate this result by saying that they are domain-relative. However, in such a case, the procedure of science is to include a qualification within the statement of the law which restores its universalistic form. Thus if the Boyle—Mariotte law of gases is found to be pretty inaccurate at low temperatures, its statement is restricted to the medium range of temperature. It then has a universalistic form that simply does not apply to low temperatures. In the same way, if it is maintained that the economics of nineteenth-century laissez-faire is one thing and the economics of the feudal system is another, so that these two systems of economics are epoch-relative, all that natural science would do to preserve the parallel would be to put in the qualifications appropriate to their application. Indeed the contention of epoch-relativism would hold only if no laws whatever could be found to apply without qualification across the board to different societies or epochs. Such a situation is wholly unlikely. It possibly gains any plausibility it may have from not being stated as such, but by being an unnoticed extension of a misunderstanding about laws in natural science to do with unstated restrictions on their applicability.

Epoch-relativism is a guess, although an understandable one. It should be noticed, however, that epoch-relativism can be maintained without also maintaining holism or historicism. The converse is much less likely if not impossible; holists and historicists are likely to be epoch-relativists. The importance of epoch-relativism lies in two factors. One is that it is used by some as a means of supporting holism or historicism. The other is this. For those who hold epoch-relativism but are not interested in maintaining holism or historicism, the doctrine is used as a weapon against science, as a means of opposing the application of science and scientific method to the study of society. Social investigation is then shorn of any way of studying society unless it embraces holism or some form of intuitionism.

Epoch-relativism has been included in this group under holism, because it implies that an epoch is a whole on its own, and because it has loose associations with holism and historicism. What then, is the overall position about these holistic schemata? Reminding ourselves that they have to be understood in their extreme forms if they are to be of any interest as guidelines for the social sciences, their most important consequence is that they rule out significant influence upon human and societal action by individual persons. In this lies the huge importance of holism as an interpretative schema of social science. And, if it is true, it is of enormous importance even if there should be no way of establishing it. From a common-sense point of view, if it is universalised it seems to be obviously false, but this is no solid disproof. If we consider the enormous influence that individuals have sometimes had upon this world, a holist would certainly be equal to the task of showing that this was compatible with holism, and there would be no way of providing a decisive disproof. Holism is a schema that attracts many to its flag; it is a schema that many others find completely repellent. It has the ostensible demerit of demoting the significance of the individual. Has it then any corresponding merit which would be recognised even by those who find it anathema? I will suggest later the existence of a factor in holism, whether detachable from the rest of it or not, that may prove of enormous importance especially as it has no counterpart in any of the other schemata.

Forms of Individualism

Holism is a schema taken for granted in some societies or in whole epochs to such an extent that individualism is there regarded as an absurdity. Equally, we find that large societies will take individualism for granted as good common sense and regard any form of holism as backward, naïve, authoritarian or mystical.

Those who live among millions of people who live by the one schema often can scarcely grasp that millions of people who live by the other schema can really swallow it. So one of the surprises is to find so many forms of individualism. Four will be discussed below. Another of the surprises is to find such odd bedfellows as Popper and Wittgenstein, not to mention the phenomenological version. There is also a Freudian version which provides an even stranger bedfellow. Only two of these, as we shall see, the Popperian and phenomenological, are of basic significance for social science, though the others make minor contributions.

A third group of forms of individualism (after Popperian and phenomenological) constitutes another interpretation about the nature of the overt societal situation or an extension of it. (There will also emerge a fourth form to be added to Weber's and Popper's, which will be detached and discussed separately later.) Its four constituents are:

1 psychologistic, typified by Freud (1921);
2 social activity, conceived as 'rule-following' by individuals originated by Wittgenstein (1953);
3 the phenomenological approach (Berger and Luckmann, 1966) to the notion of a social role, with special variants, principally Blumer (1969); and finally
4 a form of individualism which I have described as situational individualism due to Weber (1964) and Popper (1962, pp. 91, 324; 1964, pp. 136, 157−8).

These are discussed below.

Psychologistic Individualism

According to this conception, institutions are interpreted, at least in some cases, as enlarged pictures of the individual person or of the nuclear family. This may be illustrated by an example given by Ernest Jones which would almost certainly have been accepted by Freud. On this interpretation, in the institution of the constitutional monarchy, the king is the focus of sentiments directed towards the individual's good father whom he can look up to and admire and from whom he can seek protection and wise counsel. Since the individual in Freud's theory splits the father image into one that is good and one that is bad, a receptable is needed for the bad father image, and this may be conveniently located in the person of the Prime Minister, who after a while, when he can be no longer tolerated, can be changed, whereas the good father image is perpetual (Jones, 1936). If we seek a psychologistic illustration from Freud himself (1922) we shall readily find one in *The Future of an Illusion*, in which the institution of religion itself hinges on interpreting God as a focus for streamlined attitudes towards the father.

No doubt there are a few examples of social institutions that can be interpreted in terms of unconscious attitudes in this kind of way, but restricted to a *symbolic* object (or a fairly simple displacement). It would seem to be an inordinately difficult task to interpret the welter of social institutions along these lines. However, even if this should be possible the approach may still be social psychology rather than sociology. Indeed one could say that Freud, despite his colossal genius and insight into the morass that constitutes the individual unconscious mind, when he turned in the direction of society did not really treat social science as *social*; and this is the basic criticism being made here of psychologistic individualism. Where an institution can successfully be given meaning in terms of the unconscious individual or in terms of a nuclear family, what this does is provide the *meaning* or at least part of the *meaning* of the institution, and this may be a tremendous insight. What it does not do is to explain the *function*; and for purposes of social science the function of an institution is of cardinal importance. In other words, this approach provides a limited truth so far as it goes, but as an overall schema it is far too limited. This is not to say that psychologistic interpretations might not be developed further along more elaborate lines; but in its present form the psychologistic schema is not an overall schema for social science.

Rule-following Individualism

The Wittgensteinian approach is that individual action takes place in accordance with social roles: for instance, we eat with a fork not a knife; we drive on one side of the road; we adopt standards of time common to a large area; when we speak, we follow linguistic rules. This unspecific and allusive view has been subject to annihilating criticism by Gellner, but a couple of remarks may be appropriate here. The approach is of limited application, for though it is obviously true that individuals do follow rules it does not cover the huge mass of situations in which there are no rules to follow (not to mention situations in which rules are violated); but the main and overwhelming deficiency is that *the rules themselves need to be explained by social science*. This is perhaps more obvious if we notice that 'rules' in this context are *conventions*.

It is worth adding that, on the Wittgensteinian approach, all explanations are given in terms of person-initiated change. This presupposes that persons are totally outside the sphere of naturalistic explanation and causation. Societal explanation, however, if it is not to be pre-Copernican, or at least pre-Darwinian, must treat persons in some contexts as one with other natural phenomena.

Social Roles and Encounters in Terms of Individualism

The philosophy of phenomenology was developed by Husserl as an epistemology and was directed into a sociological channel by Schütz (1962). Following him is a development that follows the original phenomenological form: it is designed to explain how social roles can be constructed, or alternatively reduced to, the phenomenological

116

experience of the individual in a life situation (Berger and Luckmann, 1966; Holzner, 1968). Also inspired by Schütz comes a crop of 'post-phenomenological' approaches. One is symbolic interactionism, according to which the basis of action and of society is *interaction* between the individuals but that the 'things' with which people interact are the meanings ascribed to them in the course of interacting (Blumer, 1969). A person may go on to manipulate these meaning-things and thus add to this meaning. Another post-phenomenological development is ethnomethodology (Garfinkel, 1965): in this development, the stress falls on the fullness of actual lived experience which is cut short by commonplace descriptions that depend on mutually understood shared experiences. In yet another, inspired by economics but with stress on the individual's experience, all social encounters are forms of social and personal trading in a market, not of wares and money, but of experiences (desires, forfeits and so on) (Blau, 1964). Some of these approaches are personal, but I will include them all under 'inter-personal'.

These aspects of the approach, whether they attempt to see social roles and encounters as extensions of the phenomenological experience of the individual, or the interpretations of attitudes, or the phenomenological experiences of interpersonal interaction, can be rich and valuable. In some, even if small, degree, they provide an explanation of human and social activity and even contribute to the explanation of societal change, which cannot be said of many alternative schemata. They also provide a graphic, intimate and human sense of what is actually going on. But, most strikingly, they deal with the development of social reality resulting from the interplay between person and person. This asset at the same time reveals what is lacking in the approach: that is, it constitutes *what needs explanation*, for in the end social science wants to know about the more or less permanent features of social roles, which almost certainly cannot be wholly absorbed by the phenomenological experiences of the individual; it also wants to understand the social reality behind the interpretations that the interpretative schema produces, on the assumption that these also cannot be wholly reduced to the sum of individual phenomenological experiences. On the other hand it must be emphasised that there is a current phase of controversy because of the interpersonalist revolt against science.

A cautionary comment should be made on all of these three forms of individualism. It is not to be denied that in all of them there is some feature of society that has some social reality over and above that of individuals; but all of them seek to reduce that social reality to the experiences of the individual or at least treat individual experience as the overwhelmingly dominant factor in the explanation of social action.

Situational Individualism (Ascertainable)

The overt societal situation might very reasonably seem to contain all the possible constituents of any possible societal situation; it would be easy to suppose that nothing has been overlooked. However Weber (1921) and Popper (1962, p. 93; 1964, p. 158), who have adopted a schema closest of all to the overt societal situation, have found the need to include a further factor missing from the map given above. The Weber–Popper schema places enormous emphasis upon the *unintended consequences* of human actions. It is not that they were the only social scientists to consider this notion important, it is also (as pointed out by Popper, 1962) given great stress by Marx, but its special role for Weber and Popper lies in its connection with the overt societal situation, which gives it a more important part to play than it had in the theories of other social scientists.

The overt societal situation provides determinants for a person's decision/action; but, as Weber and Popper realised, other things happen in society that are not simply actions by individuals. To illustrate with a variant of an example of Popper's: a man wants to buy two identical houses in a certain street, he begins by buying one of them, then finds that in so doing he has driven up the price of the other one. This was not his intention but it is an unintended consequence of his initial action. What is important to Weber and Popper is that they trace such happenings to the *unintended consequences* of individual people's actions.[1] Further, the Weber–Popper thesis is that there is no other kind of social change not accountable in terms of individual actions and their unintended consequences.[2]

For Popper's term 'unintended consequences' I will substitute Weber's and Secher's, 'unintended by-products'.

The question now arises whether unintended by-products can be incorporated as a further constituent of these societal situations. One thing the notion is not — it is not overt. If you look around the societal situation to see what you have to take into account you do not find this factor. What addition must be made, therefore, to the map of the societal situation? Popper points out that, by taking a deal of trouble, some unintended by-products can be anticipated. While this is a matter of the utmost difficulty in practice there is nothing to suggest that he sets a limit to it in principle. He regards it as a practical consideration of practical importance, for if one is to act effectively it is a necessary part of one's thinking to try to anticipate what will happen as a result of contemplated action, thus

118

anticipating what may go wrong and thus possibly avoiding some mistakes, and this means trying to anticipate the unexpected. Other limits to what can be done may exist — I have argued elsewhere that there are theoretical limits (Wisdom, 1970) — but that is not the present issue. It is to be admitted that some anticipations are possible and therefore a person contemplating a decision/action must take them into account. Hence the Weber–Popper schema must enlarge the overt societal situation so as to include them. That is why I characterise the Weber–Popper schema of situational individualism by the epithet 'ascertainable'.

There is more than one possible map of the societal situation. Mankind would not be satisfied with the overt version but would include conspiracies and the influences of God/gods. To improve Popper's view we have to simplify the map in a different way. So when Popper (1962, p. 7; 1964, p. 149) spoke of the 'logic of the situation' he used an unfortunate designation, for he implied that the situation contained an unambiguous list of constituents, and he might have spoken of his interpretation of the situation. It is important to realise that the Weber–Popper construction of the societal situation is wider — and more powerful for explanatory purposes — than the initial map of the overt societal situation, for room is made for the factor of unintended by-products. It amounts to 'the societal situation with feedback', and is illustrated by Figure 8.4 in the previous chapter and by the table below.

List of constituents, groups and schemata

Individuals		(c)	Constituents of society rendered a schema below
Institutions		(c)	Constituents of society rendered a schema below
Environmental	(s)	(c)	{ Physical circumstances
	(s)	(c)	{ Biological needs
Non-contemporary	(s)	(c)	{ History, tradition, evolution
	(s)	(c)	{ Future anticipations, ideals/goals
Personal Powers	(s)	(c)	{ God/gods
	(s)	(c)	{ Conspiracies
Nature/Role of	(s)	(c)	{ Structuralism
institutions/groups	(s)	(c)	{ Functionalism
(systematic—	(s)	(c)	{ Structural-functionalism
non-holistic)	(s)	(c)	{ Conflict
Holism (general)	(s)		{ Holism (specific)
	(s)		{ Historicism
	(s)		{ Epoch-relativism or restricted applicability
Individualism	(s)		{ Psychologistic
	(s)		{ Rule-following
	(s)		{ Phenomenological/symbolic interactionist
	(s)		{ Situational (feedback)

Note: Groups are listed on the left; c stands for constituent, s for schema.

It will be realised at once that the Weber–Popper schema is wholly compatible with the phenomenological interpersonalist approach and hermeneutic schema, provided these make no doctrinaire attempt to reduce the social roles and attitudes to individual phenomenological experience without remainder. Indeed, insert the notion of unintended by-product and there is no basic disparity between these two schemata. The Weber–Popper schema provides the inventory and mode of functioning; the phenomenological approach fills this in with the richness of the interactions, and the interactionist approaches unfold the creation of social reality out of the interplay between persons — which is missing, though not in principle, from the Weber–Popper schema.

Although the Weber–Popper schema admits to the existence of social institutions over and above the aims, activities, interests, and experiences of individual persons, the schema is in an important sense individualistic in colour, and it would have no truck with any holistic force animating structures of society. Thus holism and situational individualism (with ascertainable anticipations) are fundamentally at odds with each other, they are fundamentally incompatible interpretations of social reality.

Interpretations of the 'Situation'

The Weber–Popper interpretation of situational individualism, with possible ascertainable factors included, would appear to be a maximally wide form of individualism. Its contention is that, if holism is denied, the societal situation with feedback is its complete antithesis and is sufficient to explain societal action. The broad question that arises is whether there is any possible factor, either great or small, that is missing from this form of individualism. This divides into two questions, whether some relatively minor changes might be made compatible with it and the other is whether it needs radical alteration.

As already explained, it very readily includes the phenomenological approach, provided this is not given an extreme form and made into a schema that excludes all independent reality to institutions. It is hardly necessary to mention that it includes the notion of rule-following which is but a small component of action in accordance with the broad conception of an institutional framework. It does not, however, include the psychologistic individualism of Freud and others. Popper himself deliberately excludes this because he finds psychologistic explanations anathema. But there is no fundamental reason why they should be antipathetic; it is only when the psychologistic explanation is offered as an *exclusive* schema that it is incompatible with Popper's own form of individualism, and it is only then that it is inadequate to explain societal functioning. But as a feature of some components of society at least, and not as a universalistic schema, it is a component that enriches our understanding of the social scene. Room should therefore be made for what would be called 'psychologistic hermeneutics' or perhaps 'symbolic psychologism' (to allow for the possibility that a better form of psychologism might conceivably be invented), provided the modesty of its role is borne in mind.

Thus reinforced, the Weber–Popper schema would seem to have everything packed into it short of ceasing to be individualistic; it would therefore be the widest possible form of individualism, and therefore should be accepted, provided it really is required that *all* societal change must be interpreted as fundamentally individualistic. Moreover, it should be noted that, including as it does, the notion of unintended by-product, the Weber–Popper schema is powerful, and can be put to work to explain at least great numbers of societal phenomena — whether or not it still remains an open question as to whether it explains all.

In stressing the power of the Weber–Popper thesis it should be recalled that it includes every single one of the components that lies strictly within the ascertainable situation map (the one exclusion being God/gods, a factor that is placed just outside the central map). In this regard, the Weber–Popper thesis is unlike all the other schemata and interpretations so far considered.

We turn now to the question whether the Weber–Popper schema excludes any larger kind of factor, the embodiment of which would be incompatible with it or be impossible to include. Gellner (1973b) and Mandelbaum (1955) are two who consider that the individualistic schema is not enough. Obviously, we have now reached the fundamental cleavage between holism and the Weber–Popper thesis of ascertainable situational individualism amplified to include feedback from unintended by-products.

What then, may we find in holism that has not been taken account of or has been deliberately excluded even by enlarged individualism? There would seem to be just one basic factor which might be expressed in two parts, or simply as one factor with an important characteristic requiring separate discussion. This factor might be described as consisting of hidden societal forces or constraints, and the characteristic of them that would require to be highlighted is that they are *dynamic*. Naturally, one can hardly have forces that are not dynamic, but the appearance of redundancy in the reference to dynamism is deliberate because individualism seems to lack it. Now, the Weber–Popper interpretation is opposed to this notion and the grounds of this opposition may be put in one or other of two ways though in the end they may amount to the same thing. One is that the notion would be regarded by individualists as a myth. However it might be fairly readily admitted that changes take place in society of such dimensions and beyond the reach of influence by individuals, at least in the short run, that they do give the impression of stemming from some deep structural factor. Nonetheless, so far as this would be admitted as an impression, the individualist would deny that this was a correct interpretation of social process. The answer would be given very simply that, if investigated carefully, such social processes would be found to be *reducible* to the individualistic schema, provided one attached sufficient weight to the unintended by-products of individual actions. This is the point — reducibility and, cognate with it (notwithstanding appearances to the contrary), the claim that all social phenomena can be embraced within the individualistic schema.

Parallel with this, though no one so far has considered the point, the individualist might argue that the dynamism characterising the deep structure of hidden forces or constraints in holism is an appearance taken account of by the unintended by-products of individual human actions. It is, however, worth noting en passant that no dynamic laws are to be found in the social sciences when conducted by those who are individualistic metascientists.

We see here a complete deadlock with no possibility whatever, in terms of ordinary methods of procedure to be found in science or metascience, of proof or disproof of either of the two rival schemata.

If we happen to think that our researches are likely to be fruitful, if we allow ourselves the widest possible latitude in framework of approach, then we may wish to allow a possible role for either schema. Holism certainly *seems* to be over-restrictive as regards the possible influence of individuals upon the course of society. I emphasise *seems*, because, however strong this impression and however good common sense it may be, one of the points I wish to urge is that we have no proof of it. It would be wise, however, to allow the possibility in principle and to explore it by putting it to work. Again it is worth recognising at least the possibility that there may be a fruitful component in holism. The holistic historicist schema may be overwhelmingly restrictive on the individual, but it may also have the great merit of introducing the notion of an independent social dynamics. Even Durkheim can hardly be said to have had this notion. Whether or not it is true it is the greatest merit of Marx. Whether or not it is the only component of Marxism that might survive in social science, it is surely worth preserving it within the framework of our theoretical social science and trying to put it to work.

Having just indicated that, from the point of view of fruitful research, there may be a case for utilising on occasion both schemata, the question arises how can this be done if they are incompatible. The following bipolar position is a possibility. Society might contain a hidden forceful constraint, very powerful, sometimes overriding in its effects and swamping all attempts to stem it, sometimes influential but not overriding, sometimes present but easily contained. Contained by what? By the efforts of individual people or groups. Thus, many societal situations might be largely coped with by the efforts/ decisions/actions of individual persons while many others might not be capable of being coped with in this way, and the proportion of influence might vary very greatly from case to case. Such a bipolar model would be completely flexible and allow interplay between deep-structure constraints and individuals. There would be no a priori means of knowing which was the dominant influence on any given occasion. To understand the source of social change would thus be a matter of *empirical* inquiry in all individual cases. Such an approach would thus empower us to ask a wide range of questions. This bipolar model would include the Weber–Popper schema with its eleven components, and allow also that social reality might be permeated by a hidden forceful constraint. Such a revised schema would not be contra-individualistic; but since it would admit the possibility (unproved) of a hidden dynamic factor it would be 'trans-individualistic' (Wisdom, 1970, p. 293f).

Empirical Content, Weltanschauungen, and Schemata

All natural science has weltanschauungen which are unprovable, irrefutable by observation but, as shown elsewhere, refutable by a satisfactory empirical theory. All the alternative schemata considered above are weltanschauungen, frameworks, or orientation theories, though *not* themselves empirical theories. In the present context I have called them schemata. I have sought to depict them in the societal situation map with its variations, in such a way as to bring out sharply their unprovable and undisprovable nature at least by all the classical methods of argument. If a weltanschauung or a schema can be found to be satisfactory, at least for a time, by being put to work fruitfully, it may on odd occasions be refuted by a new procedure, namely by being found incompatible with a new empirical theory that passes muster.

It cannot be too strongly emphasised that the controversy between holism and individualism cannot be settled at all by any of the classical methods of argument. What could be done would be to work within one or other framework, or within the schema of the bipolar model, so as to produce a satisfactory empirical social theory. Such a satisfactory social theory would put one of these schemata to work and, in so doing, would be incompatible with other schemata. This is a way in which the problem of schemata could be resolved.

Conclusion

Several combined aims have been welded together above: here are the contentions. The 20 possible schemata for social sciences are schemata only. They are not universal and exclusive. They are all, or nearly all, partially true. They, or most of them, can be made constituents of a unifying schema. None is provable, even the one put forward at the end to unify. The significant difference between the schemata lies in the questions that can be mounted. Most of the schemata are developed out of different interpretations of the societal situation, the one exception being holism which apparently is not. A bipolar model is proposed to combine a factor in holism with the amplified societal situation. A few — very few — criticisms have been made of some of the schemata but only for the practical purpose of dismissing one or two of the least serviceable and least interesting of them. The main point of criticism made against the various schemata is not falsity but their claim to exclusiveness.

The main bone of contention that animates 'professionals' is about whether the social sciences are solely about people (in society) or are 'scientific', structural, about the nature of society; this may resolve itself as social scientists become aware of their schemata and of the unreality of keeping schemata in watertight compartments. The problem discussed in this chapter is concerned not with such rival commitments, but with the one problem of schemata that concerns people and society in rerum natura.

Notes

1   Although Weber's work is shot through with individualism (though, like Popper, he saw individual actions as placed in an institutional setting), he only alluded to individualism, whereas Popper, however briefly, is most explicit about it. Weber (1922) said (of change in human action), 'Der ungewollte Nebenerfolg des Ablaufs sozialen Handelns . . . '. This was translated unsatisfactorily by Henderson and Parsons (1964) as 'an unanticipated consequence of a course of social action . . .' and adequately by Secher (1972) as 'the unintended by-product of a course of human

conduct . . . '. 'Unanticipated' is inaccurate, though not gravely misleading. Secher's term 'by-product' catches the spirit of Weber's, and also of Popper's, meaning better than 'consequence'.

2   Weber does not explicitly argue this (Popper does), though he explicitly assumes it, for he (Weber, 1964, p. 101) held that 'collectivities must be treated *solely* as the resultants and modes of organization of acts of individual persons': the whole tenor of his work supports this.

References

Berger, Peter and Luckmann, Thomas (1966), *The Social Construction of Reality*, Doubleday, New York.

Blau, P.M. (1964), *Exchange and Power in Social Life*, Wiley, New York.

Blumer, Herbert (1969), *Symbolic Interactionism*, Prentice-Hall, Englewood Cliffs, New Jersey.

Freud, Sigmund (1921), *Group Psychology and the Analysis of the Ego*, stand. edn, vol. 18.

Freud, Sigmund (1922), *The Future of an Illusion*, stand. edn, vol. 21.

Garfinkel, Harold (1967), *Studies in Ethnomethodology*, Prentice-Hall, Englewood Cliffs, New Jersey.

Garfinkel, Harold (1973b), 'Explanation in History' in *Cause and Meaning in the Social Sciences*, Routledge & Kegan Paul, London, pp. 1—17.

Henderson, A.M. and Parsons, T. (1964) (trans.), *The Theory of Social and Economic Organization*, Free Press, Glencoe, part 1, chapter 1, p. 135.

Holzner, Burkart (1968), *Reality Construction in Society*, Schenkmenn, Cambridge, Mass.

Jones, Ernest (1936), 'The Psychology of Constitutional Monarchy', *The New Statesmen and Nation*, *11*, pp. 141—2.

Mandelbaum, Maurice (1955), 'Societal Facts', *British Journal of Sociology*, *6*, pp. 305—17.

Mandelbaum, Maurice (1962), *The Open Society and its Enemies*, vol. 2, Harper & Row, New York, pp. 94—5.

Mandelbaum, Maurice (1964), *The Poverty of Historicism*, Harper, New York, p. 3.

Popper, K.R. (1964), *The Poverty of Historicism*, London.

Schütz, Alfred (1962), *The Problem of Social Reality, Collected Papers I*, Nijhoff, den Haag.

Secher, H.P. (1972) (trans.), *Basic Concepts in Sociology*, Citadel, Secaucus, New Jersey, para. 8, sec. 3, p. 88.

Weber, Max (1921), *Wirtschaft und Gesellschaft*, Mohr, Tubingen, Teil 1, Kap. 1, s. 8 (1956 edn, s. 21).

Weber, Max (1964), *The Theory of Social and Economic Organization*, Free Press, Glencoe, part 1, chapter 1, p. 101.

Wisdom, J.O. (1970), 'Situational Individualism and Emergent Group-Properties' in *Explanation in the Behavioural Sciences*, Cambridge, pp. 271—96.

Wittgenstein, Ludwig (1953), *Philosophical Investigations*, Blackwell, Oxford.

10 Situational individualism

One of the fundamental problems in the philosophy of the social sciences is to locate the source of power possessed by groups, if it is in any measure independent of individuals. If a group is no more than the sum of the individuals composing it, there is no problem: the power of the group is only some compound of the power of its members. But, assuming that a group is more than this, we seem forced to suppose that not all its power can derive from them. Is a dual control understandable? If not, are individuals merely the pawns of group-power? Or is there some way, after all, of seeing group-power as an outcrop of the power of individuals?

This last is the answer given by Popper (1964) through his thesis of methodological individualism. His thesis goes a long way towards solving the problem, but seems to contain a certain gap. My aim is to show that in filling it we are led to a framework of dual control. (The view of group-power as wholly overriding individuals lies outside the scope of this discussion.)

Methodological Individualism and its Dual Claims

However wrongheaded, the most natural presumption to adopt to begin with is that individual human beings began as individuals, related to one another only as individuals, and that in the course of time they banded themselves together into groups or communities. Society would then appear as a product arising from individuals. This presumption probably stems, at least in part, from the atomistic approach of western thought.

In the course of time, unacceptable developments ensue, such as severe taxation or the impossibility of disburdening oneself of a nagging wife. Individuals feel helpless before these states of affairs. The source of some of them may be, for a time, attributed to a god, but the source of others — and later on almost all others — becomes attributed to society itself. It is noticed that institutions (in a broad sense) have great effects on people which they are powerless to alter: we all have to wear some clothes; we all have to go to school; many have to follow religious observances, or to follow some social observances, such as lifting one's cap or driving on the left side of the road; all may even have to vote at an election. Whence do institutions/society derive their power? If to begin with the power is supposed to reside in a god, such a belief becomes attenuated with the (gradual) growth of secularism. It is a natural development for the power to be located firmly in society itself. Thus Marx (1906) regarded the way large numbers of individual workers were exploited as a manifestation of the institution of exploitation and explained such exploitation as a consequence of the institution of capitalism.

Thus the locus of power, as we see it, shifts from individuals to society. In extreme forms it is not shared: in the extreme form of individualism society is a mode of individual operations and partakes of no independent power; in the extreme form of what, following Gellner, we may best call holism, societal power overrides individuals who have no share of it (beyond being for Marx midwives (catalysts) or brakes).

Thus we reach the idea of an institution or of society as an *independent* source of power. Doctrines of holism, historicism, group-minds, a collective unconscious are (nearly always) versions of the idea of society with wholly independent power. Institutions seem to have a life of their own.

Then holism itself suffers a twist of the screw. Secularism, which has given up a belief in transcendent gods above, begins to doubt that any form of god is even immanent in society. A dash of empiricism and liberalism salt the scepticism. And Popper, spokesman for English distrust of the doctrinaire, for English liberalism and minimum interference with *laissez-faire*, reacts against holism[1] with the assertion that institutions do not have aims — only individuals have aims, interests, needs, intentions, or take decisions.

This thesis is one of Popper's most important contributions to the philosophy of the social sciences. But unlike nearly all his other ideas in print, his account of it is sketchy, and the Popperians have not sufficiently filled it out. Agassi's (1960) masterly exegesis almost completely succeeded, but still, I think, left a basic point obscure. This would be of no moment if the intuitive idea were wholly clear; but the very significance of it lies in the combination of two factors that, on the face of it, are incompatible.

For methodological individualism looks like a 'reductionist' theory, for it holds that institutions (or social wholes) consist of individual aims, intentions, interests, and power; but this does not quite correctly represent Popper, for he holds that institutions can never be expressed wholly in terms of individuals. So he is saying that there is nothing in society but individuals and their motivations, and yet that institutional activities have a life of their own. If this position is not explicated fully in such a way as to dispel any appearance of contradiction, the likelihood is that an account of it will achieve coherence at the expense of leaning towards one pole of the thesis or the other. Thus Watkins' discussions (notably Watkins, 1957) have left the impression with some readers that Popper's theory is fully reductionist.[2] This is the interpretation to be expected, not the opposite one, because Popper so stresses the role of individuals that no one would interpret him as reducing the activity of individuals to that of institutions. In fact, Popper's view allows a place to both poles, and (assuming that this is *not* an inconsistency, and I hold it is not), the first task is to dissect the thesis and present it free of apparent contradiction (cf. Scott, 1961).

Forms of Reductionism

Popper himself recognises that institutions have in some sense a life of their own. He is fully alive to such facts as that successive British governments in recent times intended to protect sterling currency. The problem that opens up is that of squaring such facts with individualism. And the most obvious way of trying to do so is by means of the device of 'reduction', by which an institutional aim is 'reducible' to that of individuals.

It is commonly supposed that there is just one process of 'reduction'; but this is not so — there are at least two. In the usual version, the broad procedure is to interpret a statement about institutional intentions as a *shorthand* for a statement about individual intentions, convenient in practice because of brevity but expendable in principle.[3]

Agassi appears to underwrite this method of 'reduction' as what Popper meant, for he speaks of the 'aims' of an institution as being a shorthand. I think, however, there is reason to doubt whether this is what Popper meant. This is a tricky point. As Agassi himself well points out, Popper allows of attributing an aim to an institution only in so far as *individuals* give it an aim. Thus, parliament legislates because we give it the aim of legislating; and, of course, we could take away this aim, as happens when a dictator abolishes parliament (or suffers it to remain, obliged to rubber stamp his measures). Now this construction does not 'reduce' parliament to the activities of ministers and members of parliament, judges and police; for it involves the activities of individuals outside the functioning of parliament, namely the members of the electorate. However, the intentions of these individuals should figure in the 'reductionist' analysis if this is to be at all adequate. So the 'reductionist' programme would mis-represent Popper only if it were too restricted as regards the range of the individuals included in it. Still it does apparently represent him correctly, that is that 'institutional aims' is a shorthand, provided the longhand is full enough. Is this really so?

The 'reductionist' programme aims at dispensing with *all* institutional wholes after the 'reduction' is carried out. Now Popper is fully aware, I think, that this is impossible, for you can dispense with one or even more institutional wholes, but *only in an institutional setting* (Popper, 1963, 2, p. 90). This is one of the factors unstressed in existing accounts of his methodological individualism.

For ease of reference I propose to reserve the expression 'reductionist' or 'reductionist individualism' for the extreme form of individualism, according to which all institutional wholes are 'reducible' without remainder to terms concerning the purposes of individuals, that is, all institutions are epiphenomena of individual purposes. 'Reductionist individualism' is a position sometimes attributed to Popper, the position sometimes put upon Watkins' accounts. In my view, although this is a misinterpretation of Popper's position, his view involves a partial reduction, in which any one institutional whole is 'reducible' though not all such wholes at once. That is to say, when any given institution is 'reduced' to the aims of individuals, this is effected only at the cost of introducing some other whole, which in turn can be reduced but only at a similar price. Thus, the social whole, the government, can be replaced by an individual, Mr Gladstone, when 'the Government decided . . . ' is replaced by 'Mr Gladstone signed an order . . . '; but this can be done only because Mr Gladstone acted in his institutional capacity of Prime Minister. The reference to a further whole may be covert, but it is present. Thus, with 'reduction' in this form, whatever whole is 'reduced', some whole is always left over 'unreduced'. This I take to be Popper's position. And I propose to call it 'situational

130

individualism', to bring out that for him individual aims exist only in an institutional situation, that is, that there are two poles in his thesis.

Unintended Consequences

I wish now to turn to a different facet. Popper (1963, 2, p. 324; 1964, p. 65) has laid great emphasis on the significance of *unintended consequences*, discussed in Chapter 9. By this he refers both to individuals and to institutions; he is more concerned with the unintended consequences of our individual actions than with those of institutions, but both occur and are important. We all know they occur, but few may agree that they have theoretical importance. For Popper they are basic and are inevitable.

I will first argue for a conclusion of Popper's that there must always be unintended consequences of our actions, which he did not trouble much about, leaving it as empirically obvious; but it is significantly more than that.

Unintended consequences commonly take the form of what I would describe as stable side-effects. Now supposing that the number of consequences were definite, they might or might not be all foreseeable. But an institution has an indefinite number of effects. Hence, even if *each* consequence were foreseeable, *all* would not be — just as *every* whole number is countable yet *all* whole numbers are not countable. This might be expressed by saying that unintended consequences may be *distributively* predictable but are not *collectively* predictable.[4] All of which is just a logical way of bringing out the point that whatever effort we make to foresee unintended consequences and however successful we are, there must logically always be some we shall have failed to foresee.

The reason why I have introduced the logical argument is that it enables a decisive point to be made. The unintended consequences that are not foreseen are of the same kind as those that are actually foreseen. So totally unknown consequences no longer have the aura of stemming from a mysterious origin. Their origin is the same as the origin of foreseen consequences, and these may not seem so mysterious. In fact, we may consider regarding an institution as a concatenation of individual intentions plus unintended consequences of individual intentions that are unforeseen. Then an institution would be made up of intentions and their consequences only and yet be more than actual intentions. This, I think, explains the point made by Popper, that only intentions and their consequences produce a certain institution, yet no one may actually have intended to produce it. Otherwise expressed, an institution is not a complex of goal-directed activities but results solely from goal-directed activities.

It is now easy to see that this construction of unintended consequences is identical with the construction put upon 'partial reductionism'; and we could say that 'situational individualism', which I attribute to Popper, is 'distributively reductionist', while 'reductionist individualism', which I claim Popper rejects, is 'collectively reductionist'.[5] For the unforeseen consequences of our actions are severally, though not collectively, 'reducible' to individual intentions and their consequences.[6] The sense of these rather abstract terms may be more easily retained in mind if we replace the two kinds of 'reductionism' by 'piecemeal reductionism' for Popper's view and 'global reductionism' for the misinterpretation of his view.

Thus the independent power of every institution lies in the capacity to produce unforeseen unintended consequences; but these are the results only of individual intentions, so that nothing over and above the individual intentions and their consequences is needed for building up the content of institutions. Thus Popper can maintain a position with two poles, which are apparently incompatible, namely individualism and institutionalism.[7]

I shall, however, introduce a far-reaching modification later.

Methodological Problems

The problems I wish to highlight are now beginning to emerge.

1   The foregoing exegesis of Popper's 'situational individualism' aims at removing a misunderstanding of his position by distinguishing (a) a faulty interpretation of it, namely, 'global reductionism' or 'reductionist-individualism', which allows no independence to the power or aims of institutions over and above what is possessed by individuals, from what he really seems to hold, namely, (b) 'piecemeal reductionism' or 'situational individualism', which does admit of such an independence in some measure. This distinction enables us to square Popper's individualism and reductionist tendency with the fact that he undoubtedly recognises that institutions have in some sense a life of their own. Whether or not his thesis understood in this way for institutions, is satisfactory, I suspect that for groups the thesis is not fully adequate.

2   There is, however, a closely connected problem to do with unobservables. It is not certain that these entities exist in the social sciences; when reviewing Brown (1963), I was under the

impression (Wisdom, 1964) that he had found an example in Simon (1957), but it turned out not to be one.

It seems evident that Popper's metatheory of 'situational individualism' precludes the existence of unobservables in the social sciences. Now it is undesirable that a metatheory should impose restrictions on the kinds of entity that shall appear in a hypothesis. Indeed the policy I nail my flag to is that certain sorts of problems will not give up their secret without them, many more than in the natural sciences.

In order to discuss these problems, I need an example, and, since there is none that I know of readily available in the literature that is clear-cut outside economics, apart from Bion's, and the evidence relating to his is difficult to specify, I have had to put one together. It is in the area of social psychology.

The problem I propose to consider concerns the social pathology of Great Britain. I put this forward first as two talks, on 8 and 13 August 1966, on the BBC Third Programme, and they appeared in *The Listener* for 18 and 25 August 1966 under the title, 'The Social Pathology of Great Britain'. They are rearranged, somewhat rewritten, with one part telescoped with a small addition, but there is no basic alteration. The articles are reproduced in updated form below. While one or two insertions have been made for clarification, no attempt has been made to alter the content, or to bring it up to date.

'The Social Pathology of Great Britain'

There is a problem about the ills from which Great Britain is suffering. The stimulus for tackling it was a special number of *Encounter* edited by Arthur Koestler in 1963. Distinguished contributors made some distinguished contributions: their aim was a diagnosis of the condition of Britain. I do not think they reached a diagnosis, but I think that one may be made, and after tracking down the illness the question of prognosis will arise.

I will make a list of the main complaints the nation seems to be suffering from. The first is epitomised strikingly by Koestler under the heading of the lion and the ostrich. The nation was like a lion over the Battle of Britain, but like an ostrich over the Nazi threat. Koestler has coined a nice new expression 'struthonian' from the Latin for an ostrich. I would prefer to add to this, to bring out the bipolar nature of the attitude, and speak of leo-struthonianism — after all those who wear the Old Struthonian tie might agree that one can afford to be struthonian if, when real need arises, one is really leonine. This attitude, I am afraid, is not well adapted to the battle of living during times of peace.

A whole crop of manifestations of leo-struthonianism can be found. There is a striking failure to cope with peace. This manifests itself through many examples of ineptitude. The space-time coordinates of trains, for example, are disconcerting. It is true that the space co-ordinates are usually satisfied, for trains usually turn up at the right place; it is the time coordinate that has that happy-go-lucky character that English people so enjoy in other countries. Efficiency, after all, is chilling. Roads will undoubtedly be satisfactory in ten or twenty years' time — because we shall probably have ceased to use them, that is as we do now, when we have hovercraft lorries. This solution relies on an old method: solving a problem by failure.

Housing, with doubtful justification, lags behind needs, and con-tinues to take a lion-hearted and struthonian view of the climate. It was picturesque to see village pumps set up all over London during more than one recent winter — no doubt a tribute to the resourceful-ness of the people in time of stress, but hardly a tribute to post-war plumbing. Turning a blind eye to the telescope is one thing; flouting the climate is not a realistic example of it.

Hotels have improved but basically they still expect you to accept your holiday stoically. As for cooking — I have heard of a landlady who told a prospective new lodger in the most reassuring tones that she provided only English cooking; the room was declined.

Parliament fails to make time for important measures. Reports on important matters from royal commissions are pigeon-holed; occasionally they seem to be intended to find out only what is already well known.

There are firms that make new products without even considering what intended sales might be. Hard-headed realism this; and there are firms that do not even know about relevant diplomas in tech-nology.

Trade unionism has a structure like a stage coach with an internal combustion engine attached — based on crafts rather than on industries, as Lady Williams has put it, for a factory worker may not carry out something involving a different craft within the overall industry of his works. On the other hand it is notorious that manage-ments lack initiative on a widespread scale.

Absenteeism needs no comment. Nor do unofficial strikes, often from grotesque causes.

This long list consists of variants of one symptom — that of in-competence and lack of realism. A struthonian attitude is widely adopted towards it. Where is the élan?

Now for a different sort of symptom. Many things continue to be done by the government or the nation directly against the national interest. Here are some: in relation to other countries, there has been more than one highly self-damaging action. One candidate for this would be the refusal to accept the advances of the Common Market countries over a decade before actually joining. Economic policy, whatever the merits of the arguments either way, has been self-effacing for perhaps 15 years.

In education a major revision of school policy about the eleven-plus dragged on and on. Universities are losing teachers (a celebrated Old Struthonian who renounced his coat of arms for a new one notable for its 'bore rampant' has said that professors have been seduced away by the United States, overlooking one of the facts of life that one who is happy at home will not usually be seduced out of it); and in this connection there has been a struthonian policy of expanding university education without providing the means of doing it. Research, which may be vital to maintaining a reasonably good form of society, is a Cinderella. An interesting example of 'safe' action, promoting incompetence and highly self-damaging, concerns the devaluation of 1949: what it did was to enable incompetent firms to export more easily without recourse to more economical production. Thus, there was no incentive towards improvement, only a respite for the lazy. A tax on failure to achieve a reasonable export coefficient would have been a spur to efficiency. The government directly protected inefficiency and indirectly promoted national damage.

This list of deficiencies forms the next symptom, also like the last one characterised by ineptitude, but perhaps it was more directly self-damaging.

Great Britain's isolation from the Common Market was also the most tangible sign of deliberately abdicating from her role of international leadership, disparaging her own prestige, achievements, influence, contributions, and developments, as being of no importance. A feature that is insufficiently studied is the callousness and dishonesty to be found in political life. Governments seldom bestir themselves over inadequate allowances for the old and the conditions of their lives. Yet there is hardly a member of any recent government who would be equally callous in his private life.

Governments have dishonoured agreements or have used sharp practice in the honouring of agreements with professional bodies, in a way that probably not one minister would dream of doing as an individual. Ministers in the House of Commons have lied or given information so misleading as to be morally and psychologically equivalent to a lie for political purposes, and yet as individuals you could trust them with your safe. You may say this is not striking, that political dishonesty is universal, and so on. But there is a peculiarity here, for there are very few countries in which the personal integrity of ministers is so high. In many other countries there would be nothing to note, for the political behaviour would match the private; but in Britain the point is that the political dishonesty does not match the personal but is split off from it. It is not political dishonesty that is an ill, but the peculiarity that ministers of unimpeachable honesty as individuals become dishonest as a group.

The rise of crime, the backward state of prisons, and the gross inadequacy of psychiatric services require no comment. Surely, too, a fine piece of struthonianism is the failure to accept the fact that teenagers are now in practice sexually active and to provide them with the assistance they need in their new morality. By contrast there is no change in boarding schools. It is still taboo for a boy to show too much active interest in girls; and if by chance he misinterprets this and takes an active interest in boys he soon find himself ostracised socially or physically. There is little sign of tackling the problem, arising from the fact that teenagers are now sexually mature much earlier than they used to be, of what boarding-school boys and girls are to do about it. Failure to tackle it must produce a split in the community between the highly sexualised teenagers outside the boarding school and by contrast a kind of asexual product inside — a split indeed that might be more serious even than the existing split due to class-distinction.

The Gentleman–Amateur Complex

Britain is a country consisting of citizens first-class and citizens second-class. The fact is less marked than it used to be, but it remains to a significant extent a fact. Exactly where the boundary lies (or whether there are subsidiary boundaries) is not the point here. But many people now think that a class-distinction like this is an imperfection. I am not concerned with the value-judgment but with the significance of a split in society and with the untoward consequences that flow from the split. There is a parallel attitude about foreigners. Individuals are of course charming, but as a group foreigners are regarded as slightly quaint; they therefore do not even approach resemblance to citizens first- or second-class.

I want now to consider a particular expression of this: the dichotomy between amateurs and gentlemen on the one hand and, on the other, professionals and players, even though the mere mention

136

of such a subject will make some people as uncomfortable as in former days they would have been at the mention of sex. This dichotomy has been vividly portrayed by Austen Albu. To my mind it is of fundamental importance, so I want to bring out something of its nature.

Why Gentlemen are Prized

The conception of a 'player' refers to a professional performer or a performer with expertise, and a player has no other virtues. There is something machine-like about him and he has a one-track mind. An engineer or any technologist, with the possible exception of doctors or lawyers, is a player; he is an expert at managing gadgets and thus ministering to part of the material comforts of his 'betters'. A gentleman, on the other hand, is held to have the gift of flexibility and improvisation, which is highly prized: expertise is not needed by the gentleman because his powers of improvisation will cope with any problem that turns up. But, more than that, expertise is despised, and the reason, if we could find it, would surely be important.

Parallel with this we find the dichotomy between character and brains: brains are unbecoming to a gentleman because they smack of expertise; character, on the other hand, is an absolute value; but it has, I think, a special meaning over and above dependability, loyalty, and so on, namely to cope flexibly with the unexpected. In other words it is the improvisation attribute of the gentleman all over again. Expertise, like drill, is just for 'other ranks'. Apprenticeship is a form of drill and leads to expertise. So expertise is a drill-skill, and leaves no room for improvisation. Further, contempt for expertise leads to the opinion that inefficiency is satisfactory; and Goronwy Rees is right to call this the cult of incompetence.

It will surely occur to you that this is not wholly right. And true enough there is an exception about what the gentleman is allowed — the writing of Greek verse. But such an accomplishment is hardly the thin end of the wedge of expertise. Could it be that Greek verse is something that players, other ranks, and mere technologists cannot write, so that there is no risk, even if expertise is indulged, of being identified with the craftsman — especially as to write Greek verse requires no manual skill?

Further disastrous forms of the cult of incompetence, must be emphasised.

The way Great Britain wastes its most outstanding public men is startling. Although it is to go back further than the post-war period I am concerned with, the tendency is worth tracing back. After World War I, no use was found for Lloyd George; in the 1930s

Churchill was kept on one side; in the 1950s and 1960s Butler was warded off; Grimond though not actively barred, was not bothered about. Does the country enjoy such a plethora of great men that it can afford to do without the distinctive contributions such men could offer? This is hardly the implication of the long line, with hardly an exception, of second-rate rulers, irrespective of political persuasion, that have held power for generations. The explanations for these cases are of course easy to find in the situations of the times; but nothing in the group structure has opposed the tendency — quite the contrary, the group structure has confirmed the tendency. For the country does not like really able men. One or two of those cited have been written off as 'too clever by half'. Certainly the country's distrust of the expert who has no vision is sound. But no one could maintain such a charge against these men. The country distrusts not only the 'mere expert', but distrusts expertise altogether, however leavened by the imagination of the amateur.

This extraordinary national misuse of talent could have been classified under struthonian incompetence, or self-damaging procedures. But I think it belongs more closely to the gentleman—amateur complex, because most of these men were shut out for being too able and they combined the gifts of the amateur with expertise.

We have now a list of nine groups of disabilities. Let me add that I am not concerned with value-judgments that might be made about these symptoms in themselves. Whether you or I think any one of these symptoms is a good thing or a bad thing is not relevant to the thesis I am developing; what I am concerned with is that these symptoms are likely to give rise to undesirable strains in society and to find their source. You may perhaps wonder if, in making this list of inefficiencies, I am not simply criticising too harshly because of applying impossibly high standards. Certainly there are many countries that fare worse. But of the advanced countries Britain is, in most of the respects listed, at the bottom of the class, while less than a century ago she was at the top. So the standards used are only those that were once adopted by the nation.

But we need not harp solely on a long list of lugubrious failings. From the present point of view certain shining examples of national character that lead to no dire consequences may be of significance. Let us briefly glance at a few. There are the polite police. The public cooperate with the police. The public is helpful to strangers and even good-mannered; as a colleague has put it, if you ask someone the way he almost carries you there. The public is orderly. All men are equal in a queue. The British willingness to compromise is a genuine and not a pathological formation, though it may have been functioning too well of late. There is a general sense of decency in behaviour and fair play that reveal a healthy sense of responsibility. Where there is a crisis consisting of a physical threat to himself and others (that is, of course, to *some* others) John Bull ceases to be struthonian and becomes leonine. The welfare state is more or less a success, though it may have some undesired consequences that were unintended. And so is the development of atomic energy and the development of electronics. I hasten over these features because there is less to be learnt from them, but we shall see that there is something to be gleaned.

Reverting to the first list, it consists generally of leo-struthonianism; then in particular of incompetence, lack of realism, self-inflicted damage, discrepancy between honesty in political and private life, ineffectual efforts against the seamy side, the shunning of sex among adolescents, all of which have a struthonian aspect; and then finally a muted arrogance against second-class citizens, foreigners, and experts, together with the gentleman's cult of the amateur, which are forms of a split in society.

We have now a formidable list of failings, falling broadly under the headings of leo-struthonianism and the cult of the gentleman-amateur.

Diagnosis

Now, if I met an individual with this set of disabilities, I would regard them as a syndrome, and I would make a diagnosis of *depression*, though I would qualify this as *sub-acute* (that the depression is sub-acute is because the intensity of the symptoms, or more correctly signs, is not great, and virtues exist that could not be present if the depression were deep). My thesis is that Great Britain is a group suffering from sub-acute depression — although there may be no more depressives among the population now than at any other time. (And I mean this in the psychiatric and not in the economic sense.) I am putting it forward not as an individual but as a group hypothesis.

I am not arguing by analogy. Argument by analogy does not hold. It is invalid to argue by analogy from the individual to the group. I have simply made a hypothesis , which I have taken over from a psychiatric diagnosis about individuals, and have *applied* it to a group. The question of the success or failure of the hypothesis will depend on whether it can be used satisfactorily or not, but it does not depend upon argument by analogy; that is to say, it will depend on whether it can be applied and *independently tested*.

I have thus put the numerous ills from which Great Britain is suffering under two complexes, leo-struthonianism and the gentleman—amateur complex; and these are interpretations of the facts as Koestler and others have found them. Koestler and Albu have virtually given these interpretations. I have gone further in suggesting that these two complexes are basic to the syndrome. And I have added a diagnosis of this syndrome and the complexes (namely, sub-acute depression).

We have now to examine depression as a group-psychiatric phenomenon.

The Diagnosis applied to Leo-Struthonianism

The core of the structure of depression in a person consists of ambivalence, that is, hostility to what he values most highly, and he becomes weighed down by a sense of guilt at his unkindness to the object of his greatest concern. Most characteristically, the weight of guilt removes the sunshine, makes nothing seem worthwhile, and leads to self-reproach and even self-punishment and self-inflicted damage. Already you will see a couple of the symptoms I have described falling into place, the muted *élan* and inefficiency, and the list of policies carried out against the national interest.

A person has various means of defence, all of which must be based on detaching the hostility from the object of value. In an extreme case, a person might blind himself altogether to the hostility and indulge in a burst of elation. But milder alternatives are open, for instance the denial that the hostility does any real harm, which is likely to be accompanied by a damping down of hostility generally, even where it is needed, and thus lead to giving in all round, however unsuitably. How does this apply to Chief Enahoro, who was deported from the United Kingdom at the request of the Nigerian Government? Individuals thought he was wrongly treated — and indeed that a British value was set at naught — but the nation, or at least the government of the country, as a group, acted on the claim that he would receive a fair trial when he reached home, though it was pretty obvious he would not. The British government appeared unable to give offence and show ordinary firmness to the Nigerian government. The parallel with an individual depressive is very close. The depressive is not a liar, but he is sometimes apt to use various kinds of rationalisations, prevarications, excuses, and justifications, to defend himself against reproach (which is not incompatible with self-reproach), and to him they may be convincing, while to the outsider they may appear rather thin. Despite what appeared to be the fatuousness of the government's statements about the Chief's freedom to have counsel of his choice, although the one he was known to prefer was a lawyer who would not be permitted to land in Nigeria, it would seem quite probable that the government regarded their action as morally justified.

140

Thus the hypothesis of sub-acute depression can account for a further symptom in the presumed syndrome.

Further it explains why the ostrich becomes lionhearted when physical danger actually develops; for *hostility can focus on a real enemy without ambivalence, and once the hostility is thus withdrawn from cherished values ambivalence is dispelled for the duration.*

What of crime, prisons, and psychiatric services? I will mention only one small point: the depressive is not in a position to cope with the seamier aspects of his being; if he were able to, he would not be depressed. So far from coping, he even tries to deny their existence; and this is just what the nation does about these matters — it averts its gaze.

Split attitudes and inhibition about sex again are usual in depression.

The Diagnosis applied to the Gentleman–Amateur Complex

The gentleman used to be one of the chief values of Great Britain. Now a depressive structure could not permit its values to be sullied. Hence, to prevent overt depression, it was vital to keep a sharp split between the gentleman and the player.

In the past it was easy to maintain this split. But after the war this was no longer so, and we have to enquire into the change.

There came the not-at-all surprising developments of the welfare state, increased literacy among other ranks, increased authority among other ranks, depletion of the gentleman's means — there were plenty of changes that helped to put the gentleman off his pedestal. Hence the split between gentleman and player could no longer be maintained.

Connected with this is a factor of a different sort. One of Britain's basic characteristics, which was pointed out by Renier (1933), was that it was a ritualistic society. The idea of taking pleasures sadly means that *playing* the game, important though that may be, was more important than *enjoying* the game. That is to say, playing the game was not fun but ritual. Now the effect of the democratisations resulting from the war, in dethroning the gentleman, was to break down his ritual. And this must lead to an upsurge of the state of affairs controlled by the ritual. We are thus faced with the question of the functions of ritual. Put very generally, what ritual controls involves aggressiveness; so, if ritual breaks down, the problem is how to contain it. For the nation, neither open aggressiveness nor paranoia are in character, and depression seems to be the only alternative open for containing aggressiveness.

Further, a contributory factor lies in an unintended consequence of the welfare state. For the care he bestowed on his inferiors (some inferiors, for example, servants and subjects of his charity) was part of the role of the gentleman, and you can hardly deprive a man of his altruistic activities without making him depressed. The transformation of a colony into a dominion would have in some degree the same effect. The outcome was that the gentleman lost his function and lost therefore his confidence.

Indeed, these days it is sometimes hinted that gentlemen are disappearing. Now this is physically impossible in the short time that has elapsed. So what must be meant is that the gentleman is no longer prominent, no longer counts for much. And, indeed, it is sometimes felt that to be a gentleman is 'square', and there are some who try to efface the manifestations of their type. Thus, there is ambivalence towards one of the country's most prized values — and the ambivalence emanates not just from the envy of others, which is not new, but emanates from gentlemen themselves, which is new. There is, in short, a national ambivalence — hence, the depression.

The Gentleman's Reaction to Ambivalence

Now, the gentleman's loss of prestige does not mean that the split between citizens first-class and second-class is overcome, for the gentleman has lost value to gentlemen without his being reconciled to players.

There seems to me to be interesting confusions underlying this phenomenon.[8]

With the growth of the self-reproach of being a gentleman, it has not occurred to him that a gentleman is a complex of several different kinds of qualities, and if he now feels ashamed of snobbery, for instance, he need not overlook the fact that some characteristics of the gentleman can function well. Indeed there are several of these. The gentleman had a code of decency in day-to-day behaviour (subject to limitations and exceptions, but it existed), a code of manners, a standard of taste. Naturally these would all be bogus if they owed their existence to the need, for example, to maintain snobbery: but has the gentleman questioned whether they may not have another source? Does he regard it as impossible to value these qualities while jettisoning the attitude to citizens second-class, to foreigners, and to professionals and players?

A Valid Conception of the Amateur

It seems to me that the reason why he cannot do this is because he clings to the idea of the amateur in a faulty way. The expert, as I shall call the professional and player, he conceives of narrowly as drilled to carry out one task with precision. No doubt this is what a number of experts are now actually like. But the conception overlooks an important methodological point: that *where a new problem is involved the expert is always an amateur* — it is precisely because a problem is new that the expert has not got a drill ready to hand for dealing with it. So the idea of the amateur is not wholly misguided. In fact, all original scientists have to have this character of the amateur in them. Einstein was very much the amateur. Engineers developing atomic energy, with nothing in previous experience to guide them, can only be amateurs in their new work. But this does not mean that they can afford to neglect expertise.

Expertise without the leavening of the amateur cannot cope with anything off the beaten track. By contrast, the amateur without expertise may range from being incompetent to being irrelevant. The one can perform, but only on tram lines; the other is off the rails. Our question is not whether to go on the rails or off them, but whether we can dispense with them. The question for the gentleman, then, is whether he can revalue the amateur, not as a hot-house plant, but as a rose grown upon the briar of expertise. If he could, this would overcome the ambivalence, the split with citizens second-class, and the depression.

The problem is a crucial one. Many other countries do not have it because they either never had, or they have got rid of, that group allied to the upper middle classes and merging into the upper classes. But Britain has to handle the problem. Elimination of the gentleman, even if practicable, say by educating them not to be gentlemen, would not eliminate the national depression, because it would not eliminate the ambivalence in any reasonably short run. But the idea of the expert-amateur (not the amateur-expert, that is, the specialist who does not know his job) could transform this state quite quickly.

Prognosis

Let us now turn to the question of *prognosis*.

There are several possibilities and the prognosis is a conditional prediction. It is, however, possible to weigh the likelihood of the several possible conditions and therefore to select the most likely outcome.

Broad possibilities for the depressive are: getting worse, becoming chronic, or getting better. If he gets worse, he may do so by adopting schizoid defences; if he gets better, he may do so by effecting neurotic adjustments of a more or less workable kind; if he becomes chronically depressed, this may be because his adjustments work badly.

What about getting worse? This would be indicated if the signs were that the overt disorder was not the central disorder but a defence against one; in that case I would look for activities designed, not simply to prop up the patient, but to protect him from something that is not actually present. So I would look to see whether such protective measures were attended by anxiety. And with depression what would have to be protected would be the core of the personality against being broken up. Arresting the nuclear disarmament squatters is, it is true, a minute sign of such protective measure, aimed at preventing the group of squatters from developing into a fragment broken away from the rest of society. But we should have to see repressive measures against riots and the like before the depression would get worse.

Now there are other possibilities that, on the surface, look more satisfactory. Thus the nation might become more struthonian, to the degree of believing that all is right with its world. But this would produce an irresponsibly elated national life, which might feel good but which would be unstable and a fool's paradise. However, such a development would seem to be wholly out of character. Another possibility is that confidence might be recovered by imagining grave national threats to be emanating from many quarters of the world.[9] This would undoubtedly set the country on its feet; but it is not a serious alternative for a genuine depressive, and also it would seem to be out of character. Great Britain has displayed nothing like the anxiety of some other countries, for example, France, Germany, Russia, and the USA, at threats, real or imagined, from abroad. Indeed she has often underrated these; and, although this might conceivably be a disguised indication of a paranoid trait, it would be very much a paranoid trait under control. An interesting possibility, which does seem to be real, would be an access of obsessionality, in an attempt to control aggressiveness caused by the disruption of ritual, for ritual is a controlled form of obsessionality. Nonetheless, I do not rate the chance of such an outcome very high, because it would depend on national aggressiveness threatening to get out of control; and, while the Suez episode was evidence of this, Britain does not look like repeating such a thing.[10] The protectorate may have been an obsessional interregnum, but look what it took to produce it; and as a whole it seems somewhat out of character. All these alternatives are notable for affording ways of producing an outward show of recovery. But, in fact, they would be unstable psychotic or neurotic defences against getting worse — the first manic, the second paranoid, the third obsessional. Although unstable, they could work reasonably well in the short or moderate run. Still they are not a likely choice for Britain.

If the depression is to be chronic, I would expect it to be an acceptable, though not welcome, settlement with fate on the (national) assumption that any move to improve things might make them worse and dare not be risked. There has been some evidence of this shown by several examples of refusal to take a bold line, for example, over the Common Market, town planning, and so forth, but some against it as shown by examples of enterprises; for example, the welfare state, atomic power stations, new universities and so on. This depressed attitude is reflected in the deeply ingrained conservatism of the nation and of all sections of it, and it is a danger, but I do not think it wholly characteristic, because offset by some refreshing activities.

What about recovery? The prime condition to be satisfied for genuine recovery, and not the façades referred to, would be to come to terms with the national ambivalence. The national ambivalence has two facets, the disparagement of its own values — the gentleman — and the split in society between gentlemen and players. How might this be tolerated or alleviated?

The national ambivalence would be controlled by the growth of the expert-amateur. For such an image would undermine the distinction between citizens first-class and second-class, promoting economic efficiency, removing the tendency to act nationally against the national interest, acting with more forthrightness politically, and allowing Old Struthonians to fade away or remain as eccentrics; it would undermine leo-struthonianism. The mind should not look down its nose at its hand. The main manifestations of ambivalence would be removed or smoothed.

To satisfy this condition is difficult. But certain things suggest that it is a reasonable possibility. Gentlemen in the past have shown their own characteristic of the amateur in changing their own way of life. Thus they moved into some forms of commerce — no doubt with heart-searching but the upper lip stiffened, they did it, and got over it. Let us not underrate that step; it meant accepting the humiliation of earning money instead of having it as a natural endowment. It should be no worse a step to accept the degradation of becoming versed in expertise. What may help to bring about such a change of attitude most effectively and most quickly is perhaps the new universities — provided the new enterprise they display is not smothered at birth by getting under the control of Old Struthonians. This is a great challenge to the new universities, and it would reflect a great change, in view of the country's reprehensible history over education, if the new universities should save it from itself. If this eventuality should make you too optimistic, you could enquire whether, and how far, standard vintages are being given new labels.

Since getting worse and pseudo-recovery seem to be out of character and to depend on conditions that do not seem to hold, I would say the choice lies between remaining chronically depressed and recovery. There are some developments that would militate against chronicity. On the other hand, the condition for coming to terms with ambivalence, the growth of the expert-amateur, is fraught with difficulty, that is to say, national resistance to it is bound to be very strong. I would put the odds on recovery slightly higher than on chronic depression; but more likely still, I would think, would be a partial recovery, a compromise formation between the two possibilities, quite good enough to make most people proud, but disappointing in comparison with what might have happened.

What would favour chronicity is the conservative ingrained fear of taking enterprising and bold measures; against it there is the fact that some initiative is left. What would favour recovery is the flexibility of the gentleman, who might be able to evolve a new conception of his type, together with the institutional development of the new universities, which might foster a new development of his type; against it there is the distrust by gentlemen of both gentleman and player. Since the conditions for all four possibilities are all present, I would expect a measure of each to ensue; and hence, say over the next fifteen years, I would expect to find a mixture of chronicity and recovery. [Written not later than the summer of 1964.]

A favour prognosis lies neither in Kipling nor Cousins,[11] but in culture grafted upon craft. I would expect the graft to take in some measure; but that we shall find also the conservative spirit of Kipling and of Cousins in some measure still present.

The Problems Further Specified

That completes my example, of a social psychological kind, with which to make certain points. (i) The diagnosis of a community depression seems to attribute an 'irreducible' purpose to the nation, in a sense running counter to 'situational individualism'. (ii) The diagnosis makes use (at least ostensibly) of a concept of an un-observable. The hypothesis is testable, for it yields a prognosis asserting that (within a limited span) there will be a mixture of some chronic depression with some recovery, subject to the conditions (a) that class distinctions retain some of their sharpness, to provide for the retention of social conservatism, and (b) that education under-goes radical alteration, to provide relief from national ambivalence.

The general relationship between (i) and (ii) is more complicated than it looks. For though 'reductionist individualism' is obviously incompatible with the use of unobservables (since a 'global reduction' removes everything except observables), it is not so obvious that 'situational individualism' is incompatible also (cf. Morgenbesser, 1967).

We shall have to consider whether the example of a social depression requires us to modify or go beyond 'situational individualism' and involves an unobservable.

Notes

1   Popper (1963, 1964) has made a sustained attack on holism. For me also it is untenable, but it cannot be examined here.

2   Popper himself opens the door, though only very slightly, to this misinterpretation. The following passages convey it. 'We must try to understand all collective phenomena as due to actions, inter-actions, aims, hopes, and thoughts of individual men, and as due to traditions created and preserved by individual men' (Popper, 1964, pp. 157–8); '. . . the "behaviour" and the "actions" of collectives . . . must be reduced to the behaviour and to the actions of human individuals' (Popper, 1963, 2, p. 91).

3   This method of reduction has a noble history containing some exquisite examples. Dedekind (1963) 'reduced' irrational numbers to rationals, thus solving the two-thousand-year-old Pythagorean problem of the incommensurability of the two sorts of numbers. Whitehead (1920) 'reduced' points and lines to Chinese nests of boxes, thus liquidating the two-thousand-year-old contradiction in the Euclidean concepts. Broad (1933) 'reduced' propositions to co-referential judgments in an attempt to eliminate from propositional logic any shadow of a Platonic idea. The method is excellent in mathematics and logic. One of the great failures was in philosophy, in the phenomenalist theory of perception, according to which physical objects are 'reducible' to families of sense-data. The most influential use of the idea in philosophy was Russell's (1920) theory use of descriptions ('The author of *Waverley* exists' 'reduces' to 'One and only one man wrote *Waverley*'), in which a description denotes no Platonic idea or object but is 'reduced to', or disappears on translation into, phrases denoting two objects (man and book) and one relation (writing). In relation to the present theme of 'reducing' in-stitutions, Russell's theory of descriptions ('logical constructions' and 'incomplete symbols') was adapted by John Wisdom (1933, 1934) before he entered the Wittgenstein orbit, when he worked

along the lines of Russell and Moore. He (1933) 'reduced' 'England in a monarchy' by translating it into 'Englishmen acknowledge a monarch', and (1934) 'reduced' 'Some nations invaded France and some did not' by translating it into 'There were groups of people each with common ancestors, traditions and governors such that the members of each group selected from among themselves soldiers and those soldiers forcibly entered the land owned by Frenchmen.' ('Groups' he eliminates similarly.) These 'reduce' the institutions, England, monarchy, nations and France, to individuals, Englishmen, monarch, and Frenchmen.

4   At the risk of oversophistication, it may clarify for a few readers to say that unintended consequences are 'simply predictable' but not 'omega-predictable'.

5   Or respectively 'simply reductionist' and 'omega-reductionist'.

6   Popper's criticisms of 'reductionist individualism' are that it has difficulty in accounting for the relations of institutions to one another and to individuals, for the independent power of institutions, for their unintended consequences, and also for the facts that some institutions originated unintentionally, and that some persist against individual intentions; and it would have to operate with that dubious concept, the beginning of society. 'Situational individualism', on the other hand, has no such difficulties.

7   It is clear from the above discussion that the objects scheduled for 'reduction' in Popper's theory are primarily existents or facts. Nonetheless natural science is concerned to explain natural phenomena; social science to explain institutions. And Popper's theory of 'situational individualism' is a *metatheory* stating the kind of theory an explanation of social institutions ought to be, namely that laws about institutions are 'distributively reducible' or 'partially reducible' to individuals. Thus his theory applies both to existents or facts and also to laws.

8   Psychiatrically they involve faulty schizoid identifications and splits.

9   This mechanism has been used by certain totalitarian countries.

10   And in fact has not repeated it in a case (Rhodesia) where it could be claimed to have some justification.

11   Frank Cousins, a belligerent trades union leader of the day.

148

References

Ayer, A.J. (1954), 'Phenomenalism', *Philosophical Essays*, London.

Agassi, Joseph (1960), 'Methodological individualism', *British Journal of Sociology*, 11, pp. 244—70.

Albu, Austen (1963), 'Taboo on expertise', *Encounter*, 21, ed. Arthur Koestler, pp. 45—50.

Bion, W.R. (1961), *Experiences in Groups*, London.

Broad, C.D. (1933), *Examination of McTaggert's Philosophy*, vol. 1, chapter 4.

Brown, Robert (1963), *Explanation in Social Science*, London.

Campbell, N.R. (1921), *What is Physics?*, ref. to Dover edn, 1952, pp. 85—6.

Dedekind, Richard (1963), 'Continuity and irrational numbers', *Essays on the Theory of Numbers*.

Gellner, Ernest (1936), 'Explanation in history', *Proc. Arist. Soc.*, suppl. vol., 30, pp. 157—76.

Goldstein, L.J. (1956), 'The inadequacy of the principle of methodological individualism', *Journal of Philosophy*, 53, pp. 801—13.

Koestler, Arthur (ed.) (1963a), *Encounter* 21.

Koestler, Arthur (1963b), 'The lion and the ostrich', *Encounter* 21, ed. Arthur Koestler, pp. 5—8.

Mandelbaum, Maurice (1955), 'Societal facts', *British Journal of Sociology*, 6, pp. 305—17.

Marx, Karl (1906), *Capital*, New York, chapter 24.

Morgenbesser, Sidney (ed.) (1967), 'Psychologism and methodological individualism', *Philosophy of Science Today*, 163, New York.

Popper, K.R. (1963), *The Open Society and its Enemies*, vols 1 and 2, New York.

Popper, K.R. (1964), *The Poverty of Historicism*, London.

Renier, G.J. (1933), *The English: are they Human?*, London, chapter 9.

Rees, Geronwy (1963), 'Amateurs and gentlemen', *Encounter* 21, ed. Arthur Koestler, pp. 20—5.

Russell, Bertrand (1920), *Introduction to Mathematical Philosophy*, London, 167ff., esp. 177.

Scott, K.J. (1961), 'Methodological and epistomological individualism', *British Journal for the Philosophy of Science*, 11, pp. 331—6.

Simon, H.A. (1957), 'Mechanisms involved in pressures toward uniformity in groups. Mechanisms involved in group pressures on deviate-members', *Models of Man*, New York, chapters 7 and 8 with H. Guetzkow.

Watkins, J.W.N. (1957), 'Historical explanation in the social sciences', *British Journal for the Philosophy of Science*, 8, pp. 104—17.

Whitehead, A.N. (1920), *The Concept of Nature*, Cambridge, chapter 4.

Wisdom, John (1933), 'Ostentation', *Psyche*, 13, pp. 175—6.

Wisdom, John (1934), 'Is analysis a useful method in philosophy?', *Proc. Arist. Soc.*, suppl. vol., 13, p. 96.

Wisdom, J.O. (1964), 'Review of Brown (1963)', *Economica*, 31, pp. 219—20.

Appendix I: psychological individualism

Contrasting with 'situational individualism' is psychologism, which is a form of individualism that Popper rejects.

Psychologism (or psychologistic individualism) is the thesis that an institution (or society) is a purely psychological product, manifestation, expression, or symbol of human nature, which, moreover, has to assume a life of its own even though composed of nothing else; or, in short, that society depends on the 'human nature' of its members (Popper, 1963, 1, p. 83), or more explicitly is the product of interacting minds (Popper, 1963, 2, p. 90).

Psychologism differs from 'methodological individualism'. Some critics have understandably been unable to see the difference. Psychologism refers to human nature, that is, the nature of a person or a mind, mental processes, or to the psychological theory of what these are. 'Methodological individualism' refers to none of this structure or explanatory factors but only to human purposes, and so on, which are attributes of human activity — the facts, if we like, about human beings (for which the factors coming under psychologism consist of theory or explanation). Thus for Popper, it is not psychologistic that parliament depends upon the intentions of many people to have the country governed; it would be psychologistic to interpret parliament as a societal manifestation of individual intentions to run their lives in an orderly fashion.

What sharply discriminates methodological individualism from psychologism is, I think, the *level* of psychology invoked. When

Popper describes methodological individualism in terms of the goals, decisions, actions, and so on, of individuals, he is obviously utilising some psychology. What he makes use of may appear to be simply common-sense knowledge of people's minds. But such a characterisation does not adequately bring out the nature of the psychology. How it may be characterised is as knowledge that can be expressed as laws or generalisations — in other words, not theories. What I suggest is that what is characteristic of psychologism is *psychological theory*; that is, theory of human nature, theory of mind, theory of the inner nature of our minds. Following on this discrimination, it is necessary to add that the generalisations allowed in methodological individualism have a definite function: to describe the operations by which an individual's decisions, and so forth, lead to unintended by-products; whereas a theory, on the other hand, does not explain the working out of such by-products, but is more probably used (by would-be exponents of psychologism) to describe an inner psychological reality that is 'expressed' or 'reflected by' or 'projected on to' social reality, that is, by social institutions. What I think Popper is rejecting in psychologism is the broad notion of an *inner psychological reality* being *manifested*, like a cine film being shown on a screen, in society.

Since the issue of psychologism lies on the fringe of the present investigation, it will suffice to say here that Popper gives, in my opinion, a valid criticism of the doctrine (though he leaves a loophole, which I believe could be closed). Nonetheless, although institutions are not to be interpreted purely psychologistically, there is a social whole, which is just as fundamental as the social institution, that may have to be interpreted thus — namely the social group.

One example of a group is a set of people who go to the same college. Another is a set of doctors. A group may, but need not, meet. We all have great experience of groups, but hardly any articulate knowledge. Fairly recently, however, a great advance has come from Bion (1961), whose work, *Experiences in Groups*, is perhaps the most important yet written on group psychology.

It is noteworthy that Bion eschews, at least by implication, all attempt at constructing a psychology of the group upon that of the individual. Just as for Popper, an individual is always an individual in a setting of institutions, so for Bion an individual is always a member of some group (usually several). Group activity is not 'reducible piecemeal' to individual activity; group psychology is not 'reducible piecemeal' to individual psychology. We shall have to consider whether group activity is even distributively reducible to individual activity.

Analogous to the situation described by Popper, though not

discussed by Bion, there are unintended by-products of group activity and of individual actions in groups. But again analogously, a group has no source other than individual activity; its origin, persistence, and development involve no other ingredients. Thus far a group has the same sort of structure as an institution. Moreover, it can be claimed in occasional cases that an institution is a projection or expression of the deeper layers of our minds.

But there is a difference. An institution does not have intentions; a group, according to Bion, does. It also has a catalogue of things like desires, fears, hopes, anxiety, guilt feelings, self-preservation tendencies, and so on. An individualist would, of course, claim that a group intention is formed only out of individual intentions and deny that a group intention is not reducible, even 'piecemeal', to individual activity, which would violate Popper's presupposition that only individuals have intentions. All I need for the moment is the existence in a significant sense of a group intention, and that there is a theory of its action, for Bion gives not just a concept, but a theory of group intention, which is in some measure testable.

Appendix II: the rationality principle

Popper (1945) has commited himself to the view that social activities, and the social reality they constitute according to the individualistic schema, conform to what he has called the rationality principle. He has written very little about its meaning, but it is not difficult to see roughly what he had in mind. There may be said to be two parts to it. The first concerns conscious decisions about actions to be taken to realise certain goals. The briefest illustration will suffice to illustrate such an obvious idea: in order to become a doctor, a person must decide to go to a medical school, and to take such subsidiary steps as are needed to implement entry, such as studying required preliminaries and saving or earning the fees. The second is more interesting. It concerns preconscious (what is often for convenience lumped under the heading of 'unconscious') wishes and conflicts. Any of Freud's works on psychopathology will provide examples. Thus if a person who wants to become a doctor wastes his savings or cannot concentrate properly on the study of prerequisites such as chemistry, then (except where this is due to a longstanding deep dislike of the prerequisites) we are likely to interpret the person's behaviour as a preconscious conflict between wanting to be a doctor and not wanting to be a doctor. Assuming that the conflict can be unravelled or even surmised, then we can understand the person's avoidance of study of the subsidiary subjects, and we understand it as a rational activity designed to avoid a path he does not want to take.

As thus portrayed, rationality is straightforward. But questions arise.

It hints at a suggestion that everything is caught in its net, for either the net is widened or the mesh narrowed to accommodate anything that might escape. Is the principle synthetic a priori? It can hardly be purely analytic or a tautology. Assuming that the synthetic a priori cannot be sustained, we begin to wonder what might an action be like that did not fit the principle.

Avoiding a direct comment, let us note that rational *discussion* (within a country, a society, a university, a department, a more or less indoctrinated group) permits criticism — but always only within the schema tacitly assumed. It is (usually) taboo to go against the schema.

I would suggest there is another dimension to rationality — the rational right to challenge a schema. Irrationality is an idée fixe ostracising challenge of schemata.

Reference

Popper, K.R. (1945), *The Open Society and its Enemies*, London, Routledge & Kegan Paul.

11 The poverty of individualism

Poverty does not mean the starvation line. It means only 'not having quite enough for all eventualities' while having enough to seem quite comfortable for the most part.

Individualism has a good deal to bless itself with. Great numbers of circumstances in ordinary life come satisfactorily under its aegis. As an example of a large-scale phenomenon familiar in the western world after World War II, we have the use of bank rate by major governments. When a government such as the United Kingdom or the United States is in difficulty about foreign exchange and they cannot handle it by the measures they might wish to use, they have recourse to the bank rate. Specifically, when there is a large drain on the currency, the government of the day puts up the bank rate sharply. This is the fiscal alternative to controlling wages and prices by law. The use of the bank rate may fall unevenly and unfairly but it has a particular advantage. If the law is invoked, there will be a lot of tension and even strife aroused by the control of wages, and also to a certain extent by the control of prices. Moreover, these two measures do not work very efficiently. What happens, then, with bank rate, so far as it produces the same results (and in some measure it does not), it does so by curtailing the drain on foreign currency reserves; but, more importantly, it curtails credit within the home country. The effect of this is to reduce the overall money supply available to nearly everybody, producing a drop in private and public spending, and thus a reduction, among other things, of imports. However, all this means is that the people at large get less of the things they want, as would also happen, of course, had wages been directly controlled by law. Now comes the crucial difference: the effects of bank rate are felt slowly and inconspicuously; people have no one they can put their finger on to blame for their straitened circumstances. All they know is that they are not so well off as before, whereas, with direct control of wages, they could blame the Minister of Labour or the government as a whole. To bring this fairly simple story to its close, bank rate functions smoothly in the sense of not arousing personal tensions, by avoiding the possibility of the finger of accusation being pointed against any one person or any group of people, so that the mechanism of bank rate appears to be societal rather than individualistic.

Now, the above point is concerned with societal smoothness of operation; but, as regards individualism, the operation, however inconspicuous, stems from the individualistic decision to increase bank rate and leave it to work out its insidious consequences. Here it rather resembles the theory of deism which arose in the eighteenth century and even at the end of the seventeenth century, according to which God imposed the laws of the natural world upon it and then left it to its own devices to run itself in accordance with them. The long-term or perhaps the medium-term operation of bank rate can easily be seen to be the consequences, and indeed the predictable and even foreseeable consequences of the measure to increase bank rate.

Here we have, I think, an excellent example to show an individualistic decision having large-scale social consequences which, looked at superficially, might appear holistic. Examples could be multiplied and it is even possible that the individualistic schema would, or could, cover the great majority of social phenomena that we meet with.

It is worth considering, however, whether there is more to it than this. Who is it that takes the decision to increase bank rate? The rough answer is that it is taken by the government as a whole, but largely on the advice and argument of the Chancellor of the Exchequer and the Governor of the Bank of England, for example, with the Prime Minister closely involved. We may suppose that they all agree on the measure as appropriate to the circumstances; why then do they reach this conclusion? They have come to the conclusion, rightly or wrongly, that alternative measures are not desirable, because of the fact that they do not work very well, and that they give rise to a lot of friction, or they may consider that alternative measures are not politically viable at the time in question. Leaving this on one side, we still have the question of the store of knowledge they have that gives them a rational ground for the effects they anticipate. What is it that provides them with this show of rationality? It is the economic theory that applies to a fiscal policy. No doubt, one could attempt to formulate a version of this in brief terms to the effect that there is a true generalisation asserting that increase of bank rate damps down the economy and therefore reduces the country's need for foreign exchange (thus reducing the overseas run on foreign exchange). When formulated thus, the generalisations can superficially look like holistic truths about the economy as a whole, but the individualist will be quick to reply that closer inspection of the generalisation is needed and that such inspection will show that the damping down of the economy is simply a global *expression* of large numbers of individual decisions and actions taken by individual people; their decisions consist of curtailing their own expenditure because they have less money available. Thus it will be claimed that the operation of economic generalisations can be seen to be basically individualistic.

So far as I can tell, this individualistic claim is valid; in other words, I do not find it easy to press this kind of example home, in such a way as to reveal a genuinely holistic phenomenon at work (though I do not want to exclude such a possibility absolutely).

If individualism can function well and cover perhaps even the great majority of social phenomena, wherein lie its possible weaknesses? I will first point to a practical weakness, although this might be overcome, and may be a theoretical point without much force in it. The schema of individualism may well strike social anthropologists as inappropriate to their inquiries. An anthropologist in the field is apt to be especially struck by the apparently holistic nature of ritual, witchcraft, and the like, and easily feel that individualism has no relevance to such phenomena and even to feel that individualism would militate against his research. Now all this may constitute a practical disadvantage of individualism. But it is no disproof of individualism to find it disadvantageous because of its *psychological* effects on certain groups of research workers; for the psychological effect may be no more than due to a misunderstanding by them and due to taking too little cognisance of metascientific considerations. I think the point is worth a mention, but should not be taken too seriously.

When it comes to controversy between individualists and their opponents, that is, holists, the controversy does not as a rule get off the ground. This appears to be because, whatever example is taken by the one can be squared by the other so as to fit into his own schema. This suggests that there is something nebulous about the individualistic and holistic claims or schemata which prevents us from getting a grip on the precise point at issue between them.

However, the individualistic schema impresses its opponents as something that prevents them from formulating holistic hypotheses.

It is true that the individualist may reply that a holistic hypothesis may indeed be formulated and that he will himself be happy to accept it, but that he will always be able to show that it can be reduced to individualistic terms. On the other hand, the holist continues to consider that his holistic hypotheses are not being taken fully seriously. In my opinion, examples can be found that justify the latter in this assessment. One example that I would give concerns group psychoanalysis. In one of his greater contributions, Freud (1921; Wisdom, 1978), elaborated a number of group analytic generalisations which he took over from le Bon. In fact, he took over le Bon's generalisations completely and applied them to explain various group phenomena. He jibbed however, at one thing; le Bon had an additional view of groups as holistic, that is, that groups as a whole had certain characteristics, and Freud, who was nothing if not a totally committed individualist, could not accept this. Indeed, Freud went to considerable lengths to show how certain group phenomena, which appeared holistic, could be explained by him — as individualistic by means of the generalisations alone. Now, this was an able and valuable enterprise, but it militated against the possibility of considering seriously the existence of holistic group phenomena; and, in fact, its striking advance to more general kinds of groups took place at the hands of Bion (1962; Wisdom 1978, 1979) when he quite overtly (even if oblivious of the matter of scientific revolution he was causing) used holistic hypotheses. What led him to this revolutionary idea I do not know, but he could not have done it if he had been overwhelmed by Freud's individualism. It is perhaps worth adding that Bion's holistic hypotheses are as testable empirically within the operations of the group as are Freud's individualistic ones; in other words, Bion's hypotheses stand or fall by empirical tests and not by controversy between the individualistic and holistic schemata. Another example is that referred to in the previous chapter, in which a holistic hypothesis is made about Great Britain as a whole. Under the domination of the individualistic schema it would have been impossible logically to entertain the possibility of looking for such a hypothesis.

Now it is overtly agreed, and indeed maintained here, that the possibility is not excluded that these two holistic hypotheses should ultimately prove amenable to individualistic interpretation. I know of no way of showing that this is not so. All that is maintained is that in their apparently holistic form, they provide a line of investigation and, indeed, testing that would not be open under the individualistic schema.

Now, it is a maxim of the whole of the present investigation that a schema that constricts the possibility of making empirical hypotheses is to be ruled out, even if it is true that the holistic hypotheses do not, in fact, work for whatever reason. A schema that rules out the *possibility* of investigating them is ipso facto narrow. And the reason why a narrow schema is to be rejected is because it rules out a wider one; whereas the latter, though it may very well be unfruitful, may on the other hand be fruitful, in the sense that hypotheses that come under it may be found or invented and, if they are, they would satisfy the empirical criterion of being empirically testable. In other words, I am urging that any schema whatsoever is on the way to being acceptable provided that hypotheses that come under it can be subject to the classical Popperian criterion of testability.

An interesting addendum may be given to all this. Individualism proceeds by loading the dice in its own favour, for it asserts that any hypothesis designed to explain societal phenomena must be individualistic, which entails that any hypothesis proposed that is ostensibly non-individualistic will be found on close examination *to be* individualistic. Hence, it follows that, no non-individualistic hypothesis can exist. Now a schema that precludes the existence of any alternative, simply because of its own formulation or conception, is framing itself in such a way as to be tautological. And since it is also aiming at determining the nature of hypotheses, it is synthetic a priori, and I take it that, at this stage of the debate, synthetic a priori propositions have been, or can be, shown to be without foundation.

It is perhaps worth adding that the lead into this whole way of thinking, challenging individualism in part in favour of holism, stems from a simple enough consideration. It was that breakthroughs in natural science have always come about from the invention of hypotheses containing unobservables or if you like from non-instantiative hypotheses. Now the schema of individualism permits only of instantiative ones. Hence, if one is to try to allow non-instantiative hypotheses, it will be necessary to go outside the realm of individualistic schemata — that is, to look to a holistic schema.

References

Bion, W.R. (1962), *Experiments with Groups*, London, Tavistock.
Freud, S. (1921), *Group Psychology and Analysis of the Ego*, stand. works, vol. 18, London, Hogarth.
Wisdom, J.O. (1979), 'Social crisis in a nation: caste and outcaste', *Philosophy Forum*, vol. 16.

12 On the all-powerful holistic governor

Turning from the individualistic schema to the holistic alternative, we naturally choose what is far and away the best of these, namely, that due to Marx. And we take Marx on the traditional interpretation hitherto given to him, that the basic deterministic law of society entails that society as a whole changes by its own internal inexorable laws, like the unrolling of a carpet, from past, to present, to future. And the exemplification of this is the unrolling of the carpet – the economic carpet – from feudalism to capitalism, to socialism, and, thence, ultimately to communism. On the classical interpretation of Marx, this is so holistic that individuals can scarcely impinge upon its operation. The most that an individual can hope to do is to act like a midwife, facilitating the inexorable change of society, hoping to bring about a birth that would ensue without her aid, or, on the other hand, slow up the process deliberately – again a process which would ensue naturally if uninterfered with – though the slowing-up can only delay matters; it cannot produce a total stoppage or other change.

To demonstrate the power of human thought displayed by such a schema, one would not turn to the air of wonderment and disbelief it evokes in the West. In the West, the individualist holds that history is the story of activity of individual men and women, and the idea that it might have to do with society as a whole would be greeted with incredulity. It would hardly be taken sufficiently seriously as to be regarded as false; it would simply be taken to be a superstition or, in

England at least, the sort of lunacy that only foreigners could take seriously. It is worth considering, therefore, how all this would look on the other side of the Iron Curtain. Suppose you asked a Communist what history was about, he would say, 'Oh, don't you know? It is about the movements or evolution of societies.' And if you follow this up by asking what was the role of individual men and women in all this, he would reply, 'Oh, very little if anything. They would be like puppets in the hands of the working out of the laws of history.' And such a representative of the holistic society would greet the individualistic schema with the same incredulity as his counterpart in the West greets holism. He would 'know' that the western social scientist was a victim of western ideology and thus he would write off individualism without more ado.

It would be extremely interesting to see how far a holist would go, or would be able to go, in explaining societal phenomena in this way. If we compared the individualistic sociologies with the holistic sociologies resulting from the two schemata, we should find that the holist was concerned with very large problems such as those concerning the change from one epoch to another, and be less inclined to give attention to smaller phenomena such as inflation. Just as his individualistic counterpart selects problems that fit nicely into *his* schema, so the holist would select problems that would fit into *his* schema. Thus we should have a living example of the old adage that east is east and west is west and never the twain shall meet.

There is no point in parading an array of arguments for western social scientists that there may be anything amiss in the holistic schema. They 'know' this a priori. The general weakness of the holistic schema may, however, be pointed out as exactly analogous to that of the individualistic schema, namely, that it precludes by its inherent nature the possibility of interpreting the phenomena to which it applies in individualistic terms; thus it sets constraints to the wider possibilities of social science investigation.

What I am concerned to bring out here chiefly consists of two points. One is the complete parallelism of the two schemata applying apparently quite widely to social phenomena that fit them. The other is the built-in ingredient of each schema that prevents the other from being entertained in mind; to which may be added the natural consequence that exponents of each living under the flag of each, can see the world and social theory in no other way and look upon their opposite number as either quaint or mad or brainwashed.

Now it is important to stress that the line of approach in this chapter and the preceding one, while designed to bring out something of the strength and weakness of each schema, is not designed to offer any kind of support for either as a universal schema applicable to all societal problems; nor yet is the aim to repudiate either as totally inapplicable. The aim is to indicate the possibility that each may be applicable in some situations to some problems, though not universally. Such an approach leaves the way open to the possibility that both schemata may be complementary, so that some combination of the two might possibly provide us with an overall schema that would be more viable than either or both simply juxtaposed.

13 Desiderata for a flexible schema: transindividualism

We may now try to come to grips more closely with Popper's thesis of 'situational individualism'.

I have claimed already that he does not mean that social wholes are 'globally or collectively reducible', that is, that in the reduction all mention of a social whole would disappear; such a version would render social wholes mere *epiphenomena* of individual activities. What I have claimed is that for him, social wholes are 'distributively reducible' in a 'piecemeal' way, that is, that any and every social whole is 'reducible' but that in the reduction there will always be some other unreduced social whole. I wish now to present this in somewhat different terms, to do with an analogous problem in twentieth-century philosophy.

It is well known that in the philosophy of sense-perception, phenomenalism, from its birth in Berkeley and Mill to its death-throes in Ayer, provided a reductionist account of physical objects in terms of sense-data, in which all reference to all physical objects would disappear and the reduction would refer solely to sense-data (many of the early criticisms were essentially of the form that attempted reductions, eliminating reference to one physical object, covertly brought in reference to another). All versions of phenomenalism attempting this could be regarded as 'globally reductionist'. In the twilight of its life-span, Ayer (1954) gave a new twist to the theory, in which he admitted openly that such a reduction is impossible in principle, and substituted a weaker form of phenomenalism in which all he claimed was that, although the reduction could not be carried out, a reference to a physical object involves nothing beyond a reference to sense-data (and their mutual relations). Thus a physical object was no longer, on this construction, 'globally reducible' to sense-data, in the sense that all of it was reducible, but was only 'reducible' piecemeal, that is, we could go on 'reducing' endlessly and so could not complete the reduction, and yet what was left would refer to nothing other than sense-data — to no other category of entity. Ayer thus replaced 'globally reductionist' phenomenalism by 'piecemeal reductionist' phenomenalism.[1]

The point I wish to bring out is that the 'global reducibility' of social wholes is analogous to classical phenomenalism,[2] and 'situational individualism' or the 'piecemeal reducibility' of social wholes is analogous to Ayer's 'piecemeal phenomenalism'. This point (a) throws doubt on whether social wholes, even in the milder form, can have the independent role we require them to have, for this is a doubt phenomenalism evokes. On the other hand, (b) if social wholes do have some source of power or function independent of individuals, the question arises, where does it come from?; for phenomenalism stimulates the question, if there is more to physical objects than sense-data, what is the nature of the additional factor? These questions arise on their own, but the parallel with phenomenalism underlines them.

A further significant point is that a physical object, not only for classical phenomenalism but even for piecemeal phenomenalism, would be an observable in that it would contain nothing that could not be 'reduced' (even though 'piecemeal') to observables; likewise on Popper's theory, social wholes, which are 'piecemeal' though not 'globally' 'reducible' to individuals' purposes, and so on, would be an observable in that it would contain nothing 'irreducible' (even though 'piecemeal') to observables. In other words, Popper's 'situational individualism' leaves no room for unobservables.

Let us turn at last to the question whether 'situational individualism' allows sufficient weight to the independent power of wholes. This theory asserts not that social wholes are 'distributively reducible' purely to individuals' purposes, but to these plus their unintended by-products. At first sight one may wonder whether this reduction does not include every feature that could be ascribed to a social whole. We may, however, find that the conception of 'unintended by-products' is narrower than might be expected.

Popper's conception of unintended by-product seems pretty definitely to refer to consequences that, though unintended, could have been intended. Popper is concerned with the way our *calculations* go wrong. For example, measures to end the slump in the 1930s led to the unintended consequence of exacerbating it (which could have been, though it was not, intended by arch-conspirators). Thus, what is denoted consists of consequences of a familiar sort. There may be plenty of surprises, but a surprise in this context is a surprise in virtue of its *occurrence* and not of the *nature* of the thing that occurs.

However, there exists a possibility of a different type of phenomenon, where there is total surprise, that is, the *nature* of the consequence is unexpected rather than, or as well as, its occurrence. Popper gives the impression of being concerned — very reasonably — with what might be described as 'things that might have turned out differently'. But it is another order of eventualities if a new structure comes along. Examples may prove treacherous but must be tried. Consider a situation in which an experimenter is trying out combinations of substances. He gets some surprises, such as that when he sparks hydrogen and oxygen he gets water (an 'expected surprise') or when he exhausts the supposed constituents from air and finds a residue (argon, an unexpected surprise). But then he puts together copper and zinc rods in sulphuric acid, and finds that a wire joining the rods deflects a magnet. The *nature* of the phenomenon, electricity, is not just a surprise in the sense of one thing rather than another, but a new order of things where nothing of that sort would hitherto have been expected at all. ('Surprise' is simply a graphic way of putting the matter; what is referred to is not the psychological effect but the logically unpredictable character of the consequence.)

Here I am, of course, discussing 'emergent properties'.[3] In this context there are to be considered 'emergent concepts' (standing for 'emergent facts') and 'emergent laws', both of which may be candidates for 'irreducibility' to the concepts and laws of the ingredients from which the emergent phenomena emerged. The supposition of emergence is that neither concepts nor laws are *deducible from* the given constituents (that is, of course without empirically established discoveries consisting of generalisations to bridge the given constituents and the emergent properties).

Now the group-structure I have conjectured, of a psychosocial depression, is an example of such an emergent phenomenon. It is not at all just a social reflection of widespread individual depression. It is not just a surprising occurrence that might have been otherwise; it is not the kind of thing at all that might or might not be expected. It is a different order of eventuality. And not only is it unforeseeable but it may even be unrecognised (like a psychological depression) after it has arisen. (And it may exercise some control over our behaviour without our being aware of it.)

Popper's conception of unintended by-products seems to be

confined to consequences that are unintended but could have been intended, that might be foreseeable but are not foreseen. Here I am considering a conception of 'emergent by-product', which lies outside his conception of unintended by-product.

Transindividualism

We are now in a position partially to resolve the difficulty arising from Popper's theory. Naturally, it seems obvious or virtually tautologous that there could be nothing in a social whole beyond individual purposes and their unintended consequences. And in the literal sense of consequence, this is so, for an emergent property is still a consequence. But it is so different in kind from what Popper seems to have had in mind as apparently to fall outside his domain of unintended by-product.[4]

I would reformulate: that a social whole may consist of individuals' purposes, their unintended by-products, and their 'emergent by-products'.

I would suggest that this last is what gives a separate character in some measure to certain social wholes, that is, social groups: it is this that endows them with the independent power I have been trying to isolate.

I could accordingly describe the position, just reformulated, as 'transindividualism'.

In describing the position thus, I do not mean the extreme collectivist or historicist doctrine Popper has so successfully attacked. But I do mean more than is ascribed to 'situational individualism'. The thesis it refers to gives specificity to the claim made by several critics of 'methodological individualism', for example, Mandelbaum (1955), Gellner (1956), Goldstein (1956), Scott (1961), who contend in one way or another for something 'irreducible', such as a 'diachronous' framework (Goldstein) or 'societal facts' (Mandelbaum). Their criticisms, however incisive and significant in many ways, lacked thrust, occasionally by minor misunderstandings but mainly by being unable to show that the supposedly 'irreducible' fact really is 'irreducible'; for Popper has never denied that some such phenomena as these exist, he contended only that they are (distributively) 'reducible'. So these critics were making no case against him merely by pointing to such facts; what they would have had to do would have been to give some argument against their 'piecemeal reducibility'. It is this problem that I have focused on. I have not tried to show that the social pathology of depression is 'irreducible' by any form of argument to the effect that we cannot see how the reduction would run; I have aimed at showing that such a depressive constellation is of a different order from the straightforward meaning of 'unintended consequence' and therefore presumably outside the 'piecemeal reducibility' of Popper's theory.

It is true that such separate constellations are further consequences of the unintended by-products and therefore a sense of 'reducibility' could be found for them; even so, a radical innovation in Popper's theory would have been made. This comes out additionally by reverting to the question of unobservables; for, while 'situational individualism' excludes unobservables, 'transindividualism' requires them.[5]

It seems clear that 'situational individualism' imposes upon Popper's theory of scientific method a restriction (noted by Scott, 1961) in addition to testability, for it constitutes a framework for theories in the social sciences which imposes a 'reduction' and precludes unobservables. In other words the general prescription, that a hypothesis needs only to be testable, would allow the hypothesis of a societal depression to be part of social science, but the additional restriction, that it has to be 'reducible piecemeal', would debar such a hypothesis from a place in social science.

Neither Popper nor Agassi have discriminated the extreme form of holism, according to which social wholes *dominate* individuals absolutely so that in principle, no one can decisively resist them, from a moderate idea, for example, 'emergent power', according to which social wholes *influence* individuals so that individual action is determined by a combination of two factors, social wholes and individual purposes, either of which may happen to predominate on a given occasion. Thus, if we revert to the three possibilities mentioned at the beginning, (i) of social wholes necessarily dominating individuals (ii) of social wholes necessarily deriving their power from individuals, and (iii) of dual control, the first would be held by Marx, the second by Popper, while the third is the view put forward here.

This point could equally be put in terms of the idea of 'organism'. The view that society is an organism is usually associated with historicism. Therefore, the idea of an organism is excluded from 'situational individualism'. But it need not be associated with historicism. And it is appropriate for describing the thesis of 'emergent power' I have been developing. I do not mean that a society or an institution is an organism but that it is only in *part* an organism. (Even the human body is not in toto an organism, for the hair and nails are not organic. I would think that a much larger part of society, a very large part, is non-organic.) The idea that society is in part organic does not have any 'ghostly dictatorship' or 'closed society' overtones; for inorganic substances can and do have great effects upon organisms, and, if society is in part organic, this does not preclude individuals from influencing it. The holistic or organic idea of society may have come in the first case from oracular, romantic, or obscurantist philosophers. But the idea may be salvaged. And I would claim to have given it a place, by means of the example of the social pathology of depression, in Popper's metascience of testability or refutability.

Historicist theories are monistic; so is Popper's. The modification I have introduced constitutes a bipolar theory (some would call it dualistic). It allows complete flexibility of explanation, diagnosis, and prescription, in that both individuals and the independent power of a group are factors in explaining a social phenomenon; in some cases one factor will be the greater influence, in other cases the other; in certain cases one factor may dominate and even overwhelm the other, and there is no a priori way of knowing without investigation which factor is the more significant in any given case. Which factor is the decisive one in any given case has to be decided empirically. If you think that women have not yet achieved emancipation or that men are still very largely adolescent, you might seek to explain such a situation (or remedy it) by investigating their individual psychologies or you might try looking for something in the group constellation.

'Transindividualism' allows equal weight in principle, or any proportion of weights, to individuals or the societal facts, in governing the course of individual life in a group or society.

Thus the bipolar schema of transindividualism allows the empirical social scientist freedom to work with either pole or any combination of them, in a way that is barred to the individualist and to the holist.

Notes

1 Ayer gives me the impression, though I cannot vouch for its correctness, that he was reluctantly conceding the failure of classical phenomenalism, and that he was desperately trying to save the theory somehow and so introduced a twist he did not quite like. He does not seem to have realised he was giving an interesting new theory, not an ad hoc twist to wriggle round a jam. The classical form made physical objects epiphenomena of sense-data; his new form apparently allowed them an independent role.
2 This parallel has also been noticed by other writers.
3 Mandelbaum (1953, p. 321n) has referred briefly to 'existential emergents'.
4 My case has been presented as holding for social groups. In this

paper I have tended to assume it is not needed for institutions, that is, to assume that Popper's theory is fully adequate that far; but this needs examination, as it may be conceding too much.

5 The critics of methodological individualism have dissociated themselves from all forms of holism, that is to say, while contending for 'irreducible' societal facts they do not wish to classify these as 'holistic'. They probably object to the conception of 'holism' because of its ideological overtones — the overwhelming domination associated with it coupled with the aura of religious or political veneration with which it is often endowed. The conception of 'emergent power' adopted here is not necessarily overwhelming or venerable.

References

Ayer, A.J. (1954), 'Phenomenalism', *Philosophical Essays*, London.

Agassi, Joseph (1960), 'Methodological individualism', *British Journal of Sociology*, 11, pp. 244—70.

Gellner, Ernest (1956), 'Explanation in history', *Proc. Arist. Soc.*, suppl. vol., 30, pp. 157—76.

Goldstein, L.J. (1956), 'The inadequacy of the principle of methodological individualism', *Journal of Philosophy*, 53, pp. 801—13.

Mandelbaum, Maurice (1955), 'Societal facts', *British Journal of Sociology*, 6, pp. 305—17.

Marx, Karl (1906), *Capital*, New York, chapter 24.

Popper, K.R. (1963), *The Open Society and its Enemies*, vols 1 and 2, New York.

Popper, K.R. (1964), *The Poverty of Historicism*, London.

Scott, K.J. (1961), 'Methodological and epistomological individualism', *British Journal of Philosophical Science*, 11, pp. 331—6.

14 How is a social whole manifested?

Let social wholes be taken seriously, either in the extreme form from which individualism is excluded or in the bipolar form just described which permits of a combination of holism and individualism. Then arise at least two questions.

The first question concerns their reality. What is the criterion of their reality and how do we recognise and identify them?

Taking it for granted that a whole is an unobservable, how do we attribute existence to it? We take a hypothesis embodying it and deduce consequences, of more than one kind — that is, along more than one strand; if these are corroborated we corroborate the hypothesis. Such is the familiar procedure for testing the hypothesis that a sterilised (that is, boiled) medium is harmless whereas unsterilised sputum may induce pneumonia. Likewise for testing the hypothesis that ambivalence in the gentleman in Great Britain used to have outlets while, after World War II, it had not because the genteleman had lost faith in himself and thus became inept. Examples could be multiplied. In these, the tests concern the consequences (respectively, pneumonia and ineptitude), that is, the hypotheses, which are functional, are corroborated. But we do not test for the existence of the pneumococcus or the national sub-acute depression. These are structural or ontological. They are 'natural' interpretations or presuppositions but not accorded the status of being corroborated. But, as explained in developing the notions of ontology and weltanschauung, such 'natural' adjuncts are natural because they are presuppositions of the functional or empirical hypotheses (which *are* corroborated). We do not *know* that these ontological entities exist. That is, we do not have, as it were, a disinfected form of knowledge that is available to us independently of all ideas or theories. In fact we 'know' of them — in some more mundane sense — so long as we accept the empirical hypotheses that *tell* us they are there.

Thus the criterion for an ontological unobservable, and in particular a social whole, is that it is prescribed by an empirical hypothesis.

It is identifiable, to the extent that we can or even wish to identify it, by being prescribed thus, where there are at least two strands of corroboration.

A much more serious — difficult — question concerns, not the road *to* the unobservable but *from* it: how does an unobservable show itself? This is no problem where unobservables like gravitational force or electromagnetic fields are concerned. But it is a problem for a social whole. For a social whole must express itself — can express itself only — through *individuals*. How, then, can we tell whether some social phenomenon is a whole manifesting itself through individuals or is merely a complex of the actions (and of course unintended by-products) of individuals? Otherwise put, how do we tell whether an apparent whole is holistic — a 'collective' — or is distributively reducible to individuals?

Do we know of any individual experiences that mankind has sometimes attributed to the working of unseen forces (meaning in principle unseen)? One example would be biblical: the disciples of Jesus received a gift of tongues, speaking in a way that was unknown to them, which was regarded as the Holy Spirit *working through them*. Religious leaders have sometimes similarly felt themselves 'possessed'. If these are positive, negative examples would be found in good people shrieking out blasphemies attributed to the work of Satan. In all such cases, the unseen powers seize possession of, and operate, the individual bodily apparatus, as revolutionaries seize a wireless station. In contemporary times it is possible to find more mundane parallels. In World War I it was common for soldiers to bolster themselves up with the fatalistic credo that you would be killed no matter what if your 'number' was on an enemy bullet. It is worth adding the qualification for its theoretical interest, that you were not therefore to assume that you could get up out of your trench and walk straight into an enemy gun-emplacement — sensible precautions might stave off the inevitable end a little and foolhardy risks might accelerate it slightly, but that was all. Behaving sensibly you would be carrying on normal activity, all under the dictates of individualism, but an unseen influence would have the last word; here, however, the influence would not be operating constantly from day to day but only once at the end. Another actual example, which I came across, had to do with a little boy who was out for the day at the seaside with the family's cook. He became strangely tired rather early and let her take him home. Early that evening there was a terrifying thunderstorm, which would have been frightening and maybe dangerous to have been caught out in. The boy eagerly acquiesced in the cook's reflection, 'God made you tired.' They both took it that God was constantly looking after him, making him tired so that he would go home early to be safe, but *working through* individualistic actions so that the entire process of going home was, from a *manifest* point of view, dictated by individualistic decisions. A variant would be that the onset of a heavy atmosphere, prelude to the storm (not actually noticed at the time), made the boy tired, on the ancient deist schema that God endowed thunderstorms with lethargy-inducing properties.

How can we tell whether there is an unseen hand operating *through* wholly rational individualistic behaviour?

We have a parallel question where a person offers a disingenuous reason for an action. You don't want to go to a colleague's seminar, so you take an opportunity of telling him that on that day you have to conduct an examination. This is in fact true and is publicly available information. But it is not the real reason for your not going to the seminar, as becomes clear if it comes out that you arranged the examination for that day as an alibi in order to avoid attending the seminar. (One may have known cases of people with genuine excuses cancelling the excusing engagement to avoid looking as though they were avoiding going to a seminar, which they in fact didn't want to go to!) This kind of case is not instructive, however, because it can in principle be resolved by detective work revealing the relevant information.

How about the other, at least more central, cases? They consist in an unseen power acting through rational individual decisions in such a way that the decisions may seem to be merely epiphenomena.

I do not think there is an *absolute* answer. But something relevant can be said. The first question to demand of the conjectured unseen power is: does it explain not only the individual decisions it induces but lead to some further testable consequence as well? The second, even more important, is: is the mechanism or process by which it leads to these consequences fully specified or specifiable (not just a vague allusion, swept under the carpet)? If not, it does not satisfy our criterion for being scientifically real, and is to be put in cold storage pending the possibility of better elaboration, if science-backed reality is what is at stake.

If it satisfies these requirements, it is acceptable. And it is acceptable even though the further testable consequences it leads to can be fitted into the individualistic schema, provided that such a consequence had not been noted beforehand — which amounts in effect to the discovery of new empirical generalisations.

This desideratum is, I think, satisfied by consequences of Bion's group-hypothesis and of my diagnosis of a case of national psycho-pathology.

15 Science versus the scientific revolution

Two Dogmas of Social Science

This excursion is concerned with two main theses and a subsidiary one: namely that the social sciences have inherited a certain notion of mechanism which needs to be replaced; that they have evolved an observationalist approach ruling out the use of unobservables; but that the latter can find a home even in the social sciences provided we utilise correctly the traditional hypothetico-deductive framework. More specifically, the first aims at showing that mechanism in the social sciences operates, as it were, as an 'insecticide', promoting the growth of a damaging 'resistant strain'; it also aims at illustrating social science free from it. Further this strain is explained by a historical thesis that the scientific revolution and science as we know it contains a 'parascientific' component; and the parascientific component is identified as a certain philosophy — that of mechanism.

According to the second thesis, as may be seen from those areas that are free of the first defect, lack of achievement is to be attributed in great measure to failure to frame hypotheses involving unobservables.

The subsidiary thesis is that the hypothetico-deductive framework is indispensable for the social sciences; but little is said about this; it is taken for granted that the hypothetico-deductive framework is the only way of proceeding known to us where unobservables are involved.

It is arguable that the parascientific ingredient has not in fact damaged the natural sciences — and even that it has worked in their favour; at all events even if it has been an impediment in some measure, immense progress has been made in them. Where the social sciences are concerned, however, it seems to have stultified progress in some areas; here my aim is to exhibit the role of the parascientific ingredient in psychology. In other words, the parascientific ingredient, even if wholly quiescent in the natural sciences, has been used to excess as an insecticide in the social sciences.

Arbitrary Ingredients of Science

The first thesis turns on an underlying question about the place of metaphysics in natural science. Attitudes may be divided into those that regard metaphysics as having an important influence on science, and those that regard it as irrelevant where present, a blemish, and something that should be eradicated. And some distinguished physicists, under the sway of logical positivism, have gone to considerable lengths to purge science of metaphysics. With the breakdown of logical positivism, however, an increasing number of authors, both scientific and philosophical, have been stressing the influence of metaphysics, for example in physics, without however noticing the intrinsic or, so to speak, natural part it plays. It has been my concern to specify its role and to delineate some of the markedly different items that are commonly lumped together as metaphysics (Wisdom, 1968*a*, 1971*a*). My thesis is that science contains *ontology*: first, an ontology *embedded* in the empirical content of a theory, which is in-eradicable; and second an (eradicable) ontology that determines empirical contents, by prescribing what sort of entity may be allowed or even shall appear in a theory and by proscribing entities that are to be eschewed, not to be counted as scientific; moreover, while the *embedded ontology* arises out of the empirical content of science itself, the ontologies prescribed and proscribed, are imposed by a *weltanschauung*, which is a mixed bag of policy and method and sometimes restrictive epistemology.

The first part of the present thesis is that certain areas of the social sciences have been victims of inappropriate ontology and weltanschauung, and of having their empirical content derivatively either proscribed or prescribed. I aim to unravel the ontology/weltanschauung at work.

The Framework of Four Hundred Years of Natural Science

But we may first ask what is the effect of such ingredients upon science as we know it, upon science as it has been for four hundred years?

There have been considerable changes in natural science ontology/ weltanschauung during the past four hundred years since Copernicus, and it may be instructive to list some of the variations that are relatively specific:

  — 'Action by contact' replaced by
  — 'Action at a distance' replaced by
  — 'Action by contact.'
  — 'Nature abhors a vacuum.'
  — 'Nothing comes of nothing' replaced by
  — 'Spontaneous creation of matter.'
  — 'Indivisibility of matter.'
  — 'Compounds are composed of elements in simple proportions.'
  — 'Science is built upon measurement/experiment/observation.'

Here, however, what is of concern is very general. Thus:

  — 'For all *physical* changes seek only *physical* causes.'
  — 'For all *physiological* changes seek only *physical* causes.'
  — 'All *physical* changes/natural phenomena are wrought by *mechanical* process.[2]

The first of these expresses the naturalism of the new era, but does not fully represent the activity of natural science. The second, which is a slightly more determinate prescription, reflects the professional attitude in all physiological research; it has yielded colossal dividends, even if it has sterilised other research that might also yield significant results. In expressing organicism it also expresses epiphenomenalism (which no physiologist believes in once he has left his laboratory), and, as we shall see, a reductionist approach. The last one, which Marie Boas (1952) and Rupert Hall (1962) have aptly called the mechanical philosophy (or the corpuscular philosophy, which rather confines it to physics), expresses the notion of mechanical process, or mechanism, which in general characterises the spirit of natural science.[3] For a long time it did characterise most of natural science in fact, for example, Galilean kinematics, Newtonian dynamics, and so on (see also Popper, 1958), but it does not literally characterise Newtonian celestial mechanics or electricity and magnetism. (Newton may not have looked on himself as a mechanist, but the Newtonians did.) This is easily lost sight of because these areas were somehow subsumed under the outlook of dynamics. It has been implicitly recognised, on the other hand, by attempts to eliminate action at a distance from celestial mechanics. Such matters, however, are hardly germane: the main point is the conception of Nature as *clockwork*, the broad conception of *mechanical process*. It serves most purposes to refer to this outlook briefly as 'mechanism'. Parallels in the social science area of psychology will be given below.

Mechanism has been a dominant part of the weltanschauung of natural science for 400 years. Whatever its deficiencies, in its debt are all the theoretical achievements that have accrued ever since. It may seem too trivial to prate about, but the scientific revolution that began in 1543 was just this — the replacement of theocentric/anthropocentric astronomy and physics by mechanism. Before that time God was regarded as a clockmaker who made and looked after his clock, Nature. Afterwards physics contained scarcely a reference to clock-maintenance, though the conception persisted in philosophical concomitants. God continued to have a role, underpinning the laws of physics, but the role was restricted to this and did not include the detailed managing of events; secularism meant just this 'dominion status' accorded to the physical world.

Mechanism originated in secularism and has been with us ever since.

The Resultant of the Philosophy of Mechanism

Our broad question now is: what does mechanism forbid? Less question-begging would be: what does mechanism appear to forbid?

Five types of conception (research work, theory), whether rightly or wrongly, appear to be ruled out:

1 Vitalism;
2 Autonomous mental activity/(not initiated physiologically);
3 Clinical psychodynamics/(psychical effects produced by psychical causes);
4 Psychosomatic medicine/(bodily disorders produced by mental stress);
5 Institutional societal effects upon organic/material bodies/(the changing face of nature brought about by society).

Not all of these are equally well accredited. In all biological circles, vitalism is out; clinical psychodynamics gets a mixed reception; psychosomatic medicine however, is in the ascendant; at the other extreme, everybody acts on the assumptions that minds really do things and that social organisation affects everything. But, good or bad, should they be ruled out by a weltanschauung?

Vitalism is rejected as incompatible with mechanism. But the answer, according to mechanism, assuming the form of organicism/epiphenomenalism, is that the second, third, and fourth are *not* ruled out, for they are claimed to be compatible with mechanism (the fifth has not become engaged in the question). This answer requires the several conceptions to be *interpreted* so as to be compatible; and, plausibly or unplausibly, however counter-intuitive the epiphenomenalist account may be, these conceptions can in principle be squared with it: any action by the mind would be but a shadow cast by physiological activity, which would be the active agency in bringing about the effect mistakenly attributed to the mind; the mind would be not an active agent, and to speak as if it were would be at worst false and at best to use a shorthand. Similarly for institutions.

So there would seem to be no problem. But there is. For the ultimate mechanist accounts cannot be stated in detail and therefore cannot be used in practice, so mechanists/epiphenomenalists in practice use the notion of an active mental agent even though all such expressions have to be qualified as being 'as if' formulations. Thus the claim is not about practical matters but ultimate considerations. It comes as a surprise to find so many pure philosophers around in the ranks of physiologists, psychiatrists, and doctors, who, on this account thus far, are in no way concerned with a practical problem about human beings in general or patients in particular but only with an ultimate question of mechanistic explanation to which the hypotheses used in practice must be reduced. However, these mechanists/organicists/epiphenomenalists turn out not to be so pure-minded, for they oppose both research and practical procedures (therapy) that are rooted in the conception of mind as dynamic. Thus *interpreting* mental activity as ultimately compatible with mechanism is not the sole objective: the whole enterprise of working with the conception of mind as dynamic is considered wrong-headed. That is to say, mechanists/organicists/epiphenomenalists make both the ultimate claim that mental activity is compatible with or reducible to mechanism and the workaday claim that mental activity does not at any level produce bodily changes. (This often does not come clearly over because of the ease with which one can pass from the practical question to the ultimate one and vice versa.)

This position — at least for those organicists who adopt it — means that the five types of conception listed are not merely ruled out in appearance only but in actual fact. Thus mechanism — in its initial and most natural sense which will be characterised below — forbids both research and practice embodying the notion of mental phenomena producing physical change. And it goes even further; it bars the notion of mental phenomena producing even *mental* change.

Quite generally: *mechanism forbids all hypotheses involving a non-physical causal agent.*

Associationism as Mechanism versus Dynamism

At this point we need to connect the conception of mechanism with its psychological cognate: *associationism.* The Hobbes—Locke tradition was of constructing compound ideas out of simple units (sensations) by association. This tradition is represented in the twentieth century by behaviourism in general and by the theory of conditioned reflexes or conditioning in particular. That associationism is a cognate of mechanism is not simply because of there being a historical conjunction over most of the period (Hobbes was somewhat later than Copernicus). The reason is that it is a process by which two ideas become connected together, a compound impressed upon a waxlike mind suited to being stamped with impressions; the notion of mechanical process is that of two or more perceptual units (impressions, sensations, perceptions) being compounded, as with clockwork, by being physically contiguous; thus *association is a mechanical process.*

Thus the ontology/weltanschauung is: replace dynamic mental agents by physical movements.

Under its dominance we are left with a choice between two modes of procedure in the social sciences. There have been, and there still are, those who maintain that these sciences must imitate the natural sciences to the letter; and those who maintain that they must go it alone. Exponents of these opposite policies may be called the *parascientists* and the *transcientists* respectively. The parascientists, a long line from Watson and Hull to Eysenck and Skinner have produced, as it were, a scholastic brand of social science, sometimes quite like science though lacking any broad explanatory power. The transcientists have introduced various new and interesting ideas, and done most important work if it is valid, but almost entirely lacking a means of assessment and apparently lacking even the possibility of being tested. On the one hand we get a brand of 'parascience', on the other hand, work of a purely intuitive character, ranging from the brilliant if untestable to the sloppy. Various forms of what I am calling parascience have been well and truly dealt with by Popper (1961) — those, for example, that aim at forecasting. Similar attacks

180

have been mounted by Hayek (1955) on the notion which he calls 'scientism'. With these I am not here concerned; I am concerned with a different form of parascience, one that stems from a weltanschauung of mechanism. It is understandable that some social scientists, wishing to 'do science' should adopt the classical strategy of working with testable hypotheses in a framework of mechanism, since mechanism has characterised science 'as we have always known it', that is, since Copernicus. Thus Harris (1968) explicitly underwrites physicalism in anthropology and thinks it will gain prestige among natural scientists. But, just as the medieval thinkers could not break new ground so long as they were enmeshed in their weltanschauung, so we might face decades (?centuries) of an avant-garde scholasticism in the social sciences if mechanism is retained, producing accurate results with little information-content. Likewise it is understandable that other social scientists, impatient with aridity and desirous of what is significant, should try to adopt some altogether new method and break with the classical strategy of science. Thus I am pointing up a polarity between 'parascience' and 'transcience' (or 'authoritative empathism').[4] If anyone can come up with a new method that gets results that are both significant and can be authenticated in some manner, many of us would be glad to welcome it. But that day is not yet — and may be more remote than the philosopher's stone. Again we might face decades (?centuries) of an a priori form of scholasticism in the social sciences if mechanism is replaced by unaided intuition.

Can we *seriously* consider the possibility of giving up mechanism as an ingredient of science? A break with a 400-year-old tradition? Risk undermining the admitted achievements of science? Or do we risk more? We risk more.

For mechanism provides a seductive rocklike base for the secularism of the scientific revolution. To charge it with even moderate inadequacy might be felt to open the door to the outlook of the Middle Ages. Where is the end? What is to rule out the notion of witchcraft?

This would be a big price. But do we have to pay it? The risks lurking in the shadows are grave only so long as they are unarticulated; when articulated there is a simple answer. Let an idea that goes beyond mechanism be woven into a scientific theory and be subjected to the classical strategy of science, the hypothetico-deductive framework; so long as an observation can be deduced from it and an empirical test carried out, the idea is earthbound. Refutation is the best treatment for false ideas, and testability for ideas that are not earthbound.

Worthy of mention is a principle that is often closely associated with mechanism, although they are logically independent. It is the highly interesting and significant reductionist doctrine 'Nihil in intellectu quod non prius in sensu', the import of which has been noted, for example, by Bunge (1954), Agassi (1966), and myself (Wisdom, 1971*b*). It meant that in the order of existent things no one could have an idea other than one that arose from sense-experience (historically it did not bear the semantic interpretation, which some present-day philosophers might wish to put upon it, that no conception could be meaningful unless it could have a reference to sense-experience). This doctrine, which is of great age, bears witness to the tendency to reduce experience to sensations — Agassi (1966) calls it sensationalism and I call it observationalism (Wisdom, 1970*a*); and in it one can see associationism implicitly. But, like mechanism, it provided a king-pin for the secularism of the scientific revolution: well-founded ideas must be *rooted in experience*. To go against this is surely to revert to the useless speculations of the Middle Ages. Once ideas independent of all experience are admitted into science, where is the end? Once again, what is to rule out the notion of witchcraft?

'Nihil trans sensum' (as we may abbreviate it) is an expression of reductionism. It does not necessarily, as Kaplan (1970) has pointed out to me, accompany mechanism; for there are mechanists who are not reductionists. Thus the examples cited from him later overtly go against reducing mind to something else, but display mechanism.

The distinction is important. Nonetheless, there is a large overlap, for reductionism is often adopted in the service of mechanism. Mechanism is the more characteristic of *natural* science, while reductionism is to be found more explicitly in philosophy and psychology, though, as Kaplan points out, not necessarily. Either way, reinforced by reductionism or not, it is mechanism basically that gets within its grip a great area of the social sciences.

So strongly are mechanism and the doctrine 'Nihil trans sensum' built into our culture that even flexible-minded intellectuals who are apparently far from accepting them react with blank incredulity to the idea that one might seriously have hypotheses about minds, persons, groups and so on, that are empirically testable by physical observation. But such an approach must be seriously entertained.

Assume, however, we can neutralise our built-in weltanschauung. Then scientific reform of the parascientific revolution, where significant, would consist in eliminating mechanism but retaining the hypothetico-deductive method of testing.

Some Ontology Ineradicable from Science

Are we, then, assuming that science can be freed of all ontology? As already indicated, I have been at pains to show elsewhere that this is impossible. Popper (1959) has shown that the empirical content of a theory may be characterised as being refutable by observation; I have been concerned with other components of science which are not observation-refutable.

A very simple example is a property that no one would ever have thought of mentioning in a textbook of classical physics, namely, that energy can exist at all levels. (This is of course interesting only because in quantum physics the existence of levels of energy may be restricted, whereas in classical physics there is no restriction whatever and you could expect to find any value whatever for the energy.) Moreover if a certain energy-level were not found, it might always turn up later with further investigation. So the proposition that energy-levels could take on all values or that energy could exist at all levels was not refutable by observation and yet it was a clear consequence of all classical physics in the sense that, if you denied the proposition you could not hold classical physics.

Another example would be that space is absolute. It is very obvious that this cannot be refuted by observation, but it is a presupposition of a Newtonian system. Examples could be multiplied but these suffice to show that there are claims of an ontological kind made about the world which permeate classical science and which cannot be tested by observation.

There is no great difficulty in seeing that all theories involve ontological postulates of this sort. They constitute what I call 'embedded ontology'. What may not be so clear is that they are not immediately testable by observation. But this is easy to see if we reflect that these postulates never enter into the body of theory or experimental work as separate components but only when filtered through the empirical content. We must now therefore consider more closely what is in fact tested in a scientific theory when a test is carried out. Is it purely the empirical content or is it something wider?

Suppose a scientific theory is refuted. For example, Newton's theory of gravitation predicts incorrectly the motion of the perihelion of Mercury. Something, therefore, is false: some one of the premises producing the incorrect prediction is false. Now suppose in the present context that no way of saving the theory is found and that the falsity is pinned on the theory itself. The question then arises of what part of that theory is false. Now divide the structure of Newton's theory into two components: the empirical content and the embedded ontology. If the compound as a whole is false, can we tell which component is false? To this question the following points are relevant. The empirical content might be falsified and could be replaced by an alternative (for example, r^2 might be replaced by $r^{2.00016}$) and yet the embedded ontology of absolute space would be unchanged. On the other hand there is no way of changing the embedded ontology and leaving the empirical content alone, by the very fact that it is embedded; thus there is no way of refuting the embedded ontology alone. Hence a refutation falsifies empirical content; the embedded ontology may be false also, or it may not — there is no way of telling. *An observation-refutation can refute only the empirical content but not the embedded ontology.*

This is a simple consequence of the fact that an ontology is non-observation-refutable. And if the empirical content of a theory contains an embedded ontology, then that theory contains an untestable component. And hence *embedded ontology cannot be corroborated.*

One might hope that science contained no further unempirical, untestable, components. But there is a further ontology to be considered.

Typically, the ontology is embedded in the empirical content of a theory and arises out of it, or can be separated off from it, as a distinguishable item. But not all ontology arises in quite this way; for some comes from a mixed bag, which I am calling the weltanschauung of the theory. (Although the term is not ideal, it has been selected as the best of a bad lot; it has no connection, however, with zeitgeist or spirit of the age, associated for example with Mannheim; as will now appear it has to do with framework, outlook, presumptive method and so on.) It is a source of ontology that circumscribes the theory with the ontology itself as a framework. For instance, however much they may have differed, Copernicus (with qualifications), Kepler, Galileo, Descartes, and Newton shared the new weltanschauung of naturalism or secularism in physical theory; the Renaissance meant relinquishing the weltanschauung of non-natural causes in physics and astronomy. The new weltanschauung, as noted earlier, could be expressed in the form of a policy: 'For all physical changes, seek only physical causes.' Now a policy directive is in a certain sense a method: it gives you an outline of what you must do to do science; or else it tells you what not to do. It tells you what will not count as science, and what will (if you follow the policy/method, you may do good science, or you may fail to do good science, but good or bad, it will be science for as long as that weltanschauung lasts). The example given is very general. A more specific one already mentioned would be the weltanschauung of the impossibility of action at a distance, yielding the policy/method 'no physical theory may include the idea of action at a distance'; while so long as such a weltanschauung dominates the scientific world, no paper using the idea would be accepted for publication in a professional journal.

Closely connected with this is restriction by epistemology: thus both Kant and logical positivism (in some of its forms) ruled out an ontology of entities outside our experience. Such an epistemological restriction may be subsumed under policy about method.

Thus the weltanschauung both proscribes an ontology and prescribes an ontology.

A prescribed ontology is not strictly embedded, for it is not generated by the empirical content; it selects the class of possible empirical contents; hence the empirical content will *conform* to the ontology without being an embodiment of it. Thus, if all physiological changes are to be attributed to physical causes, what is regarded as physiological research will conform to the ontology of physical causes.

Thus science contains philosophical components over and above empirical content, consisting of embedded ontology generated from within and prescribed ontology generated by a weltanschauung. Empirical content is testable or corroborable; embedded ontology and prescribed ontology are not, and can therefore be adopted rationally only as tentative, that is, tentative in the sense of being open to question even before a possible refutation by a new theory has arrived.

When working within an ontology/weltanschauung, this is not what we ordinarily try to test; it comes in question at certain stages, either before it has crystallised or when it shows signs of breaking down. The legitimacy of using untested an ontology/weltanschauung cannot of course rest upon the impossibility of doing otherwise; it rests, somewhat reasonably, somewhat uneasily, upon the fact that it is a harmless adjunct to corroborable empirical content; in other words *an untested ontology/weltanschauung will give service at least so long as the empirical content is corroborated.*

Ontology in the Social Sciences

There is often criticism of 'theories' in the social sciences on the grounds that they are untestable. This is sometimes due to a failure to distinguish empirical theories from what are perhaps intuitively recognised as frameworks. Once the appropriate distinctions are drawn, however, much that is put forward can be seen to be ontology or weltanschauung, and is therefore correctly regarded as untestable. But it is not correctly *criticisable* as untestable; for this is either to mistake it for empirical theory, or to condemn it as a foreign body that should have no place in science. It is now apparent both that a 'theory' of the framework kind is different from empirical theory and also that it is an ineliminable ingredient of science. But in eradicating mechanism, that is, in showing that it is not a necessary component of science, have we not freed science of ontology/weltanschauung? Not at all; a new one enters willy-nilly sometimes even unbeknownst. Better if we try — however unsuccessfully — to identify it. We should have perhaps an ontology of minds, persons, ideal personal types, groups, and even emergent properties[5] having a role independent of these entities. For brevity such entities may be said to constitute a *socio-personal ontology*.

Thus we may try to use the classical hypothetico-deductive framework in conjunction with a permissive ontology. And this could be done without falling victim to myth.

Clearly all psychodynamics has a socio-personal ontology. Included are psychoanalysis, one approach to psychosomatic medicine, and one approach to psychiatry. All this originated in psychoanalysis which arose in rebellion against mechanism/associationism. Social psychology also can be pursued from this angle, and is when inspired by psychodynamics.

Per contra, organic psychiatry, that is, the weltanschauung according to which all mental disorders are due to some imbalance of hormones, electric circuits, defective genetic inheritance, and so on, and also psychosomatic medicine conducted according to the weltanschauung ascribing disorders to faulty habits, and so forth, both operate on the basis of mechanism/associationism. Social psychology can also be pursued within this framework.

Likewise much non-clinical psychology is conducted on the same basis. Learning theory is a very obvious example. But the same is true of much of the psychological theory of perception, which has definite results to its credit.

Psychodynamics does not, of course, follow the mechanism/associationism weltanschauung, because it was born in rebellion.

On the other hand consider those areas that, despite being nurtured on mechanism/associationism, have got significant results. For some areas success is controversial, and at least far from decisively established. Those for which the claim is best justified are the psychological theory of perception and learning theory. Now the psychology of perception could be an area for which mechanism would be appropriate, or at least some problems in it: for instance the orientation and appearance of shape turns out to be governed by angles. Similarly with learning theory, provided the concept of 'learning' refers not to a critical grasp but to a process or drill such as typing.[6]

We can now see that those branches of psychology that fall within the framework of mechanism/associationism subscribe to the ontology/weltanschauung, 'Eschew hidden mental entities and replace them by observable physical movements'. (Wisdom, 1952*a*; Peters and Tajfel, 1957).

There is also good reason to think that several areas of the other social sciences have been under the dominance of this weltanschauung, though this possible extension of the thesis would have to be examined for each branch separately. It would certainly be deleterious for the social sciences to be forced to conform to such a paradigm. An interesting distinction which has been pointed out to me by Kaplan (1970) should, however, be noted, between behaviourist psychologists who eschew hidden mental entities on the one hand and, on the other hand, certain political scientists who retain them but nonetheless operate with a conception of man that is inert. Kaplan gives the following examples:

1 Social pressures and inherited beliefs lead members of a social group (for example, Catholics) to vote for the same political party.
2 When an individual is a member of two groups and these groups have differing political loyalties, he is likely to be undecided politically and is likely not to vote at all.

Kaplan is surely right that these are manifestations of inert mechanism. Thus it is possible to work with mental entities and yet utilise inert mechanism. What is wrong with behaviourism, then, is not merely the repudiation of mental entities as such, but the consequential universalisation of inert mechanism.

We now have some notion of the form the social sciences assume under the governance of mechanism: linkages are established through spatio-temporal contiguity and are imprinted upon a passive receptor. If we reflect upon the nature of a dynamic entity, we can see that, not only is the receptor notion inapplicable, but the dynamic entity itself plays a part in affecting linkages. Hence (unless interpreted as a particular case or as an approximation) an associationist theory is untenable within a dynamic weltanschauung.

What account, then, is to be given of dynamic mechanism? Does this not conflict with the notion of dynamism and with the supposed incompatibility of dynamics and mechanism? I think the answer to this lies in a strange feature of science inherited from the Middle Ages. Physical motion was not held to be caused by material factors; only God could cause motion; the appearance of mundane motion was simply a manifestation of the activity of God; *matter was inert*. Although, beginning with Copernicus, the doctrine of primary, or divinely operated, causes disappeared from physics, the dynamism was not transferred all at once from God to matter. Thus naturalistic or secular physics was based on a weltanschauung of inert mechanism. True, this was later to evolve without its being noticed into a dynamic mechanism in Newton's celestial mechanics, his theory of gravitation. But though the greatest theories of Newtonian and later physics were dynamic, the spirit of inert mechanism would seem to have persisted. Be that as it may, the representative of it in the social domain certainly reflects inert mechanism.

So when we speak of the weltanschauung of mechanism holding sway over the past 400 years, I think this should mean inert mechanism. And when we speak of a new socio-personal ontology for the social sciences, this should imply a dynamic mechanism. Otherwise expressed, 'mechanism' traditionally conjures up the model of clockwork, which is inert in that it needs an *extra*-clockwork entity to do the winding. The motion of 'dynamism' also involves mechanism but with *immanent* winding, that is, it has the very different sense of *autopropulsion*.

Unobservables in the Natural Sciences

There is further development of the programme of a socio-personal weltanschauung: it proposes to work with unobservables. Some find it difficult to realise that they are fundamental in natural science; others who realise this cannot believe they could figure in the social sciences. A deepseated reason for the latter is, I think, this. So long as we are under the sway of inert mechanism, that is of associationism in the social sciences, we can only use concepts of observables—associationism would not make sense otherwise. (This is even true of mechanism for, in its original naked form, mechanism involved the push and pull that were exerted between two things perceptually connected by the mechanism, though in the sophisticated developments of physics, mechanism covered situations in which there existed no process of push or pull, that is, mechanism involved unobservables.)

The possibility therefore opens out that, with the disbanding of mechanism/associationism, we may find unobservables playing for the first time a large role in the social sciences, just as they have done in the natural sciences (Wisdom, 1952b).

We have first to ask how we can have such entities in science? The key to this lies in a fact about natural science: its greatest and most successful theories embody such entities. (To avoid possibly unjustified hypostatisation, it is not uncommon to speak of the question of theoretical terms, that is, terms that do not designate observables; but serious confusion is unlikely to arise from speaking of unobservables.)

The following are examples. Newton's *gravitational attraction*, which is not to be experienced in the way force is when someone takes you by the arm. Dalton's *atom*. Rigid body *strain*. Thermodynamical *increase of entropy*. The *aether*. Maxwell's *electromagnetic wave*. The *electron*. Planck's *quantum of action*. Einstein's *absolute velocity of light*. Schrödinger's quantum mechanical *wave*. The biological *gene*. (Consider also the social science examples: in economics Keynes's *multiplier*; in psychoanalysis Freud's *unconscious Oedipus complex*.) It is difficult to give an accurate criterion for such concepts, but some, such as the above, are clearly recognisable, and so are those that are at the other end of the scale, such as tables, chairs, stars, and even molecules; for present purposes we do not need a refined demarcation criterion.

The *fact* of such concepts needs stressing, because they are seldom recognised, even by philosophers of science, outside the ranks of physics. Their enormous power in scientific explanation need hardly be mentioned (though occasionally one may be discredited, like the aether). It has never proved possible to dispense with them; nor is this necessary; for, despite the unobservability of what they designate, such concepts are used in hypotheses that are tested by observation. In short, the widely overlooked message is that mysterious entities can be used in the hypothetico-deductive framework culminating in empirical/observational test.

There is no reason to rule out a priori the possibility of proceeding along the same lines in the social sciences. Success through their use is not guaranteed, but it is reasonable to try them.

Existing Use of Hypotheses in the Social Sciences

It might be thought that such concepts do already occupy a place in the social sciences, for it is customary, at least in North America, to frame theories in terms of concepts such as *role*, *group*, *reference-group*, and so on. But these are expressible in terms of recognisable experiences, and therefore do not constitute unobservables in the out-and-out sense considered here (any more than do the physical concepts velocity, weight, density, and so on).

If there is a wish to adopt the procedure of the natural sciences, framing theories with unobservables would be the model to follow. As Popper (1961) has shown, existing attempts to copy the natural sciences have been misguided, because what has been taken over is irrelevant. There are indeed many social scientists who use hypotheses, but only in the trivial sense of checking whether something is a fact or not. There are, however, a very few endeavours that seem to follow our model.

Thus Hull (1964) formed a hypothetico-deductive system, with postulates but not unobservables. In it he enunciated a large number of theorems, which, whether genuinely derived from his postulates or not, form a system in line with some behaviouristic conditioning theory. These theorems may be considered under three headings.

Under the first come those — the great majority — that are wholly in line with common experience, for example:

Theorem 47: The action of a muscle repeating some performance will become modified so as to do less work;

Theorem 70: An organism placed midway between two objects will move towards the one it needs more;

Theorem 95: Organisms having to make a detour will choose the shortest distance available;

Theorem 98: An organism behind a U-shaped barrier will first try to go through it, but progressively move away from the direct line to its goal until it goes round the barrier;

Theorem 107: Complicated mazes are more difficult to negotiate than simple ones.[6]

To many it is a sign of scientific achievement, and metascientifically satisfactory to find that a theory leads to known facts. This can be true, but also can be a major delusion. Certainly a theory should do at least this much, but if it does no more it is not a serious theory. To aim at mere conformity with the evidence is one of the subtler and rarer misuses of the hypothetico-deductive system. It is felt intuitively that a good theory must accord with reality. This is, of course, true in the sense that its consequences must accord with observation; but such accordance provides no corroboration if *the consequences are to be expected in any event* — if they are also consequences of other accepted theories or if they are simply matters of common experience. Only if they are not to be 'naturally' expected, does the theory conflict with existing knowledge. Now Hull does not treat these theorems, which express what is already known, as a mere preliminary condition for having a satisfactory theory, before going on to serious work; he treats them as substantial results. Thus Hull's theory seems to lack *novelty-producing power* in that it *lacks consequences that conflict with existing knowledge*. Theorems coming under the second heading do nothing to modify this position; they are simply quantitative relations between certain processes such as that 'reaction-potential varies inversely as reinforcement-delay' which merely provide

190

elaborations. So we look to the third heading, concerned with theorems providing unexpected results. Of these there are very few, for example:

> Theorem-corollary xvii: a stimulus continued after reinforcement has ceased will evoke its response, sometimes even more strongly at first but with subsequent falling off and a falling off of learning; Theorem 105: A blind alley early in a maze is more difficult to avoid than one at the end.

These are mildly surprising, so however thin a result they constitute they do indicate some small content in the theory.

Eysenck (1955) makes a bolder attempt to infuse some content into a hypothetico-deductive theory. In one enterprise his main theorem is that 'dysthymics' (roughly obsessionals and depressives) are more introverted (to be expected also on the basis of clinical psychodynamics) and more easily/strongly conditioned than normals, and these in turn more than hysterics. The second part of the result is surprising on two counts: the relation of dysthymics to hysterics, and the bracketing of ease and strength of conditioning. If correct, these results are interesting and perhaps important. They are certainly worthy of being checked and should be repeated. Eysenck indicates that there are several other consequences also, but the few he alludes to have none of the specificity of the above.

If his theorem should hold, it would require clinical psychodynamics to rethink a small application, which indeed has little relevance to it; certainly the conditioning theorem, apart from other work in support, is far from adding a crucial experiment to decide between the theory of conditioning and clinical psychodynamics.

Social Hypotheses within Inert Mechanism

From Hull's extremely thin results and Eysenck's meagre ones, let us turn to Skinner. His approach is the same though more urbane than Eysenck's. Instead of attacking Freud he absorbs psychoanalytic results, which he regards as discoveries, by reinterpreting them behaviouristically. And in this he is thoroughgoing. Let us, then, look at some of his metascientific remarks.

> The practice of looking inside the organism for an explanation of behaviour has tended to obscure the variables which are immediately available for a scientific analysis. The variables (required) lie outside the organism. (Skinner, 1953, p. 31)

So Skinner is completely clear he is dealing with what Collingwood calls the 'outside' of an event, something wholly observable. Not only does he follow this line when interpreting Freud, but also when considering ordinary men:

> When the man in the street says that someone is afraid or angry or in love, he is generally talking about predispositions to act in certain ways. (Skinner, 1953, p. 162)

Certainly the ordinary man does at times mean to *include* such predispositions; but it is a mystery how Skinner can have conditioned himself to think — or write — that the ordinary man means no more than this. If Skinner did so, at least this is evidence that conditioning can be effective in paralysing a man's perceptiveness of people's attitudes. The most important metascientific commitment, however, is this:

> If to be thirsty . . . means that he drinks because of a state of thirst, an inner causal event is invoked. If this state is purely inferential — if no dimensions are assigned to it which would make direct observation possible — it cannot serve as an explanation. (Skinner, 1953, p. 33)

Although Skinner rightly recognises that 'inner' events must lead to observational consequences, the tenor of his statement suggests that he disregards the basic role of unobservables in science; and it would even seem that his belief in the impossibility of having scientific explanations containing unobservables is the kingpin of his behaviourism.

Conditioning is a specific form of behaviourism. Behaviourism is the study of bodily movements, the 'outside' of an event the only things 'observable' and 'scientific'. Add to this the restriction of inertness, for it is natural enough to link dynamism with the 'inside', and we get a set-up for laws of behaviour of a conditioning type. This is the weltanschauung that owes its inspiration to Pavlov. The sort of behaviour and the sort of laws that do appear to satisfy this framework are party-line reactions and propaganda, or reaction-patterns and pain-inductance. Such activities are possible and can be carried out effectively: you can get people to obey a host of political injunctions, for example, reporting the opinions of parents to the secret police, or you can stop a youngster masturbating by means of a system of electric shocks; they are standard for house-training puppies and kittens. Some of those who administer drill-skills, from propagandists like the late Goebbels to a regimental sergeant, know very well, as Skinner (1948) makes clear in *Walden II*, that the method does not work if trainees are allowed to indulge in critical reflection — which provides a hint about the function of the 'inside' of an event.

The position would seem to be this. There is at present no 'proof' that a dynamic 'inside' of an event exists. This puts the behaviourist/conditionist in a strong position where the prevailing weltanschauung does not demand 'proof' that he should provide more than a programme and explain all that clinical dynamics purports to explain. The broad metascientific status is much the same for both, with the weltanschauung supporting the conditioning programme (while time may be on the side of psychodynamics). *If* there is no dynamic 'inside' of events, the conditioning programme must be pursued. *If* there is a dynamic 'inside', then it must in some circumstances control action. In the latter case, there might be actions conditioning did not affect, or at most influenced in small degree, while there might be others where the inner dynamics was swamped by conditioning or was even totally inactive. (An example of this last *could* involve a symptom that originated in a psychodynamic inhibition but persisted either after the inhibition was psychodynamically resolved or after the inhibition ceased to relate to the symptom, on the assumption that the psychodynamic cause conditioned the symptom, so that presumably the symptom could be deconditioned.) Certainly it is plausible that conditioning could operate in some circumstances (at least concerning activity under the dominance of the old brain and probably more widely), especially as an ad hoc method of overwhelming psychodynamic factors. But as a *general* theory it carries no plausibility (apart from what our 400-year-old weltanschauung gives it): for in a nutshell the extraordinary story of mankind is its psychodynamic capacity to resist conditioning by oppression.

Social Dynamic Hypotheses with Unobservables

Strangely enough, almost the only psychologist I know of who in practice (perhaps not deliberately) made extensive use of the hypothetico-deductive framework and also of unobservables was Freud: he was constantly seeking explanation, consequences, and checks; he was unfortunate in not being able to find a satisfactory way of testing consequences.

The pursuit of psychodynamic hypotheses must involve unobservables. I have deliberately sought to put some psychological/social concepts of unobservables into the hypothetico-deductive framework and to squeeze an observational consequence out of them. I list examples briefly.

(i)   It is required to test the hypothesis of syndrome-shift. This is the idea that when a patient is relieved of a set of symptoms and soon gets another set, the same or different, the new syndrome sometimes has the same source as the first one. In other words, while some patients get two diseases in succession, others get one disease with two syndrome manifestations, that is, with a shift of syndrome. There is no firm evidence for this; and, even accepting the possibility, there is no way of telling when a syndrome is new and when it is a shift. The theory is bound up with the psychosomatic framework in modern medicine, namely that a psychological cause can be a dominant factor in producing a physical disease: the shifted syndrome is attributed to the psychological cause of the original syndrome.

My suggested investigation (stripped of all refinement) is as follows. Consider a set of children, at some suitable age such as eighteen months, who have become ill *for the first time* with a syndrome considered psychosomatic; consider also a set, at the same age, who have had no such syndrome; we could also add a set, at the same age, who have had such a syndrome say two to four times. What is the frequency with which each group will get another such syndrome? If the theory of syndrome-shift is false, all groups will be the same — the expected illness rate conforming to the normal incidence rate for children of their age. If the theory is true, the first group should have a greater expectation of developing a new syndrome than the second group (and it should conform to the rate already found in the third). This investigation could be carried out from the case records of a family pediatrician (Wisdom, 1968*b*).

(ii)   It is required to test Freud's hypothesis of primary narcissism, which is not open to inspection by any procedure whatever (even by psychoanalysis) (Balint, 1960): it is thus unlike secondary narcissism which is open to social inspection, being in effect vanity.

To be in the phase of primary narcissism is to have no personal relationship with any person (or object). The child in this phase has a non-personal relationship of need and the like, and a parent is a non-personal source of supplies and so on. Thus a person is no more than a utility. Now utilities can be equivalent; a utility is therefore replaceable; utilities are substitutable. Hence primary narcissism has as a consequence the *principle of substitutability of utilities*.

Experiment: Place before children of about 6 months old three cups/toys identical with a favourite cup/toy. On the theory of primary narcissism they will accept one as readily as another; if it is false, that is, on the theory that they do have rudimentary personal relationships, they will look to see which is really their cup/toy (Wisdom, 1968*b*).

(iii)   It is required to test not a psychoanalytic hypothesis in the

194

abstract, but an application of it, that is, an interpretation, in a therapeutic session with a patient.

Interpreting a patient's associations presupposes that their meaning is unconscious because of the patient's defences; it is assumed that, when interpreting, the analyst knows what these defences are, even though he may not be interpreting them. The main function of interpretation is to change the patient's defences. Test: an analyst could make a point of predicting change of defence; boundaries of falsification could be set (Wisdom, 1966, 1967).

(iv) An example concerning groups, which of course is much more liable to interference from innumerable factors, comes from an account of the parlous state of Great Britain given by Koestler and collaborators in 1963. I reached a group diagnosis: that the country was suffering from a sub-acute group-depression — a societal emergent property. This state was explained as due to an ambivalence in society towards a split-off component of it. This enabled me to form an estimate of the likely outcome in ten or fifteen years' time (Wisdom, 1970*b*).

Such an attempt is fraught with risk. It can be deemed to have come off if the actual outcome is understandable in terms of the theory together with whatever accidental circumstances have entered the scene. Thus no ceteris paribus clause is involved.

The Outcome

To revert to the question of the parascientific revolution and its reform, the innuendo throughout has been that the scientific revolution from 1543 to the present has consisted of the valid strategy of the hypothetico-deductive framework plus an unjustified ontology of mechanical-type processes prescribed by a weltanschauung of inert mechanism. Although this ontology apparently worked wonders for natural science (though it conceivably hampered progress with electro-magnetics), it need not have been exclusive of other types of entity. I would suppose that scientific progress would have been slower and less spectacular, but that it would have been more balanced, so that the twentieth century would not have had divinities presiding over technology and children controlling society. Be that as it may, the parascientific ingredient, inert mechanism, is dispensable, and should be eliminated if the social sciences are to flower. The main point for the future of the social sciences is to keep open certain ontological routes. Insecticides have brought farming out of the Middle Ages but kill much valuable wildlife. Our social science weedkillers can be undiscriminating; so far as they are selective, they may promote a resistant strain, a self-perpetuating useless growth, of so-called social research.

On the metascientific issue, whether to do parascience, as has been so widely practised by social scientists, or whether to go-it-alone with the transcientists, my suggestion is to try the traditional strategy of science — to eat the pudding. That is to say, while altering the ontology, to give the hypothetico-deductive method a serious trial.[8]

The only serious objection to this method is likely to come from transcientists, who may confuse it with parascience, and who are likely to regard it as incompatible with an empathic approach to the study of persons; but I hope to have shown by my example that no such incompatibility exists. Indeed further, empathy actually needs to be supplemented by being subjected to the discipline of the hypothetico-deductive framework. This amounts to saying empathy, though needed, and even vital, cannot be authoritative.

Thus, apart from certain areas where inert mechanism is appropriate, the strategy for the social sciences is the hypothetico-deductive framework with an ontology involving persons, types, groups, and even unobservables such as emergent group-properties. Let the pudding be made of any entities however mysterious, but let it be subjected to the rigours of observational testing, and let the proof of it be in the eating. Only thus can the ideal be realised, as Freud (as also Radcliffe-Brown in connection with society) has put it, of making of psychology a *natural* science.

Ontologica non sunt purganda praeter necessitatem.

Notes

1 Based on various lectures, mainly at the Creighton Club, Colgate University, New York, 27 April 1968, and seminars at The University of Southern California, February 1966.
2 A wholly satisfactory terminology is difficult to find; a good suggestion is 'mechanical process', which I owe to Mr J. Robert Bath.
3 'The essence of mechanistic philosophy in the seventeenth century was the axiom that all natural phenomena could be reduced . . . to one single kind of change, the motion of matter' (Hall, 1962, p. 101).
4 C. Wright Mills (1959) castigated the aridity of social science under the heading of 'abstract empiricism' (by which not very apt expression I think he meant observationalism, plus statistics, abstracted from context, theory, etc.), and did so most effectively.

He, too, introduced a second pole, which he called 'grand theory' (by which I think he meant ontology and framework but not empirical theory). Though correct in criticising it, I think he failed to realise that it has an authentic role and that the main contemporary error made about it is to discuss it under the belief that it is empirical theory.

5   I have suggested earlier the need to allow of emergent properties that are in no sense reducible to individual persons, their actions and aims, and their foreseeable unintended consequences (Wisdom, 1970b). Such properties thus constitute a system over and above individuals. Although I put it forward as a development from, though inconsistent with, Popper's 'methodological individualism', he would seem to have originated essentially the same idea, which he conceives of as the 'third world' (is it not rather the 'fourth world'?). He has not, as yet, revised his 'methodological individualism' in the light of his 'third world', (or alternatively shown that the 'third world' is compatible with 'methodological individualism').

6   It could be urged, as pointed out to me by Anderson (1971), that perception of shape and inculcation of typing skill are hardly *psychology*: that is to say, the success of mechanism in 'psychology' has been made possible by interpreting the subject in a non-psychical physicalistic way so that it easily conforms to mechanism.

7   These are my abbreviated renderings. In full theorem 70, for example, reads: 'Other things equal, in a heterogenous adient-adient competitive situation with the organism placed midway between the adient objects for one of which the organism has a greater need or drive (D) than for the other, the organism will tend to choose the direction of the object involving the greater drive'.

8   The present thesis may seem to be essentialistic: science, the pure untainted unchangeable method of rational enquiry; 'parascience', a kind of 'black science' practised on the witches' sabbath. The actual position here, on the contrary, goes the other way. For the theory of science offered involves three main components: the hypothetico-deductive structure, an embedded and alterable ontology, and an alterable weltanschauung; while 'parascience' involves a rigid ontology and a rigid weltanschauung. So the present approach is in fact the reverse of essentialistic: thus it is not that the philosophy of mechanism was wrong, but the fact that it was regarded as essential and non-replaceable; here it is held that that philosophy was excellent in certain areas but inappropriate and replaceable in others.

Although any one form of ontology is expendable, some embedded ontology would seem to be essential. This is, however, a small concession: all it asserts is that a theory peoples the world with whatever entities it presupposes — which is tautological rather than essentialistic.

An overtone of the discussion is that even the hypothetico-deductive framework may not be essential. About this I would offer two comments. It may be that this framework is a purely logical consequence of the notion of explanation, in which case the framework would be a component not for essentialistic but for analytic reasons. The other is that we might find a new way of 'establishing' putative knowledge about the world other than by testing hypotheses. I am not hopeful of such a consummation, I do not know what it might be like, and indeed I do not believe in it; but it is rash to hold that something is impossible, and if such a development should materialise, we should be only too glad of it.

References

Agassi, Joseph (1966), 'Sensationalism', *Mind*, 75, pp. 1—24.
Anderson, Gordon (1971), Personal communication.
Balint, Michael (1960), 'Primary Narcissism and Primary Love', *Psychoanalytic Quarterly*, 29, pp. 6—43.
Boas, Marie (1952), 'The Establishment of the Mechanical Philosophy', *Osiris*, 10, pp. 412—541.
Bunge, Mario (1954), 'New Dialogues between Hylas and Philonous', *Philosophy and Phenomenological Research*, 15, pp. 192—9.
Eysenck, H.J. (1955), 'A Dynamic Theory of Anxiety and Hysteria', *British Journal of Psychiatry*, 101, pp. 28—51.
Hall, A.R. (1962), *The Scientific Revolution*, London, pp. 205—16.
Harris, Marvin (1968), *The Rise of Anthropological Theory*, New York, pp. 231, 655.
Hayek, F.A. (1955), *The Counter-Revolution of Science*, New York.
Hull, C.L. (1964), *A Behavior System*, New York.
Kaplan, Harold (1970), Personal communication.
Mills, C. Wright (1959), *The Sociological Imagination*, New York.
Peters, R.S. and Tajfel, H. (1957), 'Hobbes and Hull — Metaphysicians of Behaviour', *British Journal for the Philosophy of Science*, 8, pp. 30—44.
Popper, K.R. (1958), 'Philosophy and Physics', *Acts of XII International Congress of Philosophy*, Venice, vol. 2, pp. 367—74.
Popper, K.R. (1959), *The Logic of Scientific Discovery*, London and New York.

Popper, K.R. (1961), *The Poverty of Historicism*, London and New York.

Popper, K.R. (1968), 'On the Theory of the Objective Mind', *Proc. XIV International Congress of Philosophy*, vol. 1, pp. 25—53.

Skinner, B.F. (1948), *Walden II*, New York.

Skinner, B.F. (1953), *Science and Human Behaviour*, New York.

Wisdom, J.O. (1952*a*), 'Mentality in Machines', *Proceedings of the Aristotelian Society*, supplementary volume 26.

Wisdom, J.O. (1952*b*), *Foundations of Inference in Natural Science*, London.

Wisdom, J.O. (1966), 'Testing a Psycho-Analytic Interpretation', *Ratio*, 8.

Wisdom, J.O. (1967), 'Testing an Interpretation within a Session', *International Journal of Psycho-Analysis*, 48, pp. 45—52.

Wisdom, J.O. (1968*a*), 'Scientific Theory: Empirical Content, Ontology, and Weltanschauung', *Proceedings of the XIV International Congress of Philosophy*, 1969, Vienna.

Wisdom, J.O. (1968*b*), 'What Sort of Ego has an Infant?', in *Foundations of Child Psychiatry*, E. Miller, ed., Oxford.

Wisdom, J.O. (1970*a*), 'Observations as the Building Blocks of Science in 20th century scientific thought', paper given at the Philosophy of Science Association, Boston, 23 October 1970, *Boston Studies in the Philosophy of Science*, Reidel, Dordrecht, Holland, vol. 8, 1971.

Wisdom, J.O. (1970*b*), 'Situational Individualism and Emergent Group-Properties', in *Explanations in the Behavioural Sciences*, R. Borger and F. Cioffi, eds, Cambridge.

Wisdom, J.O. (1971*a*), 'Scientific Theory: Empirical Content, Embedded Ontology, and Weltanschauung', *Philosophy and Phenomenological Research*.

Wisdom, J.O. (1971*b*), 'Four Contemporary Interpretations of the Nature of Science', *Foundations of Physics*, 1.

16 Finale

This chapter is not exactly a conclusion nor a summary. It contains concluding remarks which highlight the main points that have been developed in order to cast them into perspective. I suppose that Part I could be described as a softening-up process preparing the reader for the main thesis. The depiction of various forms of schemata in this section was partly to give examples, but their chief importance lies in their powerful, though insufficiently recognised, influence in determining the kind of work that contemporary social scientists do and the way in which they think. Some of these were positive schemata which social scientists use either deliberately or not, in all their thinking. Others were negative in that they interfere with the approach of social scientists, through being based on misunderstandings, leading social observers to overemphasise certain aspects of social thought and sidetracking them from genuine modes of enquiry. This section was also concerned to pave the way towards isolating one of the most important schemata of the present day, namely individualism which was taken up in detail in Part II.

Part II began by delineating, in some detail, the notion of weltanschauung of which schemata are a particularly important subset, being in fact the weltanschauungen that social scientists have used of comparatively recent times in their approach both to the social world and to theories about it. I turned to these social science schematas, of which I noted 20, and described them in some detail though possibly over-briefly. Here the overall point of importance to emerge was that social scientists have tended to hoist a flag over one particular schema in the sense that they regarded other schemata as excluded by their own one and usually not worthy of serious thought or consideration. I conducted the exegesis in such a way as to bring out as sharply as I could that nearly all of these were isolationist approaches which had no guarantee lying within them; moreover nearly all of them seem to be required in any reasonable approach to the social sciences and to theories about them. Thus large numbers of problems are undercut as being parochial disagreements. There survive, however, two issues. One of them typifies a common academic situation in which a cult has grown up; a cult of the individual encounter, and the demand that people and groups of societies shall be understood in terms of the way they see themselves. This cult is of some, though very limited, value in that it suffers from being the beginning of sociology rather than a full-blown explanatory empirical theory. It has arisen in opposition to what is conceived to be the arid dehydrated impersonal positivistic view of science. This issue, however, rests upon the plethora of misunderstandings. Their removal is necessary only to enable social scientists to do appropriate empirical work and not spend their time on a misconceived enemy and a misconceived debate. The other issue that emerges differs in that it is inherent in the structure of sociological growth. This one, which is of fascinating interest, is that between individualism and holism. It is one to which attention is seldom given because practically all western social thinkers are individualists and a few opponents are ideologues and neither tries to understand the other. Pari passu thinkers in the other half of the world are holistic, and there individualism is equally frowned on and its practitioners warded off.

I have taken some trouble to elucidate individualism, in the form of what I call 'situational individualism' due to Weber and Popper. In order to bring out its difficulties, and to sort out a basic ambiguity within it, I have sought to put it in its most plausible and strongest form. We are then in a position to consider its poverty or its limitation. Then if we grant that it does have possible limitations, we may turn to consider its contrasting rival, holism. The schema of holism, not expressible in terms of the individuals that compose wholes, or collectives as they are sometimes called, means that wholes are all-powerful in that individuals are powerless to control them. Such wholes seem to apply to different kinds of problems but to have parallel limitations in not being so applicable to certain problems which seem to be more suited to the individualistic schema. The reason why they both seem to be inadequate is that they both preclude the possibility of forming hypotheses that would most naturally come under the aegis of the other.

This kind of difficulty is no proof or disproof, according to the claim of this entire book. It is not possible to prove or disprove a schema, but we can rank schemata in terms of what they can do and in terms of what they preclude, and it is a contention here that a schema is not to be entertained if it is exclusive or forbids certain kinds of hypothesis from being entertained. In terms of this wider approach that eschews boundaries, I have proposed a more flexible schema which I call transindividualism. This schema includes components both from individualism and holism. It is a bipolar schema in which either the holistic component of the individualistic component may dominate at any one time for any one hypothesis for any one problem. Its superiority to the others would lie simply in its being more permissive of forming hypotheses in the social field. Naturally problems arise in connection with such a schema and they are similar to those that are present already for holism. One prominent problem is to understand how it might be possible for a property of a whole to become manifest in the social world. After all, the only active entities in the social world are individual people, and therefore the whole must be manifested through their actions. How then are we going to be able to recognise a whole through the actions of individuals, and decide that there is something more than simply the sum of the individual actions (or more than the complex arising out of the sum of individual actions)? To this I have proposed an answer which provides an account for reality and in particular the reality of social wholes. It seems to me that it may just possibly prove adequate.

The preceding chapter has the nature of being a conclusion to the book although it was neither constructed nor written with that in mind. It seems desirable to try to state the main points of that chapter so far as they highlight the theme of the book. Although the chapter is devoted in large part to the philosophy of inert mechanism, to try to show that this is a weltanschauung that need not be a sacred cow but can be replaced by a person-weltanschauung, it contains a still more important idea which is referred to in various places throughout the book. That idea is that in the higher regions of explanatory theory to do with powerful empirical theories on science the hallmark that can be found is that of a non-instantiative hypothesis. That is a hypothesis that contains at least one non-instantiative concept or (as it is often called) theoretical term. It is obvious that physics and other natural sciences have not been able to get on without such concepts, and here I have been at pains to claim that the social sciences will not be able to make progress until they take this lesson to heart in their own field (instead of aping the natural sciences in faulty ways which are not really intrinsic to scientific procedure). The social sciences would do better to try to follow the traditional procedure of the natural sciences by looking for empirical theoretical explanations (not rooted in mechanism) that contain non-instantiative concepts. In illustration thereof I have been able to point to a very few cases. One is drawn from the psychoanalysis of groups, due to Bion, and the other to a social-psychological hypothesis which I put forward to explain the post-war forms of disintegration in Great Britain. I have not, of course, proved that the social sciences cannot work without such concepts; I would only put forward the possibility as extremely likely, and suggest that the proof of the pudding is in the eating — that is, if one works with such concepts one may at last make some explanatory progress.

The note on which I wish to end is to point out that individualism in its most powerful form (situational individualism) would seem to preclude the use of non-instantiative concepts in social science. Situational individualism, for all its widespread and successful application, seems to have a certain poverty-strickenness through not making use of them, and ceases to focus on the notion of truth as hidden.

The thesis of the book hinges on a wider aspect of philosophy of science than simply the empirical aspect of science. This involves the use of philosophy not simply as a metascientific enquiry into the empirical component of scientific theories but beyond that an enquiry into their frameworks or weltanschauungen or here schemata. It is held that problems concerning schemata are basic to the understanding of the social sciences and their progress, and concretely that the issue of the individualistic and holistic schemata constitute a problem that is fundamental to the development of the social sciences, and lastly that in addition to a new schema being required at that point replacing the weltanschauung of mechanism by a weltanschauung of persons combined with societal wholes, the most important adjunct of all is to adopt that procedure of natural science that is rooted in the use of non-instantiative concepts.

Index

Wisdom, John, 147, 150
Wittgenstein, 110, 114, 126, 147
work, 14

Wright Mills, 196, 197, 198

Zinoviev, 98